Reader praise for Glynis McCants and her work:

"Glynis is the master guide to revealing where your numbers can take you in life. She is all about empowering YOU by sharing the meaning behind your numbers."
—Gillian Holloway, Ph.D., author of *The Complete Dream Book*

"When I met my fiancé, the first thing I did was run his numbers using Glynis' book. I found my perfect match! After four years together we still remind each other that we are built to last. Thanks Glynis!"
—Clare Graham, Texas

"Glynis has shed new light on the way I approach love in my life. My relationships are astronomically better since I found her book. I wouldn't start or end a relationship without it!"
—Kassandra Vaughn, California

"There's not enough words to express how much Glynis has helped me, and the countless others I've passed her books on to."
—Teresa Jones, Florida

"Glynis' book has changed my life! I know I am with the man of my dreams, the house that will make us prosperous and how to approach and reach out to our kids. Glynis has helped blend my mixed family and we couldn't be happier!"
—Kelley Logan, Texas

"I have shared my copy of Glynis' book with many friends. We all agree that numbers tells our own story. I am so thankful for her book because it has helped me understand myself and others more than I could have without it. Thank you Glynis, you are awesome!"
—Vicky Root, Wisconsin

"Glynis is the reason I became fascinated with Numerology years ago. I saw her on a talk show giving readings, picked up her book, and was hooked! I use Numerology ALL the time! It is especially helpful with relationships."
—Krystal Cummings, Vancouver BC, Canada

"Through the insight I gained in Glynis' book, I am not only better able to understand myself, but my relationships with family and friends as well...including my teenage daughter!"
—Suzanne Parham, Georgia

"When I started to learn about Numerology by reading Glynis' books, my whole world unfolded and made so much more sense than ever before."
—Chelsea Wickins, Oklahoma

"I have found Glynis' work to be a constant reference guide in my life where numbers are involved. If you are drawn to the subject, let Glynis be your Numerology guide—she makes it entertaining and yet profound, where wisdom, intuition, logic, and this ancient science of numbers are combined to bring the greater life to you."
—Angelika Sielken, Hawaii

BY THE

NUMBERS

Love BY THE NUMBERS

How to Find Great Love or Reignite
the Love You Have Through the Power of
NUMEROLOGY

Glynis McCants

SOURCEBOOKS CASABLANCA™
AN IMPRINT OF SOURCEBOOKS, INC.®
NAPERVILLE, ILLINOIS

Published by Sourcebooks Casablanca, an imprint of Sourcebooks, Inc.
P.O. Box 4410, Naperville, Illinois 60567-4410
(630) 961-3900
Fax: (630) 961-2168
www.sourcebooks.com

Library of Congress Cataloging-in-Publication Data

McCants, Glynis
  Love by the numbers : how to find great love or reignite the love you have
through the power of numerology / Glynis McCants.
     p. cm.
  Includes bibliographical references and index.
  1. Numerology. 2. Love—Miscellanea. I. Title.
  BF1623.P9.M38 2009
  133.3'35—dc22
                          2009021326

Printed and bound in the United States of America.
BG 10 9 8 7 6 5 4 3 2 1

I dedicate this book to my father John McCants, who passed away on September 8, 2008. Through his own example, he taught me that if I kept my focus, there was nothing I could not achieve. It is because of him I knew I could choose a unique path to help others and became a Numerologist. I love you Dad, and I feel you with me every day.

Contents

Acknowledgments

I thank my mother Gwen McCants, who is truly remarkable. She is always such a help when it comes to writing and picking out just the right word. Mom, you're such a blessing, and I feel so lucky that you are in my life. You have inspired me always and made it clear to me from a very young age that I could make a positive difference in the world.

Thanks, also, to my wonderful husband Charlie Youngblood. You are a constant support and the most consistently loving person in my life. I can honestly say that if I were trapped on an island and it were just you and me, I would feel as though I were truly living heaven on earth. God bless you, and may our true love by the Numbers inspire everyone out there to never settle for less. I love you Charlie!

I would like to acknowledge the amazing Louise L.Hay, author of the life changing book *You Can Heal Your Life*. I have been referring to Louise's book for over twenty years now, and whenever I pick it up, I feel I learn something I need to know. I have been blessed to work with Louise, and I can tell you first hand that this woman absolutely practices what she preaches. Thank you Louise for being such a phenomenal human being and for helping millions of people, including me, achieve their dreams.

CHAPTER 1

Introduction to Numerology

We come to love, not by finding a perfect person, but by learning to see an imperfect person perfectly.

—SAM KEEN

When I wrote my previous book *Glynis Has Your Number*, I had so many topics to cover that I only put one chapter about love in the book. I vowed that my next book would be dedicated to love, because I believe there is nothing more important to our well-being.

I have been practicing Numerology for over twenty-one years, and one of my greatest pleasures is to bring two people together and help them find lasting love by the Numbers. It is a blessing when we share our lives with kindness and consideration to help each other achieve our dreams. I find equal satisfaction in counseling married couples whose marriages have lost their way. Numerology has helped them to understand each other, begin to work through their differences, and fall in love all over again.

It isn't as much fun if you have a great career and achieve success but have no one with whom you can share your triumphs. I strongly believe that God did not put us on a planet with millions of people and yet doomed us to live our lives alone. It only makes sense that He would want us to be able to share our lives with the right someone else. If you are dating and looking for a lasting love, I can help you find a loving partner through the power of Numerology. If you are already in a relationship and know that it is not a healthy one, help is on the way!

• HOW IT WORKS •

Numerology, a 2,500-year-old science of numbers, was created by the Greek mathematician Pythagoras. Pythagoras believed that when we are born, we enter this world with very specific Vibrations. These Vibrations have a direct influence on our character and what our life purpose will be. Pythagoras attached a Number to each Vibration, using the Numbers 1 (new beginnings) through 9 (completion). If you have a person's first and last name, and full date of birth, you can discover exactly who they are by using the Pythagorean Number System.

There are three Numbers that come from the name (the Soul Number, the Personality Number, and the Power Name Number), and there are three Numbers that come from the full birth date (the Birth Day Number, the Life Path Number, and the Attitude Number). Below are the brief definitions of what each number tells you about a person.

The Soul Number: Defines what will fulfill your Soul.
The Personality Number: Defines how people perceive you.

The Power Name Number: Defines the strength of your character.

The Birth Day Number: Defines how you appear to people when they first meet you.

The Life Path Number: Defines your life's purpose. This Number has the biggest impact on your Life.

The Attitude Number: Defines your general outlook on life.

Here is an example of what the six numbers above look like when they are laid out:

93345*/7Attitude

When you do a Numerology Blueprint, the layout of the numbers will always be in this exact order, going from left to right. The first number will be the **Soul Number** (9), the second number will be the **Personality Number** (3), the third number will be the **Power Name Number** (3), the fourth number will be the **Birth Day Number** (4), the fifth Number will be the **Life Path Number** (5), and the sixth number will be the **Attitude Number** (7). I will always put an asterisk (*) next to the **Life Path Number**, because it is the most important Number when it comes to love relationships. However, if your Life Path Numbers are a Challenge, all is not lost because I do give you advice on how to deal with this in Chapter 14.

When you have determined the six numbers for you and your partner, you will have the information you need to create a Personal Numerology Chart Comparison and see whether this relationship is worth pursuing or ending so you can move on. This book will help you answer this question with confidence. If you are in an unhappy marriage, and your relationship is mostly Toxic but you want to save it, perhaps because you have children or just do not believe in divorce, there is information throughout this book that will give you the tools to heal your relationship.

When you do a Personal Numerology Chart Comparison, there are three ways that each number interacts with another number:

A **Natural Match Number** means you have an instant rapport and an easygoing understanding of each other.

A **Compatible Number** means you get along most of the time and can learn to agree to disagree.

A **Challenge Number** means that no matter what you say, you will be misunderstood. More often than not you will find a break down in communication, which can feel very Toxic and make the relationship difficult.

I will discuss each of these further in Chapter 3.

As time goes on, there are couples who believe they have outgrown each other, and others who say they grew much closer in later years. I believe this actually has to do with the **Maturity Number** (what you achieve in midlife) and the **Destiny Number** (where you are headed), which are two Vibrations that reveal themselves later in life. Although these two Numbers are not one of the six Numbers used in your Numerology Blueprint, they do also help you understand each other better. By learning what they are and mean, you can prepare for them with your mate; or if you are dating and find they are Toxic, you may want to reconsider the relationship.

By studying your Numerology Blueprints with your partner, you can learn a whole new way to communicate, so that your partner will actually *hear* what you are saying—perhaps for the first time.

Throughout this book, when I discuss the Numerology characteristics of a person, I will use the words **Number, Energy,** and **Vibration** when I refer to them. These three words are interchangeable.

The words **Challenge Number** and **Toxic Number** are also interchangeable.

Here's an example:

His 2 **Vibration** is a **Challenge** to her 5 **Energy.**

I could have just as correctly written:

His 2 **Vibration** was **Toxic** to her **Number** 5.

• SOUL MATE CONNECTIONS •

Love by the Numbers will cover Soul Mate relationships. The formula for a Soul Mate Connection occurs when you share three of the Six Main Numbers (not counting the Attitude Number). Surprisingly, being Soul Mates with someone is not always good news. Sometimes the connection is a difficult lesson, and the relationship is not a positive experience. Yet, it teaches you, "Oh boy, I will never do that again!"

Then there is the other, more familiar kind of Soul Mate—the one you want and who is a wonderful blessing in your life. You'll be drawn to the Soul Mate, in either case, but this book will show you how to recognize the difference between the good and bad relationships right away.

A Soul Mate Connection, whether it is good or bad, never really ends. So, if it is someone you broke up with long ago, it should make you smile that he or she still pops up in your head because of the Soul Mate Connection. I find a lot of people are able to mentally release a bad relationship from their past once they know this is so. If you are married and your partner is a Toxic Soul Mate Connection, you will want to focus on the Affirmations presented in Chapter 21 to find ways to make the relationship healthy.

Special Note

If the person you love is abusing drugs or alcohol, then no matter how great your Numerology Chart Comparison looks on paper, the relationship is not wholesome. A relationship works in Numerology when each person is living on the Positive side of his or her Numbers. Doing drugs, abusing alcohol, gambling or sexual addictions are certainly not living on the Positive side of anything, especially life. It means you are basically spending time with Dr. Jekyll and Mr. Hyde, never knowing which one you are going to get each day. I do not condone enabling a partner to stay addicted. Either encourage that person to get help or move on with your life. *You deserve great love*, and if your partner won't make the effort to get well, it means you are in last place, and that can lead to tremendous pain and unhappiness. I know great love is out there for every one of us, and no one should settle for less!

• MY LOVE STORY •

Below are the six Numbers of my husband's and my Personal Numerology Blueprints. I have put them here for the sake of telling you my love story. You will learn exactly how to find your Numerology Blueprint in the following Chapter.

Glynis McCants: 87633*/2 Attitude
Charlie Youngblood: 96664*/6 Attitude

Back in 2002, I was dating what I called the "X-Files"—men I had broken up with, but who I was still friends with. We'd still get together from time to time. So you might say we were "friends with benefits." I was not happy, and I just knew there had to be someone special for me. The funny thing is I had been matchmaking people by the numbers for years and never did it for myself. Finally, I decided I would be proactive in attracting a wonderful love relationship into my life.

I joined a dating service, and the headline I put for my profile read, "Numerologist Looking for a Man Who's Really Got My Number!" Then, I wrote down what I wanted in love, and what I wanted from the person with whom I would share my life. My favorite line from my profile was, "I am looking for a man who knows that a relationship is a *get to*, not a *have to*." I also added the fact that I am a Numerologist and to please send me their full date of birth.

A lot of men responded to the ad, probably because I submitted a topless photo (just kidding!). The first guy I dated lied about his birth date. It was funny because there were things about his personality that did not make sense, judging from the birth numbers I had derived from his fictitious date of birth. I kept thinking, "How can the numbers be so wrong?" When he finally told me the truth, I had to laugh. We are actually friends to this day.

I started looking again. Then along came Charlie Youngblood. As you can see above, his Name Numbers are a 6 Soul Number, a 9 Personality Number, and a 6 Power Name Number. He was born on a 6 Day with a 4 Life Path Number, and a 6 Attitude Number.

The Natural Match Numbers to my 3 Life Path are 3, 6, and 9, and so I was thrilled to see all of this Natural Match Energy in his Personal Numerology Chart.

His Life Path 4 is a Challenge to my 3 Life Path. However, when a number repeats itself in your chart that is not the same as your Life Path Number, it will have quite an impact on what kind of person you are.

Looking at the four 6s in his chart made me very optimistic, because the 6 Vibration is a Natural Match to my Life Path 3.

I knew the physical chemistry would be amazing, so I made the decision not to meet him in person. We talked on the phone for over four months. He'd call me morning, noon, and night. He'd phone me just to say "good morning," or, "I hope you have a good lunch, and I'll talk to you this evening." We would talk about two hours each night, and I knew I was falling for him.

I was comfortable with that arrangement because I knew his numbers, but of course he didn't know anything about Numerology and had no idea what he was in for! However, as a woman, I was smart enough to keep my deep feelings for him to myself at this stage of the relationship. After all, relationships take some time, and one should never move too fast, especially if they are looking for a lasting love, which I certainly was.

So the first time I met him in person, I was with a group of friends in a bar with a lovely fireplace. I was so nervous! But, sure enough, as soon as I saw him I knew he was the one, and I had been wise to take it slow.

Since we had talked so much on the phone, he knew all of my friends' first names and various things about them. They were all very impressed. After about an hour, my friends had all left and when it was just the two of us, I teasingly said, "There's something I have been meaning to tell you all night."

"What's that?" he asked. And then I kissed him. That kiss lasted for forty-five minutes!

The next time we got together, he cooked the most amazing meal. I just thought what a caring man he was, and how many men think they're too macho to get in a kitchen. Frank Sinatra's music was playing in the background because Charlie knew how much I loved Sinatra. He had champagne on ice (another one of my favorites). I was hooked from that night on. It has been seven years, and it has been heaven on earth for me ever since!

When I die, the first thing I will do is thank God for Charlie Youngblood. He never stops surprising me with his absolute consideration for me. You see, before Charlie, I was always the big giver in the relationship. The man would get comfortable taking and then seem surprised if I wanted anything in return. With Charlie, it is the mutual admiration society. We both respect and consider each other's needs daily.

As I said before, his 4 Life Path is a Challenge to my 3 Life Path number, so every so often he will say to me, "Glynis, the 4 in me needs to say something." Then I take a deep breath and prepare myself for what is coming next. By putting me on notice, he is letting me know that what he is about to say may feel Toxic, but it needs to be said. That kind of consideration is what keeps our love alive.

I want all of you to learn to communicate by the Numbers, so that you do not take everything your partner says so personally. In doing this, we can make our love relationships much stronger. And for those looking at a new love relationship, using Numerology as a tool can help you get it *right from the start*!

CHAPTER 2

Discovering Your Numerology Blueprint

I love you, not only for what you are, but for what I am when I am with you.

—ROY CROFT

Now that you are familiar with the Numerology Blueprint, it is time for us to lay out an actual Personal Numerology Chart Comparison. As you learn exactly how to get each Number, I suggest you grab a piece of paper and do your own chart as you go along.

As introduced in Chapter 1, your Numerology Blueprint consists of six Numbers: the Soul Number, Personality Number, Power Name Number, Birth Day Number, Life Path Number, and the Attitude Number. These Numbers are derived from a person's first and last name and full date of birth.

WHICH NAME TO USE?

Many people ask if their Birth Certificate Name matters more than the name they go by day-to-day. Numerology has many layers, and the name that you use today contains the Vibrations you are putting out when you meet someone. While it is true that the Birth Certificate Name gives you your Destiny Number (discussed in Chapter 11), it is nevertheless the name that you go by day-to-day that is most important when you are doing a Personal Numerology Chart Comparison with someone else.

The **Destiny Number** is another layer, but you will not feel that Vibration as much as you do the Numbers from the name a person is currently using. If you decide this is the person you want to know *everything* about, then it will behoove you to know the Destiny Number as well, as this will tell you where he, or she, is headed.

As I mentioned in Chapter 1, there is also the **Maturity Number** that reveals itself in midlife. That number is also worth exploring so you can understand the changes your partner may go through at that time. The Maturity Number is covered in Chapter 12.

• THE PYTHAGOREAN NUMBER SYSTEM •

In Numerology, we also need to know how to break down the numbers in names. To do this, we will use the Pythagorean Number System, which assigns a number to each letter of the alphabet.

Pythagorean Number System

1	2	3	4	5	6	7	8	9
A	B	C	D	E	F	G	H	I
J	K	L	M	N	O	P	Q	R
S	T	U	V	W	X	Y	Z	

EXCEPTION:

Sometimes the **Y** is a consonant, and sometimes the **Y** is a vowel. Here's how to determine which is which:

If the **Y** is **next to a vowel** (A, E, I, O, U) it is considered a **consonant**.

If the **Y** is **next to or between two consonants**, it is considered a **vowel**.

Example:

Lynn: The **Y** is a **vowel** because it is **between the two consonants** L and N.

Judy: The **Y** is **next to the consonant** D, and so it is considered a **vowel**.

Joy: The **Y** is **next to the vowel** O, so in this case, the Y is a consonant.

Note: if your name has a suffix, such as Jr., Sr., III, you do not include them when you break down the name.

Example:

If you go by John Smith III, you only break down John Smith.

• THE SIX MOST IMPORTANT NUMBERS •

In *Love by the Numbers*, we focus on six numbers that describe our most important character traits. As we discussed in the previous chapter, these numbers are derived from two sources: the name that you go by day-to-day and your full date of birth. These Numbers are:

1) THE SOUL NUMBER: You get this number by adding all the vowels in your name and reducing them to one digit.

2) THE PERSONALITY NUMBER: You get this number by adding all the consonants in your name and reducing them to one digit.

3) THE POWER NAME NUMBER: You get this number by adding all the consonants and vowels together and reducing them to one digit.

4) THE BIRTH DAY NUMBER: The number of the day on which you were born. If it is more than one digit, then you reduce it to one digit.

5) THE LIFE PATH NUMBER: The sum of the digits in a person's birth date, including the month, day, and full year reduced to one digit.

6) THE ATTITUDE NUMBER: The sum of the digits in the day and month of your birth date reduced to one digit.

Before I get into specifics about what each of these Numbers says about you, let's break down some Numbers together. We begin with Paul Newman and Joanne Woodward.

Paul Newman and **Joanne Woodward** make up a truly fascinating Numerology Comparison Chart that explains their wonderful love affair. I will use Paul Newman's chart first to show you how to break the numbers down, and then I will tell you the powerful love story of these two iconic individuals.

```
1+3      +5      +1    = 10 = 1+0              = 1 Soul Number
 | |      |       |
PAUL  NEWMAN
 |   | |  | | |   |
 7   +3 +5 +5 +4  +5 = 29 = 2+9 = 11 = 1+1 = 2 Personality Number
```

Soul Number (1) + Personality Number (2) = 3 Power Name Number

The Three Name Numbers:

First we take the name that he goes by, Paul Newman, and then we add the vowels across the top of his name and reduce them to one digit to get his **Soul Number.** His **Soul Number** is a **1.**

We now add the consonants below his name and reduce them to one digit, to get his **Personality Number.** He has a **2 Personality Number.** (Some of you who are familiar with the Master Numbers will notice that I reduced the Master Number 11 to a 2. To understand my thoughts about the Master Numbers 11 and 22, refer to Chapter 9.)

Now, we add the two together, to get the **Power Name Number,** which is a **3.**

Those are the first three Numbers in his Personal Numerology Blueprint.

The Three Birth Date Numbers:

Now let's get the other three numbers from his full birth date. **Paul Newman** was born **January 26, 1925. The actual day** you are born is significant. **2+6 = 8**, so that means Paul has an **8 Birth Day Number**, and that is considered his appearance number.

Then we break down his whole Birth Date to get his **Life Path Number**. To do this, take his full date of birth, and reduce it to one digit.

DOB: 1/26/1925

> 1+2+6+1+9+2+5 = 26
>
> 2+6 = 8

Paul Newman is an **8 Life Path**.

To find his **Attitude Number**, take the month and day, and reduce it to one digit:

1/26

1+2+6 = 9.

The Number **9** is his **Attitude Number**.

So now we have his full Numerology Blueprint, which looks like this:

12388*/9 Attitude

Remember, the * signifies the Life Path Number.

When I look at his chart, the first thing I see is the 1, 2, and 3, and I always say if you have the Numbers 1, 2, and 3 in your chart, you need to say out loud, "My life is as easy as 1, 2, 3," because 1, 2, 3 is a very fortunate configuration. The 1 is ambition, 2 is the ability to love, and 3 is a sense of humor and the natural performer.

Paul Newman was born on an **8 day** with an **8 Life Path**. When the Birth Day Number and the Life Path Number are the same, it means "what you see is what you get." This man was a straight shooter, and also business minded, which is a strong characteristic of the 8 Vibration. His 9 Attitude was the part of him that was a philanthropist, and if you don't know Paul Newman as an actor, you certainly know his products. He was a founder of a food company called Newman's Own, and all of the profits were donated to charity. By the time he passed away on September 26, 2008, he had given $250 million away to various causes. A phenomenal man.

Now let's take a look at **Joanne Woodward**:

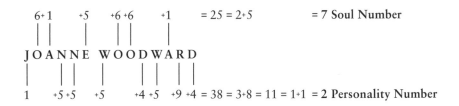

Soul Number (7) + Personality Number (2) = 9 Power Name Number

The Three Name Numbers:

First, we take the name she uses, Joanne Woodward, and we add the vowels across the top of her name and reduce them to one digit to get her **Soul Number**. Her **Soul Number** is a 7.

We now add the consonants below her name and reduce them to one digit to get her **Personality Number**. She has a **2 Personality Number**. (For those of you familiar with the Master Numbers, you will notice that I reduced the Master Number 11 to a 2. Refer to Chapter 9 for my thoughts about the Master Numbers 11 and 22.)

Now we add the two together, to get the **Power Name Number**, which is a **9**.

Those are the first three Numbers in her Personal Numerology Blueprint.

The Three Birth Date Numbers:

Now let's get the other three numbers from her full birth date. **Joanne Woodward** was born on **February 27, 1930**. The actual day you are born is significant. She was born on the 27th, **2+7 = 9,** so that means Joanne has a **9 Birth Day Number**, and that is considered her appearance number.

Then we break down her whole birth date to get her **Life Path Number.** Take her full date of birth, and reduce it to one digit:

DOB: 2/27/1930

$$2+2+7+1+9+3+0 = 24$$
$$2+4 = 6$$

Joanne Woodward is a **6 Life Path.**

To find her **Attitude Number,** take the month and day, and reduce it to one digit:

2/27

$$2+2+7=11$$
$$1+1 = 2$$

The Number **2** is her **Attitude Number.**

So now we have her full Numerology Blueprint, which looks like this:

72996*/2 Attitude

Now let's bring their numbers together, and do a Chart Comparison.

THE COUPLE:

Paul Newman: 12388*/9 Attitude
Joanne Woodward: 72996*/2 Attitude

CHART COMPARISON	Paul Newman	Joanne Woodward	Number Connection
SOUL NUMBER	1	7	Natural Match
PERSONALITY NUMBER	2	2	Natural Match
POWER NAME NUMBER	3	9	Natural Match
BIRTH DAY	8	9	Challenge
LIFE PATH	8	6	Compatible
ATTITUDE NUMBER	9	2	Compatible

Joanne Woodward said when she fell madly in love with Paul, she had no problem putting her acting career second to raising her children. It is not uncommon for a 6 Life Path female to feel strongly about her children, yet she was also able to continue to perform and win awards for her wonderful talent. Keep in mind that the numbers 3, 6, and 9 encourage performance, and both she and Paul had numbers from that Natural Match category.

So now that we have their six numbers, we can evaluate them as a couple. You can see that they share the Number 2, and the 2 is about physical love. Joanne said that when they first met, they had such lust and it was so ardent they couldn't keep their hands off each other. Other times they would fight and play hard, but there was always enormous love. You can see that in their charts.

The Number 9 is for that humanitarian instinct they both shared, caring so much about "how do we leave the world better than we found it?" And they were very successful at doing that as a couple.

In Paul Newman's acting career, he won the Academy Award for his performance in Martin Scorcese's 1986 *The Color of Money,* he won three Golden Globe Awards, a Screen Actors Guild's Award, an Emmy Award, and many honorary awards. He also won several national championships as a driver in the Sports Car Club of America road racing, and his race team won several championships in open-wheel Indy racing. I believe it was his Soul Number 1 that gave him his passion for racing and love of winning.

Most significant was his phenomenal love with Joanne Woodward. Numerology shows that if your numbers are healthy as a couple, you should both be able to achieve a lot together, as well as separately, and these two are fine examples.

Paul Newman also showed his strength in adversity. He had a son from a previous marriage, named Scott, who overdosed on drugs. In the midst of his grief, Paul created a center for drug abuse prevention in memory of his son. Clearly Paul chose not to be a victim. He responded to a tragedy by making it do some good—preventing others from dying from drugs.

This is a man who truly embraced life, and when he passed away, he had lived life to the fullest.

As I noted earlier, Joanne had three daughters with Paul and was fulfilled as a mother. As proof of compatibility, they were able to work together—a difficult feat as many actors will tell you. They did ten films, which included the classics *The Long Hot Summer* (1958), *Rally 'Round the Flag, Boys* (1958), and *The Drowning Pool* (1975).

In 1958 Joanne Woodward won an Academy Award for best actress in *The Three Faces of Eve*. She was also nominated for best actress in *Summer Winter Wishes Dreams* and *Mr. and Mrs. Bridge*. She was named best actress at the Cannes Film Festival in 1974 for her performance in *The Effect of Gamma Rays on Man-in-the-Moon Marigolds* and also won two Emmys for best actress.

Like Paul, Joanne also produced and directed. She is an Artistic Director at the Westport Country Playhouse. Joanne Woodward cast her husband as the Stage Manager in a revival of *Our Town*; the play moved to Broadway where Newman earned his first Tony nomination in 2003.

How, in show business of all professions, did these two work together in such a competitive venue and not compete with each other? It's all right there in the Numbers. When you're in a healthy relationship, you cheerlead for each other, and you are thrilled when the one you love does well.

When studying their Numerology, one could see that these two would have a vigorous old age and be together till the end—"until death do us part," literally.

Their fiftieth anniversary occurred on January 29, 2008. Here are two hugely successful actors, and arguably, no one in Hollywood was more physically attractive than Paul Newman. His love for his wife, and her devotion to him, should be truly inspirational for all of us. They overcame all the odds.

Paul Newman was once asked what had made their relationship so long and lasting and he said, "It has the correct amount of lust and respect." And it's funny, when I think of the 2 Vibration, I would think of lust; and the 9 Vibration in their charts gives them that respectful balance. Who could ask for anything more!

In the following chapter, you will learn exactly how to interpret a Chart Comparison for you and your mate.

CHAPTER 3

Is it a Love Match? How to Interpret Your Chart Comparison

There is only one happiness in life, to love and be loved.
—GEORGE SAND

At this point in the book, it is time to take a look at the six Numbers for you and the person you are interested in. Now you will learn whether each Number is a Natural Match, Compatible, Neutral, or a Challenge.

Keep in mind that although the placement of a Number may change, the actual definition of the Number will remain the same. It is the placement of the Number in your chart that will determine its significance. For example, a 3 Soul Number has the same traits as a 3 Life Path Number, but you will really notice the traits of the 3 Vibration when someone is a 3 Life Path because that number is about their life purpose. Having a 3 Soul Number is more subtle. It refers to how the person feels inside and is not as obvious.

Below is the list of how each Vibration gets along with each Vibration. This applies to every Number in the Numerology Blueprint. For example, the 7 and the 8 are a Challenge in Numerology. So if you have a 7 Life Path and your partner has an 8 Life Path, then your Life Path Numbers are a Challenge. If your Soul Number is a 7 and your partner's Soul Number is an 8, then your Soul Numbers are a Challenge. If your Personality Number is a 7 and your partner's Personality Number is an 8, then your Personality Numbers are a Challenge, and so on.

I suggest you bookmark this page, so you can always refer back to how the numbers get along. This information is absolutely essential when doing a Numerology Chart Comparison.

The 1 Vibration

Natural Match Numbers: 1, 5, and 7
Compatible Numbers: 2, 3, and 9
Challenge Numbers: 4 and 6
Neutral Numbers: 8

The 2 Vibration

Natural Match Numbers: 2, 4, and 8
Compatible Numbers: 1, 3, 6, and 9
Challenge Numbers: 5 and 7

The 3 Vibration

Natural Match Numbers: 3, 6, and 9
Compatible Numbers: 1, 2, and 5
Challenge Numbers: 4, 7, and 8

The **4 Vibration**

Natural Match Numbers: 2, 4, and 8

Compatible Numbers: 6 and 7

Challenge Numbers: 1, 3, 5, and 9

The **5 Vibration**

Natural Match Numbers: 1, 5, and 7

Compatible Numbers: 3 and 9

Challenge Numbers: 2, 4, and 6

Neutral Numbers: 8

The **6 Vibration**

Natural Match Numbers: 3, 6, and 9

Compatible Numbers: 2, 4, and 8

Challenge Numbers: 1, 5, and 7

The **7 Vibration**

Natural Match Numbers: 1, 5, and 7

Compatible Numbers: 4

Challenge Numbers: 2, 3, 6, 8, and 9

The **8 Vibration**

Natural Match Numbers: 2, 4, and 8

Compatible Numbers: 6

Challenge Numbers: 3, 7, and 9

Neutral Numbers: 1 and 5

The **9 Vibration**

    Natural Match Numbers: 3, 6, and 9

    Compatible Numbers: 1, 2, and 5

    Challenge Numbers: 4, 7, and 8

• THE LIFE PATH NUMBER •

The Life Path is the most important Number in your chart, because if this Number is not fulfilled, neither you nor your mate is going to be very happy. If you meet a person you feel you could love, and that person is not fulfilling the mission he or she has been called to achieve in life, there is a good chance you will experience lots of frustration. You may even turn to drink, drugs, promiscuous sex, or whatever else helps kill the pain.

> Remember that the words **Vibration**, **Energy**, and **Number** are used interchangeably throughout this book.

• NATURAL MATCH NUMBERS •

Each of the nine Life Path Numbers can be categorized as a Mind Number, a Creative Number, or a Business Number. These categories are called Natural Match Numbers.

1, 5, and 7 are Mind Numbers, always thinking

2, 4, and 8 are Business Numbers, always taking care of business

3, 6, and 9 are Creative Numbers, always creating

I have found that when you meet someone who is a Natural Match to you, you have an instant rapport. There is an immediate understanding, and it can be exciting to meet someone who is a Natural Match. Right from the beginning, when you meet a Natural Match, you can sense what the other is thinking and can immediately relate to one another. When you start talking about your life, you may even find that you went through many of the same experiences while you were growing up.

Every so often that Natural Match person can be wrong for you. You may look at the way they live and think, "Oh, that is not what I want," or, "That doesn't feel good to me." That means that this person is living on the Negative side of the Number, and chances are, you are living on the Positive side. So trust your gut instinct about that person no matter what the Numbers say.

The Mind Numbers: 1, 5, and 7

This is a cerebral group of people. They spend a lot of time thinking, and they are always mentally processing life. What is nice in each Natural Match Category is that all three Numbers would understand the characteristics about each other perfectly. The 1s, 5s, and 7s are all about wanting to meet an intellectual equal; they want to be stimulated by your ideas and conversation. They also enjoy movement and adventure. If you are somebody who likes to stay at home and not do much, it is best not to pursue a 1, 5, or 7 Life Path. They are probably not for you. If you crave adventure and want to cover the world beyond you, the Energy of the 1, 5, or 7 Vibration would suit you very well.

The Business-Minded Numbers: 2, 4, and 8

These are the business-minded people. They care very much about establishing a solid financial foundation. So if you fall in love with someone who is a 2 Life Path, 4 Life Path, or 8 Life Path, you should know that financial concerns are a big part of their lives.

Note on the 2 Vibration:
Although these three Numbers are in the Business Minded Number Category, the 2 is a little different from the 4 and 8 Life Paths. The 2 does "business with heart." This Number is the ultimate caretaker. They feel the need to rescue, and mediate for everybody. Also, the 2 Life Path gets along with more Life Path Numbers than any other Number in Numerology.

The Creative Numbers: 3, 6, 9

These creative-minded people are happiest with an audience. They tend to be performers, natural counselors, and teachers. On the down side I have found that the Life Paths 3, 6, and 9 attract partners who act more like patients than mates.

The 3s, 6s, and 9s are drawn to people they mistakenly think they can "fix." In truth, you can't really "fix" anyone. If you are a 3, 6, or 9 Life Path and you are attracted to someone who is emotionally distressed, always between jobs, or suffering from chronic depression, please do not let yourself fall into the trap of wanting to rescue this person. Mistaking that feeling for love is self-defeating.

• COMPATIBLE NUMBERS •

A Compatible Number will not give you the instant understanding that Natural Match Numbers have, but you will be drawn to each other right away. With a Compatible Number, you will learn the art of agreeing to disagree.

There are times you will get along beautifully, and other times you will not. There is no need to ever get in a fight with a Compatible Number. You just have to remember, "I love this person, and overall we get along, so I am going to keep the peace." You can always make that choice with a Compatible Number.

• CHALLENGE NUMBERS •

Challenge Numbers are complicated. A Challenge Number is when you meet somebody and no matter what you say, they just do not get it. It really is as if you are speaking two different languages. A Challenge Number might ask, "What are you talking about?" or they will look at you and say, "You know what I mean, don't you?" and you have to say, "No, I really don't."

It is frustrating, but interestingly a Challenge Number can often generate a fiery lust. It is not uncommon for Challenge Numbers to jump into bed because their bodies seem to speak the same passionate language. I strongly suggest that you keep your clothes on when confronted with a Challenge Number. Later, in a calmer moment, you will be able to decide rationally whether you want the hard work that goes with this kind of relationship.

• NEUTRAL NUMBERS •

When it comes to a love match, I have found a couple of interesting exceptions to the rules. There are certain Numbers that would be considered a Challenge to each other, but I have come across many couples who make it work.

The idea of a Neutral Number basically has to do with the Number 8, and how they get along with the 1 and 5 Vibrations, respectively. I have seen the 1 Life Path and 8 Life Path come together and, as I have noted, it can be terrific at first and then become volatile. This also occurs with the 8 Life Path with the 5 Life Path. These relationships can sizzle or run icy cold.

I have found that if these couples treat their love more like a business, actually scheduling their time together, because they are both so busy, doing so can work for them romantically, as well.

The 8 and 5 Vibrations, as well as the 8 with the 1 Vibrations, move fast in their own orbits and they have to make time for each other. If they are married, they should pause and say, "Hey, let's find a way to go out to dinner once a week and really catch up with each other." This kind of planning and care is very helpful for these couples.

• INTERPRETING YOUR • CHART COMPARISON

Now it's time to take a close look at *your* numbers. When you have found the Numerology Blueprint for yourself and for the person you are interested in (refer to Chapter 2 to see how this is done), compare your six Numbers using a chart like the one below. To find the Number connection, refer to descriptions of each Number Vibration at the beginning of this chapter.

CHART COMPARISON	Name	Name	Number Connection
SOUL NUMBER			
PERSONALITY NUMBER			
POWER NAME NUMBER			
BIRTH DAY			
LIFE PATH			
ATTITUDE NUMBER			

What did you discover? Take a look at your Challenge Numbers. If you find you have **zero Challenge Numbers** in your Personal Numerology Chart Comparison, then I say *you are very lucky to have found each other!* The only way it would not be a wonderful thing is if you or your mate are living on the Negative side of your Vibrations and cannot embrace the love you could have. If that is the case for your relationship, I recommend you go to Chapter 21 and do some positive Affirmations. Otherwise, this is very good news, indeed!

If you have **one or two Challenge Numbers** in your Personal Numerology Chart Comparison, it is not a big deal. You will have a good chance to find a way to compromise, because the positives far outweigh the negatives in your relationship. Note: there is one exception to this rule. If someone is abusing substances, then all bets are off! No matter how good the Numerology Chart Comparison looks, it will be distorted because of the addictions.

If you have **three Challenge Numbers** in your Personal Numerology Chart Comparison, this relationship is going to be a work in progress. If you will commit to understanding where you are different, and find a way to truly accept that fact, then the relationship can mellow as the years progress.

If you have **four or more Challenge Numbers** in your Personal Numerology Chart Comparison, you really have to ask yourself, "Is this worth it?!" Unless you are hermits who live on a mountaintop and have no worries in your life, this relationship will be tumultuous. The chances that you were originally drawn to each other, like moths to the flame, make perfect sense to me. Challenge Numbers almost always promote irresistible chemistry. However, when life throws you a curve ball, your partner with four Challenge Numbers will look at you dumbfounded and have no clue what it is you want from them. Every so often I meet a couple with four or more Challenges, and because they are both living on the Positive side of their Vibrations, they make it work through mutual respect. However, this is very rare.

Study this chapter carefully and memorize the **Natural Match, Compatibility,** and **Challenge Numbers**. You will then be well on your way to finding the love you are looking for, or enriching the one you already have.

• ARE YOU LIVING ON THE POSITIVE • OR NEGATIVE SIDE OF THE NUMBER?

Keep in mind that as you read the following chapters, you will find a Positive and Negative side to every Number. So study both sides carefully, and then ask yourself if the person you are interested in is living on the Positive side of the Number. This answer makes a big difference when it comes to a love relationship.

CHAPTER 4

The Soul Number: "The Secret Number"

Soul meets soul on lover's lips.

—PERCY BYSSHE SHELLEY

I call the Soul Number "the Secret Number" in Numerology because it is not something you can actually see when you meet somebody. This number will fulfill a person's soul. You know your own soul is content when you can't stop smiling, and you feel that life is moving along exactly as it should. In the second part of this chapter, I will define each Soul Number to give you a sense of what will complete the soul of the person you are interested in.

But first, here are some Soul Number examples with celebrity names you may recognize, and a review of how to find the Soul Number. You will see what it is like when your Soul Number is Compatible or, conversely, when your Soul Number is a Challenge to the person with whom you are doing a Chart Comparison with.

• FINDING THE SOUL NUMBER •

To find your **Soul Number**, take the vowels of your name, add them straight across, and reduce them to one digit.

Let's do **Lucille Ball.**

3 +9   +5   +1   = 18 = 1+8 = **9 Soul Number**
| | | |
L U C I L L E   B A L L

Add up her vowels, and reduce them to one digit.

From the Pythagorean Number System (see page 13), we know that U is 3, I is 9, E is 5, and A is 1.

Lucille Ball has a **9 Soul Number.**

Now let's do her first husband, **Desi Arnaz.**

5 +9 +1   +1   = 16 = 1+6 = **7 Soul Number**
| | | |
D E S I   A R N A Z

Add up his vowels, and reduce them to one digit: E is 5, I is 9, A is 1, and A is 1.

Desi Arnaz has a **7 Soul Number.**

• THE CHALLENGE COUPLE •

In Numerology, the 9 and the 7 are considered a Challenge to each other—and when you look at the history of Lucille Ball and Desi Arnaz, this conclusion sadly makes perfect sense.

Lucille Ball's Soul was a 9, which means family would be extremely important to her. The idea of family—she was famously close to her mother, until her mother's death—marriage, a lifetime commitment, would complete her as a person. She had difficulty getting pregnant and was elated when she conceived her first child. The 9 Soul Number is content when family is around, but they can also have serious issues of abandonment when the family does not stay close.

They began their life together when Desi was a bandleader and singer. He was almost always on the road, constantly traveling and performing. She pitched her TV show, which allowed Desi to be the costar, so they could spend more time together. She feared if they could not find a way to work together, their time apart would destroy their relationship.

Now, what do we get with Desi? His Soul Number is a 7, and the 7 is the Number that likes to go places and do things. Someone with the 7 Soul is happy when he or she is on the road and on to the next adventure. The 7 Soul also likes peace and quiet and to avoid conflict. When living on the Negative side of the Number, they can escape through drugs, alcohol, geography, work, or sex. Desi Arnaz was known to be a workaholic, a heavy drinker, and a notorious womanizer, and yet that did not stop Lucille from doing whatever she could to keep their relationship alive.

In his case, he was also a 5 Life Path, which also includes a desire to escape, so by having a 7 Soul Number and a 5 Life Path, his need for variety in life was intensified. If I just saw their Numerology Chart Comparison, without knowing who they were, their conflicting Soul Numbers would tell me that these two would have trouble in their relationship.

A major accomplishment for Lucille's Soul Number 9 would mean having the family all together in the same house, enjoying life.

Fulfillment for Desi's Soul Number 7 would be, "Where are we headed next? Where is the next exciting place we are going to go?"

He would enjoy being around nature's beauty and celebrating his life, but not necessarily when he's home. It would be more about getting out there and finding whatever it is he was looking for. The 7 also hungers for spirituality, and if they do not find it, that is when their vices take over. Their Personal Numerology Charts showed that problems would occur, and those problems eventually led to a divorce, even though those who knew them best believe they were always very much in love.

Now let's look at a couple that is a Natural Match with their Soul Numbers: **Bill Gates** and **Melinda Gates**.

Bill Gates:
Add the vowels straight across and reduce them to one digit.

```
9       +1  +5      = 15 = 1+5 = 6 Soul Number
|        |   |
BILL  GATES
```

Bill Gates has a 6 Soul Number.

Melinda Gates:
Add the vowels straight across, and then reduce them to one digit.

```
5 +9    +1    +1  +5     = 21 = 2+1 = 3 Soul Number
|  |     |     |   |
MELINDA  GATES
```

Melinda Gates has a 3 Soul Number.

• THE NATURAL MATCH COUPLE •

Bill Gates' Soul Number 6 and Melinda's Soul Number 3 are a Natural Match.

A contented Soul in Bill Gate's case would be feeling like the king of the castle, having a beautiful wife, kids, and being very successful in his business. Well, no one can dispute the level of success that Bill Gates has achieved. His Soul is pleased by that, and when he returns to his lovely home, wife, and children after doing some of his humanitarian work, his 6 Soul Number is content.

Melinda's Soul Number is a 3, and the 3 is more about communication, keeping things light, finding ways to keep her sense of humor, throwing parties for worthy charities, and also inspiring others to be successful. When she can give advice to Bill, and he takes it, her Soul Number 3 is delighted. Those who know the couple say that Bill has tremendous respect for what Melinda has to say and is known for taking her advice and counsel. So I am quite sure her Soul Number 3 is nourished by their relationship.

When a Soul Number is a Natural Match to a partner's Soul Number, the couple can be very successful together. These two have been a team, and no one has done better than Bill Gates in the computer and business world—in part, because he has the right partner to encourage him and help him keep his eye on the prize. These two are also known for their legendary generosity and the world owes much to their creed: *Every person on earth deserves a healthy and productive life.*

• THE NINE SOUL NUMBERS •

Now I'm going to give a brief definition of each Soul Number, 1 through 9, and I want you to keep in mind that in Chapter 3 I showed you how each Number gets along with the other: whether it is Compatible, a Challenge, or a Natural Match. So when you do your own chart comparison, refer back to Chapter 3 to see how your Soul Numbers relate to each other.

If the person you are interested in is a 1 Soul Number:
The **1 Soul Number** is fulfilled when they have a personal victory, when they have won some sort of a competition, when they feel that whatever they do is treated with respect, and when they have the courage to be just who they are and are accepted for it. If they do not feel validated in their relationship, it can turn sour real fast.

If the person you are interested in is a 2 Soul Number:
The **2 Soul Number** is fulfilled when they are in love, or they have found themselves in a harmonious environment. They are naturally intuitive and trust their instincts. When things go right, they are so happy. Sending a 2 Soul Number a special card detailing why you love them so much will go a long way. Any special efforts on your part, such as making a cup of coffee for them in the morning, or any act of caring, will make their 2 Soul Number purr with delight.

If the person you are interested in is a 3 Soul Number:
The **3 Soul Number** is fulfilled when they can laugh and have great conversation with the person that matters most to them. The 3 Soul Number is never shy about giving their advice, and if you take it, you will see appreciation in their eyes. Not to mention, they tend to know what they are talking about, so taking their suggestion is a smart move on your part! Long-lasting friendships are also very important to the 3 Soul Number.

If the person you are interested in is a 4 Soul Number:
The **4 Soul Number** is fulfilled when they have security. Whether it is financial or a relationship, they like to know that everything is taken

care of. If you are their partner and can find a way to help their money grow for the future, their 4 Soul Number will be so pleased. Having a solid plan, and knowing exactly where they are headed, is crucial. If you get in a dispute with a 4 Soul Number, trust they will not give up their position, and that the best thing to do is to end the conflict. The 4 Soul Number is very loyal, and if you reciprocate, there is nothing he or she will not do for you.

If the person you are interested in is a 5 Soul Number:
The **5 Soul Number** is fulfilled when they are on the road again, taking a look at the world and having fun. The 5 Soul Number is happy when they are honoring someone. It is all about sharing their thoughts and ideas. They embrace information and good conversation. It is a waste of time to lie to a 5 Soul Number. They love digging for the truth, and they will find out exactly what happened. If you love a 5 Soul Number, know that deceiving them is a deal breaker.

If the person you are interested in is a 6 Soul Number:
The **6 Soul Number** is fulfilled when they have children. If they don't have kids, they might just have a cat, a dog, or anything that will love them unconditionally. Their surroundings matter a great deal to them. If they live in a nice home, they are happy, and it makes them feel good. Running a large company with responsibility, and respect from others, is also wonderful for the 6 Soul Number. Gratitude is very important to them. They don't mind working hard and doing everything it takes to get the job done, but they do need someone to say, "Thank you." If you love someone who is a 6 Soul Number, offer to help them and be sure to follow through. If they trust you enough to do one of their many tasks at hand, and you drop the ball, the 6 Soul Number will find it hard to forgive you, and you will sorely regret it.

If the person you are interested in is a 7 Soul Number:
The **7 Soul Number** is fulfilled when they can get away from all the craziness that life can bring. It can be as simple as sitting on the beach, looking at the ocean. They are happy when taking a trip, perhaps taking a nature hike, or any time they are alone with nature. A beautiful sunset can take their breath away. Their soul is also strengthened by answering the profound questions of why we exist. Once they feel they have found something that rings true, they are elated. It's like, "Eureka! I found it!" If you love a 7 Soul Number, and can contribute to this quest, the 7 will be appreciative. The Soul Number 7 is all about discovery, and the journey is often within themselves.

If the person you are interested in is an 8 Soul Number:
The **8 Soul Number** is fulfilled when they work hard and are well compensated. When they come up with an entrepreneurial idea, and turn it into money, they are content. The 8 Soul Number feels strongly about many things, and when they have an opinion that is valued, and see justice prevail, their Soul Number 8 is satisfied. The 8 Soul Number appreciates a beautiful home, a luxury car, impressive collections (think Elizabeth Taylor and her jewels) and memorabilia of all sorts that hold meaning for them from the past. When the person they love helps create a beautiful safe environment, their 8 Soul Number feels serene.

If the person you are interested in is a 9 Soul Number:
The **9 Soul Number** is content when whatever happened in their past is forgotten, and they find a way to forgive and forget. Their 9 Soul is then at peace. The 9 is also satisfied when family is nearby and they are embraced by a nurturing environment. Giving back to society by doing charitable work is also rewarding to the 9 Soul Number. If the person with the 9 Soul Number has profoundly affected other people and has improved

their lives in some way, they feel so grateful. If you love someone with a 9 Soul Number, always ask if you can ease their life by helping out, because they will never expect it and will be pleasantly surprised!

• UNDERSTANDING SOUL NUMBERS •

Keep in mind that the Soul Number is not something you see when you meet somebody, especially if the Soul Number is in conflict with their Life Path or Attitude Number. Unless there are other numbers in a person's chart that are the same as their Soul Number, you will not pick up on this Vibration when you first get to know the person.

That is why you always want to break down the first and last name the person uses day-to-day. The Soul Number you find from that name will help you understand him or her better.

As I wrote earlier, some Numerologists believe the Birth Certificate Name gives you someone's Soul Number. But I disagree. I have researched the question thoroughly and believe the name a person uses every day reveals their current and most important Soul Number. The Soul Number does change when you use a different name. Your Birth Certificate Name gives you your original Soul Number, but it is a layer and changes when you alter your name. The traits of the original Soul Number will not be as strong as the current Soul Number that is for the name you go by today. In some cases, people will find that the name they go by today has the same Soul Number as their Birth Certificate Name, but this is uncommon. What makes the Birth Certificate Name so important is that it is the name that gives you your Destiny Number, which is the one Number in your name that can never change. The Destiny Number subconsciously pushes you forward to achieve certain goals before your life is over, and only your Birth Certificate Name can tell you what it is. Chapter 11 covers the Destiny Numbers in depth.

CHAPTER 5

The Personality Numbers: Do You Click, or Do You Clash?

Love is friendship set on fire.

—JEREMY TAYLOR

When you do a Personal Numerology Chart Comparison with someone who is your significant other, or someone who is a candidate to be your significant other, you definitely need to learn how to find their Personality Number. How your Personality Numbers get along with each other will help you in understanding your relationship better. The Personality Number is one of the six Numbers that make up the Numerology Blueprint, and it is derived from the consonants of the name you go by, added all together, and then reduced to one digit.

This number tells you how you appear on the outside; that is to say, how the world sees you. It is not as significant as the three numbers pulled from the birth date numbers, but it does give you valuable insight into a person's character.

Let's take a look at two different couples and their Personality Numbers, one that is a Natural Match and one that is a Challenge. We will use **Will Smith** and **Jada Pinkett Smith** as the Natural Match **Personality Number** example.

Will Smith:

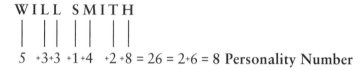

W I L L   S M I T H

5 +3+3 +1 +4   +2 +8 = 26 = 2+6 = **8 Personality Number**

Take the name Will Smith and add the consonants straight across below the name: 5 for W, 3 for L, 3 for L, 1 for S, 4 for M, 2 for T, and 8 for H. They add up to 26. Then reduce 26 to one digit, and it becomes an 8.

Will Smith's Personality Number is an 8.

Jada Pinkett Smith:

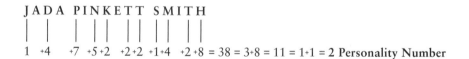

J A D A   P I N K E T T   S M I T H

1 +4   +7 +5 +2 +2 +2 +1 +4   +2 +8 = 38 = 3+8 = 11 = 1+1 = **2 Personality Number**

Again, add the consonants below the name: J is 1, D is 4, P is 7, N is 5, K is 2, T is 2, T is 2, S is 1, M is 4, T is 2, H is 8. It first adds up to a 38. Reduce it to one digit, and it becomes a 2.

Jada Pinkett Smith's Personality Number is a 2.

The Natural Match Couple

Will Smith's 8 Personality Number tells me is that he is business minded. He indeed has had the most amazing career. Virtually every movie he has made has been a blockbuster. Jada Pinkett Smith has the Personality Number 2. The 2 is about love and encourages romance. I would think she does what she can to keep the love alive in the relationship. Jada is also business minded. Financial security is important to both of them, and keep in mind that the numbers 2, 4, and 8 fall into business-minded Natural Match category.

Both of them are so dynamic, attractive, and appealing together, that all eyes follow them whenever they appear in public. Their Personality Numbers help explain why people are so drawn to them as a couple.

Now I know that in their complete Personal Numerology Chart, there are some Challenge Numbers, but their Personality Number is one of the Numbers that is strong for the relationship and encourages them to be good partners and find ways to stay together and keep their relationship thriving.

To Read Will Smith and Jada Pinkett Smith's complete Chart, refer to Chapter 23.

Now let's take a look at the Personality Numbers for **Julia Roberts** and **Danny Moder**.

Julia Roberts:

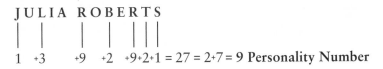

JULIA ROBERTS

1   +3   +9   +2   +9+2+1 = 27 = 2+7 = **9 Personality Number**

J is 1, L is 3, R is 9, B is 2, R is 9, T is 2, S is 1, so it adds up to 27 and reduces to a 9.

Julie Roberts has a 9 Personality Number.

Danny Moder:

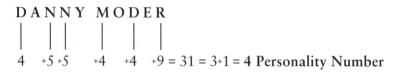

DANNY MODER

4 +5 +5   +4   +4   +9 = 31 = 3+1 = **4 Personality Number**

D is 4, N is 5, N is 5, M is 4, D is 4, R is 9, so that becomes a 31 and reduces to a 4.

Danny Moder has a 4 Personality Number.

The Challenge Couple

In this case, their Personality Numbers 9 and 4 are a Challenge, which I do not find remotely surprising. Let's look at the relationship. First of all, it is very private. Very few people know about Julia Roberts and Danny Moder's relationship. Occasionally there are rumors of trouble in the marriage. I have observed when Julia does major movie premieres, more often than not, she shows up without Danny. Sometimes, she'll be with her movie producer, director, or with some friends, but not with Danny.

Her personality is a 9, which is a bright light, and that is why you notice her big smile and sparkling eyes, and it's a face that seems so welcoming towards the world. She just opens up her arms and people want to love her. Her Personality Number encourages this trait, whereas her 7 Life Path number does need privacy.

Danny's Personality Number is a 4, and the 4 Vibration cherishes its privacy; crowds can make them uncomfortable. Danny Moder avoids public affairs because his 4 Personality Number does not welcome all that attention, yet he'll be there for Julia when she gets home. He definitely cares about the family and having a partnership, but he won't be controlled. His 4 Personality will not put on a big bright smile if that is not what he's feeling. Yet Julia Roberts 9 Personality Number understands when it is "showtime, folks!" Whether she is feeling it or not, she can turn it on when necessary. I believe the clash in their Personality Numbers has caused some stress in their relationship.

Through the years I have been asked to study the Julia Roberts/ Danny Moder relationship, and I am aware that they have many Challenge Numbers in their Chart Comparison. Challenge Numbers always promote great chemistry, but they do not make it easy for communication.

A couple can have Challenge Numbers and still make their relationship work. The 9 Personality Number wants to keep the family together, and the 4 Personality Number is committed to their family. Also, Julia Roberts is working hard on this relationship and truly wants it to last. She wants to be a good mom to her children and a loving wife to her husband. But these are very different people, and their differences are clearly reflected in their Personality Numbers.

• PERSONALITY NUMBER DESCRIPTIONS •

If the person you are interested in is a 1 Personality Number:
People notice the **1 Personality Number.** They have an air of confidence and you'll see that in them. They want to be successful, appreciated, and valued in a relationship. They bring a lot to the table and can be an asset to your life. If they think they are right, they will not give up their position. This can be a great Personality Number because these people are so alive! The 1 Personality asks, "What's the next step? What is going on?"

The 1 Personality is a multitasker, and they try to accomplish a lot in a short span of time. If you are even a little bit lazy, know that the 1 Personality will not tolerate it. They will call you on it and keep you moving forward, whether you like it or not! When the 1 Personality feels as though they are a major player in this thing called life, they are happy.

If the person you are interested in is a 2 Personality Number:
The people with a **2 Personality Number** are gentler, more relaxed. They value harmony, tranquility, and love, above all else. They make friends easily. Once they do befriend you, they are loyal. They are not aggressive, unless other numbers in their Numerology Blueprint encourage them to be so. If a 2 Personality Number has a strong person in their love relationship, then they will do whatever they can to help their partner succeed. This is true especially if it is an endeavor that helps a lot of people at the same time. The 2 Personality cares deeply about their fellow man. This Vibration can be too sensitive and needs to measure their emotional involvement in other people's misfortunes. Unless they maintain an emotional distance, they will find themselves unable to effectively lend assistance.

If the person you are interested in is a 3 Personality Number:
The **3 Personality Number** has a sense of humor that will get your attention. They usually stand out and you may notice their eyes, voice, or warm smile. In love, they will try to keep the relationship upbeat, and if it gets too serious, the 3 Personality will express their disappointment.

When you praise the 3 Personality or compliment them in various ways—such as, "I like your outfit," "You look great tonight," or "You smell good"—you will definitely see their Cheshire cat grin. They have plenty to say, and when they become upset, the mood is usually fleeting. All it takes is hearing the right music, or seeing a friendly face, and they are happy again. The 3 Personality is happiest when they have your complete attention.

If the person you are interested in is a 4 Personality Number:
The **4 Personality Number** is serious-minded and sensitive. There is intelligence here, and they are always learning. This is a Number

that wants to be the best at what they do. You can count on people with a 4 Personality Number, and they pride themselves on doing a good job.

On the Negative side of the Number, the 4 Personality can have trouble sleeping. It is very hard for them to just relax, and sometimes to obtain relief they may resort to alcohol or prescription drugs. One of the things you can do as the 4's mate is to help them learn to take it easy in beneficial ways, such as immersing themselves in a hot bath or getting a foot rub or back message. The 4 Personality will always tell you what they are thinking; they are very direct and candid. If you are dishonest with them, doing so may be the biggest mistake of your Life!

If the person you are interested in is a 5 Personality Number:
The **5 Personality Number** is a whirlwind of energy, and you can feel their vitality. There is an excitement there and you may not know exactly what it is, but you can see the intensity in their eyes. If you choose to love them, fasten your seatbelt because there will never be a dull moment. The 5 Personality Number has so many ideas swirling around in their head that I actually call the 5 Vibration "the Human Popcorn Machine." They are always popping off with a new idea or plan for the next exciting thing to do.

If the 5 Personality Number is not having fun, they can fall into the martyr mode. You might meet a 5 Personality Number who is lamenting that life is unfair. Just know that those 5s are living on the Negative side of the Vibration. They are the exception, not the rule. If you looking for exhilaration in your life, you need look no further than a 5 Personality Number.

If the person you are interested in is a 6 Personality Number:
The **6 Personality Number** is usually nicely put together. They wear

attractive clothes, and they take pride in their appearance. People with the 6 personality are magnetic, and others are drawn to them. They take charge and like to get the job done. They are responsible, and yet they need to know that it is okay to ask for help, and that no one has to do it all alone.

If you are in love with someone who has a 6 Personality Number, praising that person and letting the individual know how much you appreciate everything he or she does for you will do wonders for your relationship. They like their homes to be well kept and have a cozy feeling. A 6 Personality is a dynamic Energy. They are involved, and they like to keep you involved as well. The 6 Personality Number will always do more than their fair share when there is work to be done, but if you want to score points with them, do things to ease their life. It could be as simple as picking up the dry cleaning, making dinner unexpectedly, or surprising them by taking them to their favorite restaurant. The 6 personality will always appreciate that kind of thoughtfulness.

If the person you are interested in is a 7 Personality Number:
The **7 Personality Number** is an enigma. It will take some time to get to know this Personality Number. They are observers and at first they will not necessarily want to tell you what it is they are thinking or feeling. Once they feel they can trust you, they will open up and tell you what is on their mind. They have a strong need for privacy, and if you invade their space, it can end an otherwise good relationship. The 7 Personality is intriguing. I find that other people are drawn to the 7 Personality because they are not an open book, so it becomes a goal to find out "what can I do to crack the code? How do I break through?"

The 7 Personality Numbers have a love of nature and need some time by themselves. They can't always be social with others. If they have faith, then listening to them talk about it can be hypnotic. If they do not, they can be bitterly sarcastic, and that can lead to sorrow for those who care about them. So if you encounter their need for solitude, and you sometimes feel excluded, don't take it personally. It is just the way the 7 operates.

If the person you are interested in is an 8 Personality Number:
I call the **8 Personality Number** "the Politician Number." That does not necessarily mean they are actually into politics, but they do have very strong convictions about what they believe and what they think. You can rest assured that they will tell you, and with any luck at all, convert you to their point of view. They are going to be direct and blunt. If they are successful with money and saving for the future, the 8 Personality will appreciate that quality in you. However, don't be too frugal when it comes to them. They do welcome an occasional luxury gift from their mate.

The Positive side of the 8 Personality is that they are incredibly hard workers and want to make a good living. If the 8 Personality is living on the Negative side of the Vibration, money can slip through their fingers. If you are in love with an 8 Personality that falls into the latter category, make sure you are in charge of the household finances. They also like to look their best physically and expect the same from their partner. If this is not the case, then something is not working in their life, and they may have shut down.

If the person you are interested in is a 9 Personality Number:
The **9 Personality Number** has a lot of wisdom and is charismatic, so you will notice them when they enter the room. If you give them an assignment, they will get the job done. They are the ones you will

think you may have met before. You will look at one and think, "Do I know that guy? Do I know that girl?" Subconsciously there is something that automatically makes us look up to them.

Because of this innate power, sometimes when they speak and they are just expressing their opinion, they sound patronizing to the listener. That is something that a 9 Personality has to be aware of. What the 9 Personality Number wants most is to feel that they are making a positive impact on the world.

If you are fortunate enough to share your life with a 9 Personality Number you will find they are very protective of you and the family. They are aware of what their parents did wrong when they were young and will do whatever they can to get it right. It is not easy for a 9 Personality to ask for help, so if you are already married to one, or you are falling in love with a 9 Personality, be sure to check in on them emotionally. If something seems wrong, come right out and ask them how they are doing. The 9 Personality will be beyond grateful that you even noticed because, although they truly welcome your caring, they have become very good at hiding their vulnerability.

CHAPTER 6

The Power Name Number: Who's Got the Power?

There is no remedy for love but to love more.

—HENRY DAVID THOREAU

The Power Name Number says a lot about a person's character, and it is the most revealing number of the three Numbers found in your name. You can gain a lot of insight about your partner by studying this Number. How do you get the **Power Name Number?** Take the **Soul Number** and the **Personality Number** from the name you use, **add them together and reduce them to one digit.**

Let's use **Ava Gardner** and **Frank Sinatra** as an example of when the Power Name Number is a Challenge in a Personal Numerology Chart Comparison.

Let's break down Ava Gardner first:

```
1   +1   +1      +5                    = 8 Soul Number
|   |    |       |
AVA  GARDNER
|   |  |||  |
4   +7 +9+4 +5  +9 = 38 = 3+8 = 11 = 1+1 = 2 Personality Number
```

8 (Soul Number) + 2 (Personality Number) = 10 = 1+0 = 1 Power
Name Number

Now, let's break down Frank Sinatra:

```
1       +9  +1    +1 = 12 = 1+2        = 3 Soul Number
|       |   |     |
FRANK  SINATRA
||     ||| |  ||
6+9   +5+2 +1 +5  +2 +9 = 39 = 3+9 = 12 = 1+2 = 3 Personality Number
```

3 (Soul Number) + 3 (Personality Number) = 6 Power Name Number

The Challenge Couple

The 1 and 6 Power Name Numbers are considered a Challenge to each other. The 1 Vibration does not want anyone telling them what to do. The 6 feels there must be order in the relationship and says, not always gently, "This is what I want." The 6 believes in home, family, and prefers to stay in one place. The 1 Vibration enjoys the adventurous life. They want to explore the world and need to feel that no one is tying them down.

The Power Name Number could help explain the tremendous difficulties in the Frank Sinatra–Ava Gardner relationship. Frank was madly in love with her, and yet he was married at the time to another woman he could not bear to hurt. He had to go through a very difficult divorce to be with Ava, and they were married immediately after the divorce.

Ava was working on a movie when she discovered she was pregnant. She decided not to have the baby and hid her decision from Frank. When he found out about it, it broke his heart. The 6 Vibration is the Parent Number and usually embraces having children; and this was very true for Frank Sinatra. He wanted a beautiful wife, loving children, and a fine home. He achieved this with his first wife Nancy, and he really wanted this with Ava.

Ava defied Frank because of her 1 Power Name Number, which is all about having independence. Not only were their Power Name Numbers Toxic to one another, but so were their Life Path Numbers 4 (Frank) and 5 (Ava) (refer to Chapter 8 to read about Life Path Numbers) so the odds were very much stacked against them.

Ava and Frank's torrid love affair demonstrates how Challenge Numbers can promote nonstop chemistry, but also make understanding one another's needs very difficult.

Now let's use **Tom Hanks** and **Rita Wilson Hanks** as an example of the Power Name Numbers that are a Natural Match in a Personal Numerology Chart Comparison:

Let's break down Tom Hanks first:

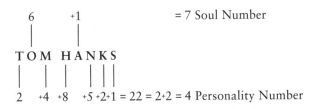

7 (Soul Number) + 4 (Personality Number) = 11 = 1+1 = 2 Power Name Number

Tom Hank's Power Name Number is 2. That explains why he is such a fine actor, who has such command of his emotions that he can go to such vulnerable places on film.

Rita Wilson Hanks:

When Rita Wilson married Tom, she took on his last name, so sometimes she goes by Rita Wilson and other times by Rita Wilson Hanks. In this case we will look at the married name because it gives them a Natural Match Connection and is actually better for their relationship.

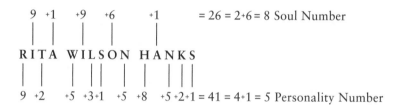

8 (Soul Number) + 5 (Personality Number) = 13 = 1+3 = 4 Power Name Number

Rita Wilson Hanks' Power Name is 4.

The Natural Match Couple

Now, here is what makes this such a wonderful partnership in Numerology: The 4 and the 2 are considered Natural Matches, so these two have a real understanding of each other. Just for the record, their other Chart Numbers also match up well.

For one, Rita has the 5 as her Personality Number. The 5 Personality is the person with the ideas. After she went to view the one-woman show *My Big Fat Greek Wedding*, she talked Tom into investing and making the one-woman show into a movie. The Power Name Number 2 will listen to their partner, especially a business-minded partner with the Power Name Number 4. Tom invested $5 million, and that movie went on to become the highest grossing independent film of all time. It made over $300 million.

Rita and Tom have a really loving, respectful relationship. It is not that they have to agree on every issue, but they know how to listen to each other. When Rita uses Tom's last name and takes on the Power Name Number 4, it is very good for them as a couple. The 4 Vibration gives her a sense of security and belonging. Their Natural Match Power Name Number has helped make them a stronger couple. As you study this chapter, you may find your Power Name Numbers are Toxic, and you may consider changing your name to make your relationship more compatible. We do cover this topic in Chapter 18.

• POWER NAME NUMBER DESCRIPTIONS •

If the person you are interested in is a 1 Power Name Number:
Those who have the **1 Power Name Number** possess a strong desire to be the best. They are critical of themselves; therefore, they are critical of the people in their lives. So if you love someone with the 1 Power Name Number, you need to be aware of that. They are not trying to be hurtful, they just have high standards for themselves, and they are trying to bring out the best in everyone, including you.

It is important that the 1 Power Name Numbers find a way to be respected and not feel controlled. They are entrepreneurial and it is best that they run things themselves (or at least think that they do). If they are interested in sports or intense workouts, this is a smart way for the 1 Power Name Number to release their stress.

If the person you are interested in is a 2 Power Name Number:
When the **2 Power Name Number** does business, they do so with their heart, and it has to be something they believe in. They don't want to

just make money for money's sake, because that would not satisfy them. The 2 Power Name Number does not necessarily want to lead; they enjoy working with others,

If you meet a Power Name Number 2 who is very competitive, that trait originates somewhere else in their Personal Numerology Chart. The Number 1, for instance, would give them more ambition and drive than what is normally found in the 2 Vibration. They want to get behind and be supportive of the people they respect in the workplace and also in a love relationship. They can intuitively pick up on what is going on with the people in their life and should always trust their incredible gut instincts. It is when they second-guess themselves that they end up regretting it later. When you look in their eyes, you will see a gentle spirit that tells you that you can count on them.

If the person you are interested in is a 3 Power Name Number:
A person with a **3 Power Name Number** is called upon to be a communicator on some level. It could be on a stage, teaching, radio broadcasting, behind-the-scenes writing, or counseling. The Power Name Number 3 encourages those with that Number to express themselves. In love, the Power Name Number 3 will make their partners laugh, and they appreciate your wit, too.

A realized Power Name Number 3 will find a job where a round of applause is forthcoming. They need people, and they do see the world as their stage. If you love someone with the Power Name Number 3, and they are not good at expressing themselves, that tells me that they did not have the support they needed when they were young from one, or both, of their parents. If you are willing to be their audience, and encourage them to be their best self, the smile on their face will make it well worth it!

If the person you are interested in is a 4 Power Name Number:
If you love someone with the **4 Power Name Number**, realize that this is someone who prefers logical action—they want to know what the plan is. They seek knowledge, and once they learn a skill, they can show you how to do it. Actually, just try to stop them. The 4 Power Name Number has to be careful not to use their mouths as blunt instruments. These people can be abrasive. So if you love someone who has the 4 Power Name Number, and they seem harsh or critical, understand that they are just trying to be helpful. They can over-think things. You tell them a great idea, and then they will start pointing out why the idea would be difficult for you to achieve. Just thank them and move on. They really don't want to be wet blankets; they feel they are just giving you valuable advice. The 4 Power Name Number is a direct Vibration, and a responsible person.

If the person you are interested in is a 5 Power Name Number:
The **5 Power Name Number** is high energy and a very dynamic personality. They are fast thinkers and are usually loaded with ideas. When you love a 5 Power Name Number, know that they must have the freedom to come and go as they please. If you understand this need, your relationship will go much more smoothly. If you try to control them, the 5 Power Name Number will exit stage left, and they could exit permanently if you are too controlling.

They love to celebrate life. They can be found anyplace people congregate for fun. They love people and are fascinated by their comings and goings. The 5 Power Name Number always digs for the truth and is not satisfied until they find out what is going on. They love a good story. They can be very giving. The Power Name Number 5 loves to give you the perfect gift. They must be careful not to give so much that it makes it impossible for someone to reciprocate. This can put them in the "martyr" mode. When the 5 Power Name Number is well adjusted, they create a joyful ambiance wherever they go.

If the person you are interested in is a 6 Power Name Number:
The **6 Power Name Number** is a magnetic Vibration. These people care about how they look, from the clothes they wear to their posture. This is a responsible energy, but they can overdo it, because their fear is, "If I don't do it, it will never get done." In love, the Power Name Number 6 must learn to ask for help when they need it. They also have to learn to trust that life is going to be okay, that everything does not have to be a crisis.

Their partner must know the 6 Power Name Number is very good at damage control, and so if you are in trouble, always let them know. Knowing that they have once again "saved the day" puts the 6 Power Name Number in a very good mood. They need to feel useful. If the 6 Power Name Number has children, they can become obsessed with being a "perfect parent," and they have to learn that there is no such thing as a "perfect parent." The 6 Power Name Number is a dynamic vibration, and someone you will not be able to ignore.

If the person you are interested in is a 7 Power Name Number:
When it comes to the **7 Power Name Number**, do not waste your time trying to figure out exactly what it is that makes them tick. They will *never* let you know all that there is to know about them. The 7 Power Name Numbers need to feel they have not revealed their whole self to anyone. It is just their way. If you are in involved with a 7 Power Name Number, you must not take this characteristic personally. It is just a part of who they are.

The Power Name Number 7 is also an astute observer of what is going on around them. They may be the people at the party who are quiet, but when they finally open up, what they have to say is usually fascinating, and their perceptions are accurate. When a Power Name Number 7 chooses to be a spiritual teacher, he or she is unusually profound. A good career for this Vibration would be teaching others what they believe in themselves, such as eating healthy foods, or becoming a personal trainer who gives guidance on taking better care of the body. People with this Vibration are also good with animals, because they often trust them more than they do people.

If they are not tapping into their sacred, or altruistic, side, they have to be careful not to become too pessimistic. Because a pessimistic 7 Power Name Number can take their loved ones down that trail with them. So if you become the partner of a 7 Power Name Number, find out if they have faith, and if they do not, try to guide them in the right direction. They will ultimately be very glad that you did.

If the person you are interested in is an 8 Power Name Number:
If you love someone with an **8 Power Name Number,** make a note to yourself that they are strong, opinionated, and usually have very specific thoughts on what is wrong in any given circumstance, and what should be done to fix it. When an 8 Power Name Number is living on the Negative side of the Vibration, they must avoid thinking that when they have some bad luck, it is someone else's fault, or that someone is out to get them.

The 8 Power Name Numbers usually care about their appearance, and they like quality things, not because they cost a lot, but because they are drawn to the best that life has to offer. They are dependable and very direct. Sometimes they will not edit their words, and they can seem to be targeting you unfairly. Defending yourself would be a waste of time because, really, it was not their intention to offend you in the first place.

If an 8 Power Name Number is in business, increasing their personal wealth will be a priority. If you are involved with someone with the 8 Power Name Number, look at how they handle the financial side of life. If the 8 Power Name says, "I enjoy working hard and making good money," that is a Positive 8 Power Name Number. But if the Power Name Number 8 says, "I don't really care about money," unless he or she is a trust-fund baby, I would be really concerned. He or she could be very comfortable *spending your money*.

If the person you are interested in is a 9 Power Name Number:
If you are interested in, or already involved with, a **9 Power Name Number**, know that it is natural for this particular Number to be compassionate and care deeply for the people in their life that matter to them most. The 9 Power Name Numbers are old souls, and even as children said things that were way beyond their years.

Gandhi comes to my mind when I think of the Number 9, because he learned how to win independence for his people without violence. He used fasting as a way of nonviolent protest, and he used nonviolence to unite India and end British rule. The 9 Power Name Number really has the strength and the gift to change the world for the better and would welcome a partner to join in this journey.

CHAPTER 7

The Birth Day Number: Is What You See Really What You Get?

Happiness is love freely given and joyously returned.

—ANONYMOUS

When someone meets you, the first thing they notice is a reflection of your Birth Day Number. I often refer to it as the "appearance number," because the day you are born is how people will perceive you at first glance. The Birth Day Number is easy to find; it is determined by the day you were born reduced to a single digit. It is important to know that someone can come into the world on a day that is a Challenge to their own Life Path Number. When that happens, *what you see is not what you get.* Here is an example of a Birth Day Number that is a Challenge, using **Brad Pitt** and **Angelina Jolie:**

Brad Pitt was born on 12/18/1963. Reduce his **Birth Day Number** down to one digit.

$$1+8=9$$

Brad Pitt was born on a 9 day.

Angelina Jolie was born on 6/4/1975.

$$=4$$

Angelina Jolie was born on a 4 day.

The Challenge Couple

Technically, the Numbers 9 and 4 are considered a Challenge to each other. But since Brad is a 4 Life Path, when Brad met Angelina, he looked at her and saw himself. He saw something familiar and thought, "Wow, we really have a lot in common."

But behind Angelina's 4 Birth Day Number is a 5 Life Path. A 5 Vibration is very different from a 4 Vibration. So Brad was in for the ride of his life from the minute they got together. Again, it was the 4 Birth Day, not the 5 Life Path, that he saw when they first met.

What Angelina observed: Brad was born on a 9 day. That is the humanitarian Number. He feels called to do some humanitarian work to effect a positive change in the world, and Angelina's own good works are legendary. Furthermore, his 4 Life Path had a calming effect on Angelina's 5 Life Path. It made her think that "this is someone I can spend my life with, someone who would ground me. He would certainly want to be the father of my children." This is a case of two people in a relationship, born on days that are technically a **Challenge** to each other, and I am quite sure their relationship takes a lot of work and compromise.

Our Next Birth Day Number example is a Natural Match Combination with **Catherine Zeta-Jones** and **Michael Douglas**.

Remember to reduce the **Birth Day Number** to one digit:

Catherine Zeta-Jones was born 9/25/1969

2+5=7

Catherine Zeta-Jones was born on a 7 day.

Michael Douglas was born on 9/25/1944.

2+5=7

As you see, Michael Douglas is also born on a 7 day.

The Natural Match Couple

Not only were **Catherine Zeta-Jones and Michael Douglas** born on the same day, they were also born in the same month. Michael has said that the minute he met Catherine he told her, "I want to be the father of your children." As almost anyone would, Catherine just laughed off his remark. Of course, Michael pursued her, and little by little she became fascinated by him.

They ended up having two children together. I would say that although there is a 25-year age difference between them, they have a very special connection because of their shared birth date. It also explains why they are such a dynamic-looking couple.

• BIRTH DAY NUMBER DESCRIPTIONS •

Remember that the Birth Day Number determines what a person appears to be, and your expectations will be geared to this perception. Sometimes we are shocked to find someone to be radically different than our original vision of them. So to be safe, always check all six numbers of their Numerology Blueprint before moving ahead.

The 1 Birth Day Number

If you are interested in someone born on the 1st, 10th, 19th, or 28th:
Those who are born on a **1 Day** will attract your attention. They stand out from the crowd and seem to command instant respect. They like their opinions to be listened to. When they think they are right, it is hard for them to give up their position. If you love someone born on a 1 day, and want to keep them off guard in the middle of the debate, just say, "Hey, you are right. What was I thinking?" They will never see it coming.

The 2 Birth Day Number

If you are interested in someone born on the 2nd, 11th, 20th, or the 29th:
One of the first things you will notice about people born on a **2 Day** is the sensitivity in their eyes, and when they are hurt, it is obvious. They have an air of kindness about them and usually want to help others out on some level. They are good listeners, loyal in friendship and love. You can count on a 2 to come through for you, especially if you are their loved one or someone they view as a good friend.

The 3 Birth Day Number

If you are interested in someone born on the 3rd, 12th, 21st, or 30th:
Those born on a **3 Day** tend to be upbeat and playful. If they do any form of public speaking, they are sure to use humor. They will try to get you to understand a serious subject, and then they will throw in a punch line. And guess what? You suddenly get it. They must be free to express themselves, so only good listeners need apply to be the mate of the 3 Birth Day Number. If that is you, you will have a wonderful time.

The 4 Birth Day Number

If you are interested in someone born on the 4th, 13th, 22nd, or the 31st:

When you first meet someone born on a **4 Day**, you will see a certain seriousness about him or her. There is intensity to the 4 Vibration. They may have other Numbers in their Personal Chart that lighten them up, and they can be very amusing, but this is a strong personality who very much would like to be in charge of their future. You never want to lose the trust of anyone born on a 4 Birth Day. Absolute honesty is the rule.

The 5 Birth Day Number

If you are interested in someone born on the 5th, 14th, or the 23rd:

You will experience a certain electricity when you first meet someone born on a **5 Day**. These people have inquiring minds and they love to be in the know—so if you have a secret, be advised: they will find out what it is. They are high energy, easily bored, and like to stay busy. It is not uncommon for them to have all kinds of hobbies, and travel is a big plus for them. It is actually best that they stay occupied, so make sure that's okay for your own needs before you pursue them.

The 6 Birth Day Number

If you are interested in someone born on the 6th, 15th, or 24th:

A person born on a **6 Day** is usually responsible and would rather be instructing others on what needs to get done than taking orders from someone else. The 6 is also considered the Nurturing Number in both males and females. If they have children, they care deeply about doing a good job as a parent. They take care of their mate as well, but they must have that pat on the back, that well-deserved "thank you." They like to have their days planned out, and are people who work hard. It is not easy for them to tolerate laziness, so if you are one who likes to take it easy, be aware of this.

The 7 Birth Day Number

If you are interested in someone born on the 7th, 16th, or 25th:
There is something about people born on the 7 Day that is quite appealing. You will be drawn to them, but they do not automatically let you in. They tend to study and observe what is going on around them before they express what they think and feel. They have to be careful with their lethal tongues, because they are honest and sometimes forthcoming to the point of unintentional rudeness. This Vibration will always need time to themselves, and yet they will love you deeply. A person born on a 7 Birth Day would appreciate a lover that does not need constant reassurance.

The 8 Birth Day Number

If you are interested in someone born on the 8th, 17th, or 26th:
Someone born on an 8 Day is typically business-minded and efficient. It is not surprising to see both the men and women with tasteful jewelry, finely tailored clothes—always something that tells you that they appreciate quality. The 8 Birth Day is outspoken, and you never have to wonder what is on his or her mind. You must be willing to give them the floor when they need to express their opinions. Help them understand that "stuff happens," so if things go wrong they know they are not the target of a conspiracy. This would be a good mate for an upbeat person who is also a natural cheerleader.

The 9 Birth Day Number

If you are interested in someone born on the 9th, 18th, or 27th:
Those born on a 9 Day give people the impression they are in control and know what to do. The 9 does not necessarily want to lead, but

the people in their lives push them to the head of the line. Others will assume that they are in charge of whatever is going on. They may come up and ask them for directions if the 9 Birth Day Number is walking the street, and address them in the native tongue of whatever country they may be visiting, or even try to pay them if they are waiting in line for some event! What is interesting is that the 9 will actually assume responsibility. They will want to come through for those who are depending on them. They usually have a nice smile and an air about them that makes it difficult to ignore them.

CHAPTER 8

Life Path Number: What Each Life Path Offers and Desires in Love

How do I love thee? Let me count the ways...
—ELIZABETH BARRETT BROWNING

The Life Path Number matters a great deal in a love relationship, and it is the most important number in the six Numbers you can find in your Numerology Blueprint. Things go a lot more smoothly in a relationship if the two Life Path Numbers are a Natural Match or Compatible. On the other hand, if the Life Paths are a Challenge, it is important to be able to understand where your partner is coming from so that, though you are very different people, you can solve the problems of life together. You get the Life Path Number by taking the full date of birth and reducing it to one digit. If your Life Path breaks down to an 11 or 22, please study the 2 Life Path and 4 Life Path, respectively. We will discuss the Master Numbers in Chapter 9.

You learned how to find your Life Path Number in Chapter 2, but I'll also review it here. Let's find the **Life Path Number** by using **Clark Gable** and **Carole Lombard's** birth dates, and see the kind of influence the Life Path Numbers played in their relationship. To find the Life Path Number, take the full date of birth and reduce it to one digit.

Clark Gable was born on:
2/1/1901
2+1+1+9+0+1 = 14
$$1+4 = 5$$
Clark Gable is a 5 Life Path.

Carole Lombard was born on:
10/6/1908
1+0+6+1+9+0+8 = 25
$$2+5=7$$
Carole Lombard is a 7 Life Path.

The Natural Match Couple

Clark Gable: 7291**5***/3 Attitude
Carole Lombard: 1126**7***/7 Attitude
Note: * denotes the Life Path Number

It has come down to us in Hollywood lore that Clark Gable was crazy in love with Carole Lombard and would never have left her in this lifetime. Although she was his third wife, he had never met such a wonderful woman and he called her his Soul Mate. From a Numerology perspective, he was absolutely correct! They shared three numbers (1, 2, and 7), which gave them a Soul Mate Connection.

Most important, their Life Path Numbers were a Natural Match to each other. Clark Gable was a 5 Life Path. Carole Lombard was a 7 Life Path.

I know that made their connection very powerful. He loved her youthful spirit. He was only 7 years older than she, but that was enough for him to be slightly shocked, but totally enchanted, by her outspokenness. Carole's four-letter-word vocabulary was legend in a town that was pretty good at it. She just said what she thought and, I can tell you, having that double 7 in her chart, which was her 7 Life Path and her 7 Attitude, would encourage her to do just that.

Carole helped the war effort in World War II by flying around the country and urging people to buy U.S. War Bonds. It was nighttime and the twin engine DC-3 in which she was flying crashed into a mountain. The crash occurred on January 16, 1942, and Clark Gable was inconsolable. Not only did he lose his beloved wife, he lost his mother-in-law, with whom he was very close, and MGM staff publicist Otto Winkler, who was the best man at Gable's wedding to Lombard.

Clark Gable went on to have a distinguished military career during the remainder of the war. But he began to drink more heavily. He married two more times, the last time successfully, but the love of his life was Carole. At one point he was quoted, "You can trust that little screwball with your life, or your hopes, or your weaknesses, and she wouldn't even know how to think about letting you down." That's praise any of us would want to hear.

Again, what they shared was a 1 for their ambition, the 2 for the ability to love and great chemistry, and a 7 for their love of nature and each other's intellectual equality. By the way, Clark Gable was a Republican and Carole Lombard was a liberal Democrat, and yet they didn't let their politics get in the way of their love. If anything, they just enjoyed each other all the more, probably thinking the other was mistaken.

The Life Path Numbers play a very important role in a relationship, because it means that you and your loved one are on the same path. It is a meeting of the minds when you live on the Positive side of the Number.

Clark Gable was, by all accounts, a macho man. When he first got together with Carole Lombard, she was actually making more money than he. Her annual income as a freelance performer exceeded his studio salary until he starred in *Gone with the Wind*. Then they finally both earned comparable salaries. This is the kind of blending of the Numbers that you seek and hope for in Numerology. Despite the tragedy at the end, it was a true blessing for Clark Gable to have loved Carole Lombard, and it was the Numbers that made their connection so powerful.

The Challenge Couple

Robert Wagner   83217*/3 Attitude
2/10/1930
Natalie Wood   11223*/9 Attitude
7/20/1938

Note: * denotes Life Path Number

In this chart, we have an example of Life Path Numbers that Challenge one another. Always be aware that if your Life Paths are a Challenge, there is usually fiery chemistry, but it is often accompanied by a breakdown in communication. Robert Wagner and Natalie Wood were a solid example of this, and they married not once, but twice.

Robert and Natalie had a Soul Mate Connection. When you have three numbers in common out of the six main Numbers (not counting the Attitude Number), it is considered a Soul Mate Connection. They shared the numbers 1, 2, and 3: the 1 for their independence, the 2 for their chemistry, and the 3 for communication. But, unfortunately, when your Life Path Number is Toxic to your partner's Life Path Number, big problems can arise. When you become stressed out, you will have difficulty understanding each other.

I believe that is exactly what happened on the night of November 29, 1981, when Natalie Wood drowned after falling off their yacht *Splendor* near Catalina Island. Robert Wagner and Christopher Walken may have gotten into some sort of argument about Natalie. The rumor at that time was Robert may have even felt that Natalie was involved with Christopher Walken.

Natalie Wood had expressed time and again how afraid she was of the water. She couldn't swim, and yet she tried to get on a dinghy, the small boat attached to the yacht, and fell into the water and drowned. Her willingness to put herself in such a precarious situation has led people to assume that she was drunk.

Again, when your Life Path Numbers are Toxic, it may cause emotional conflict. Here is what I've learned about the 3 Life Path with the 7 Life Path in a relationship. The 3 is a big communicator, and sometimes the more they try to share or explain things, the quieter the 7 becomes. The 7 simply shuts down and doesn't want to talk, so then the 3 keeps pushing, and they provoke one another.

In this case, there was a tragic ending and the Numbers, of course, do not foretell that. I do not look to the Numbers for this kind of ending, but the Numbers certainly tell me that, when your Life Path Numbers are in conflict and life gets difficult, you will look at your partner as if you are speaking two very different languages.

Regarding this incident, the two men on the *Splendor* waited about 90 minutes to call for help after they discovered Natalie was missing.

So that does lead me to believe that there was some sort of falling out that night on that boat that helped cause this tragedy.

The first time Robert Wagner and Natalie Wood were married, Natalie was 18 years old and Robert Wagner was 26. They got married originally in December 1957, and then four years later they got a divorce because Natalie felt Robert was too critical of her friends. In May 1969, Natalie married again, but got divorced, and when she ran into Robert again they reconciled, and they remarried in July 1972. This is not surprising, considering they had a Soul Mate Connection in Numerology.

I believe they both fervently wanted this relationship to work. But when anybody escapes through any unhealthy addictions, it will blow apart the most compatible of numbers. Toxic Numbers and substance abuse make for a lethal combination.

Everyone on that boat that night was drinking. There were accusations bandied about, tremendous jealousy, both Natalie and Robert are reported to have thought the other was unfaithful. The Toxic Life Path Numbers would encourage this lack of trust. It didn't stop the fact that they loved each other, but it certainly produced an unstable relationship. Most likely, if she had lived, without major changes in their lifestyle, they would have divorced again.

• LIFE PATH NUMBER DESCRIPTIONS •

Now that you have taken a look at two Life Path couple examples, I am going to give you insight into each Life Path Number, 1 through 9, and how they interact in love.

The 1 Life Path in Love

We are most alive when we're in love.

—JOHN UPDIKE

The 1 Life Path welcomes a partner who will cheerlead them into becoming a success in whatever profession they choose. It is even better if you can find work where you both can share being victorious. The 1 Life Path strives to be their best self and, if you are feeling down, they will encourage you to get back up again. The saying "Never give up, and never surrender" could easily have been first said by a 1 Life Path. You will definitely feel the love and support when a 1 Life Path believes in you.

When it comes to romance, if you praise the 1 Life Path, they will dazzle you in ways you never imagined. Like drinking cool water in the hot desert, telling the 1 Life Path how special they are replenishes their very soul. So turn on the charm and the praise when your 1 Life Path comes home. And you will get everything you could ever hope for in a love relationship.

The biggest pitfall for a 1 Life Path in a relationship is that they spend so much time processing everything in their mind. They have to learn to acknowledge what is going on in their heart and express the love they feel for the people in their life. When it comes to being intimate with their partner, they can run hot and cold. When they don't want a relationship to continue, they can be completely unavailable, but when they do want it to happen, watch out baby!

I think this has a lot to do with that perfectionist streak of wanting everything to be perfect. If there is any discord in the relationship, the 1 can shut down sexually. If they are willing to learn to trust that setbacks with their partner are temporary, then the sexual relationship can become a form of healing for the 1 Life Path. It's all on how they deal with everyday life.

Most 1 Life Paths need to learn to control their tempers. They are opinionated and often have well-thought-out ideas on how things should be. So when they suddenly blow up over something that bothered them, it can be overwhelming and can hurt their partners more than they intend to. The 1s, typically, can become upset, and then they will get right over it, but their partners won't recover as quickly, and these outbursts can interfere with what could be a satisfying relationship.

This is especially damaging if the 1 Life Path is with someone who's a Challenge Number to them. At least a Natural Match like the 1, 5, 7 has a better understanding of what is going on with the 1 Life Path because they are also Numbers who are very cerebral. The other Numerology Life Paths might assume the outbreak is somehow their fault and ask themselves, "What did I do wrong?"

The 1s tend to be pretty intuitive and do not hesitate when it comes to giving advice to others. They really want their partners to succeed, so sometimes the partner will feel criticized. But that's not the intention of the 1 Life Path. They really just want their loved one to be successful, and incidentally, they wish the same thing for themselves. They can be hypercritical about themselves, and when you are critiquing yourself, how hard is it also to critique your partner? Not hard at all.

NATURAL MATCH NUMBERS: *1, 5, and 7*
COMPATIBLE NUMBERS: *2, 3, and 9*
CHALLENGE NUMBERS: *4 and 6*
NEUTRAL NUMBERS: 8

The 2 Life Path in Love

There is only one path to Heaven. On Earth, we call it Love.

—DAVID VISCOTT

When it comes to relationships, the 2 Life Path is someone you can usually count on. These are people who want to make sure everyone gets along. For example if you have a family and two of the siblings are fighting with each other, the 2 Life Path would behave as the mediator. That is why they often become counselors or social workers. They just want to bring peace to everyone. Unless they have numbers in their chart to make them more aggressive, they will follow whomever they consider a good leader. They don't have a problem if they think you are good at what you do.

When it comes to love, or moral support, if the 2 Life Path is living on the Positive side of this Number, this can be the most loving of all the Numbers. They really don't want to fight. They are also extremely intuitive. They can just feel the truth of a situation, and if they learn to trust that inner voice, they will soon learn how often that voice is right.

The Negative side of a 2 can lead to the 2 feeling miserable when they give too much (they can be the ultimate codependent) and feel responsible for everyone. The 2 must be careful not to allow that to happen in their relationships. If you love a 2 Life Path, try not to take advantage of their generosity. They can be very giving, and you should try to reciprocate even when you get comfortable with all that they have to give.

Surprise them occasionally with flowers or a night on the town, something that tells them how much they matter to you. Otherwise your relationship will ultimately backfire. Remember, there are two sides of every Number, and when they live on the Negative side, the 2 can worry too much, become physically stressed, and as a result may become physically exhausted. So they must express themselves, get it out of their body to feel better.

But when it comes to love, in all of my research in Numerology over 21 years, I have found that the 2 Life Path is the love Number. If you meet a 2 who is cold or aloof, that is not coming from the Life Path Number. It is coming from other Numbers in their Personal Numerology Chart.

It is interesting to note that sexually they can be incredibly giving to their partner, doing exactly what their partner wants, but, because of their innate desire to please, the partner may not notice that they have needs as well. This can cause trouble because the next thing you know the 2 shuts down, doesn't want to be touched or loved, and becomes frigid because heart-to-heart conversation is completely at a standstill. That is where counseling can help. If you are willing to work with the 2, you can get it back to the love that it once was. Such an outcome is always possible because the 2 loves being in love, and they really don't want it to end and have to move on to somebody else.

NATURAL MATCH NUMBERS: *2, 4, and 8*
COMPATIBLE NUMBERS: *1, 3, 6, and 9*
CHALLENGE NUMBERS: *5 and 7*

The 3 Life Path in Love

Love is the master key which opens the gates of happiness.

—OLIVER WENDELL HOLMES

When in a relationship, the 3 Life Path is very alive and passionate. When living on the Positive side of their Number, they can easily communicate what they feel. Their emotions are obvious. You can tell what is going on with them just by the sound of their voices. A healthy 3 is someone who laughs, has a great sense of humor, and has picked some kind of career in which they can creatively express themselves for a living.

If they're an unhealthy 3, they can feel sorry for themselves or complain about what is wrong with their world, or how unfair life has been. But that is not the norm. The 3s, by the way, are known for developing emotional crushes. They can be married or dating, and suddenly they have become obsessed with an actor, a political figure, or a business associate. They'll eat, sleep, and breathe the one they're fixated on. Be assured it doesn't mean a thing. If you love a 3 Life Path, you need to know that's just what they do. They have huge hearts and they really love people, and if they think someone they care about is being mistreated, they may obsess about it, because it really troubles them. Ride it out because it will pass.

Their love for you is genuine. The 3 Vibration is loyal, and they want to love you forever. What can shut them down is the fear that you don't care about them. They might feel that most of the love is coming from their side. This can cause a problem in the relationship, but if you tell each other what you think and feel, the relationship can remain stable.

The 3 Vibration makes these people very appealing, and they are also good at dealing with trouble. They can handle a dramatic crisis because they like it when their life is never dull. If you love a 3, don't be surprised when they appear overly dramatic. It is just their way of processing their lives. If you are involved with a 3 Life Path, take steps to keep the romance alive. A lovely restaurant with soft music playing is a good idea. If you normally are a little thrifty, splurging on the 3 Life Path is a wise decision. They will be grateful and want to do something special for you in return.

NATURAL MATCH NUMBERS: *3, 6, and 9*
COMPATIBLE NUMBERS: *1, 2, and 5*
CHALLENGE NUMBERS: *4, 7, and 8*

The 4 Life Path in Love

If you judge people, you have no time to love them.

—MOTHER TERESA

When a 4 Life Path is in a relationship, it is important that they are respected for taking care of their loved ones. They want to do a good job, and providing financial stability is important to them. If they can't find a way to make ends meet, it will interfere with their love relationship. The 4 is direct. They will tell you what they think and feel, and often they need to learn the art of communication, to find a new way to express their thoughts, so as to not hurt their partner's feelings.

When it comes to being intimate, success lies in their willingness to let go. A part of them is so logical, they go through all the emotions and know what they are doing, but they don't necessarily surrender to passion and that is something a 4 Life Path needs to work on. The more they are willing to get into the moment, the better it is for them and their partner. The 4 likes the things in their environment to be organized and everything in its place. For example, if a 4's home is messy, that is not the norm for the 4 Life Path and tells you that something is troubling them. If you live with a 4 and are somewhat sloppy yourself, clean up your mess without them asking you to do so. You will score so many points, and the pleasantly surprised look on their face will be well worth it!

The 4 must watch what comes out of their mouth (often a lethal weapon) and the 4 has to think before they argue with their partners. They should ask themselves, "Is this worth fighting over?" 4s always say they don't want to fight, but somehow they know just what to say to provoke an argument. They do so because they are honest, and do not edit themselves when they speak. Also, 4s don't always tell you what they are feeling. Sometimes they shut down emotionally, and that is something they need to stop doing if they want to sustain a life long relationship.

You can count on 4 Life Path. Unless there are many Numbers in their chart to the contrary, they are very reliable. Another plus, they don't like playing the field. They really do want a partner for life. Their home matters a great deal to them, and they usually have a way of making it cozy for all who visit.

These people love to learn. The more they learn, the more they are fulfilled in life, and dispensing useful information to others makes them feel valued. They need their partner to encourage them to take some chances in life. Otherwise they'll stay in a dead-end job just for the security of a paycheck. A 4 welcomes that kind of input from their partner. Their loved one's encouragement is important to them.

NATURAL MATCH NUMBERS: *2, 4, and 8*
COMPATIBLE NUMBERS: *6 and 7*
CHALLENGE NUMBERS: *1, 3, 5, and 9*

The 5 Life Path in Love

Love one another and you will be happy. It's as simple and as dif-
ficult as that.

—MICHAEL LEUNIG

If you are in a relationship with a 5 Life Path, or considering one, this is what you need to understand. First and foremost, 5s need to feel they have "freedom," and it is your job to help them define exactly what that means. When they are single, the 5s may think they don't want children. They can constantly change careers and often express a desire to move to different locations. Ultimately though, that might sound like a free spirit, but it is not. When the lights go out at night, they feel unhappy and wish they had someone with whom to share their life.

That's where you come in. The 5 can get married, have a settled life with children, and thrive. Still, there's a trick to it. Sometimes they will feel as though the family with all of its wants and needs is depriving them of their "much needed space." This is your cue to seem more independent, yourself. Help to keep the relationship lasting by encouraging the 5 to take a couple of days away from the family. There is the other kind of 5 Life Path that does not like the trappings of marriage and family. If they tell you that, you should listen. It is their truth. And pushing a 5 Life Path to do something they do not want to do is like pushing a rope. It does not work and will cause you great frustration. If you give the 5 Vibration plenty of space, they will happily come running back to you. A few days on their own will help them regain their balance.

The Number 5 is often gifted at many things. If you are in love with a 5, encourage them to focus on one thing at a time, and complete it, before moving on to the next. Then, if you see them getting antsy and feeling, "Oh, you are trying to control me," let them go and see what they do, because, again, they will come back, and trust me it won't take too long. But if you try to restrict them, or tell them what to do, or how to feel, it will backfire with the 5 faster than with any other Number in Numerology.

NATURAL MATCH NUMBERS: *1, 5, and 7*
COMPATIBLE NUMBERS: *3 and 9*
CHALLENGE NUMBERS: *2, 4, and 6*
NEUTRAL NUMBERS: *8*

The 6 Life Path in Love

Love at first sight is easy to understand; it's when two people have
been looking at each other for a lifetime that it becomes a miracle.

—SAM LEVENSON

The 6 is a strong, capable vibration. If anything, the 6 needs to learn
that it is okay to ask for help. They must learn to trust and count on
others, especially in love. On the other hand, it is not uncommon for
a 6 Life Path to idealize their life partner, making them larger than
life. As a result, the reality of their partner, who is only human, sets in
and it is as if the rose-colored glasses have been suddenly yanked off
their face. That beautiful golden haze the 6 was in when they first met
their mate will clear away, and once again they will decide that they
are the only capable one.

In all truth, if you need help, the 6 will make sure it gets done.
They are good at damage control. In fact, it is when things are out of
control they are at their best. They don't even know what to do when
things go well.

The 6 Life Path should try to find a way to either own or manage
a company. If the 6 Life Path you love is working for someone else,
it may cause them unhappiness. I advise you, as their partner, to
encourage them to use their creativity and launch their own business.
If you do, they will feel supported and better about their current situation because they will know you believe in them.

In a relationship, they have a lot of trouble with criticism because
they have such high standards for themselves, and they have this inner
dialogue that is so demanding, that by the time their partner interjects
with anything that sounds negative, it can upset them greatly.

The other thing about a 6 Life Path is that sexually they really want
to please their partner, but then when it is time for the partner to

reciprocate, the 6 might not realize that their partner has no idea of what they want. So a 6 must learn to communicate their needs and desires in bed, because if they are unsatisfied, they start to feel rejected by their partner. In the worst-case scenario, they can completely shut down sexually. It is important that a 6 Life Path finds a way to talk to his or her partner more intimately, and keep the love alive.

NATURAL MATCH NUMBERS: *3, 6, and 9*
COMPATIBLE NUMBERS: *2, 4, and 8*
CHALLENGE NUMBERS: *1, 5, and 7*

The 7 Life Path in Love

> *Loving people live in a loving world. Hostile people live in a hostile*
> *world. Same world.*
>
> —WAYNE W. DYER

How a relationship with a 7 Life Path succeeds really depends on whether the 7 has found a spiritual answer that has fulfilled them, or whether they are still seeking it. If they are still looking, you will find that they are hungry for knowledge. Whether it is picking up a book, attending a New Age conference, or exploring a variety of religious institutions, they are looking for the answers to life's puzzles. They want to know why they are here and what their life's purpose is. A word of caution: when you love a 7 who is abusing drugs or alcohol or engages in any other obsessive behavior, you will not know him or her as their true 7 Life Path self.

When they are on track and have found the spiritual answer they have searched for, the 7s are so loving and willing to give of themselves. Still, there will be times when they have to dig within themselves to get the answers to the questions they seek and get very frustrated in their quest for a sacred truth, and during those times they can be hard to live with. When they finally realize that the ability to discern truth lies within them, and they have a breakthrough, they are a gift to all who know them.

Nature usually plays a big role in their lives. They enjoy the scenic beauty and serenity that nature has to offer. Any large body of water such as a river, lake, or ocean can have a calming effect on them. If you can live near the water as couple, it is good for the relationship.

If they find a spiritual truth that they can believe in, it will be a joy to listen to them talk about it. The 7 Vibration often has a soothing voice that is pleasant to listen to, and because this is true, make great radio broadcasters. Since they have such a love of nature and enjoy their solitude, being a captain of a ship or an airline pilot are also healthy career choices for them to make. If a 7 is happy in their career, it has a profoundly positive impact on their love relationship. When it comes to a loving relationship with you, once they surrender to being in the moment, it can be exhilarating. The sexual relationship will become fulfilling, but if the 7s get too cerebral, it will become your job to bring them back to earth.

NATURAL MATCH NUMBERS: *1, 5, and 7*
COMPATIBLE NUMBERS: *4*
CHALLENGE NUMBERS: *2, 3, 6, 8, and 9*

The 8 Life Path in Love

Treasure the love you receive above all. It will survive long after your
gold and good health have vanished.

—OG MANDINO

If you are looking for love with an 8 Life Path, the first thing you need to know is that most 8 Life Paths must overcome their feelings about image. They generally have an opinion of what things are supposed to look and feel like and have a real need to keep up with the Joneses. That is a problem because the truth is, no matter how many material things they have, and most of them are good at acquiring them, that is not what is going to make them happy.

Then there is the other kind of 8 Life Path, those who actually have issues about possessing money and are apt to put down those who have it. Theirs is a reverse snobbery. The first thing you're going to want to know with the particular 8 you're interested in is what's going on with the financial side of their life, and how do they handle income?

The 8s that work hard and are prosperous can be very generous, but there are others who panic, rush to put their money in the bank, and don't want to spend a dime of it. Again, this is one of the first issues you've got to look at with an 8.

When the 8 Life Paths make love, they sometimes get caught up in this perfection streak of what they think it is supposed to be like. These are the 8s who get caught up in performance anxiety. These 8s are not in the moment; they are not releasing and not able to let go. This is something a loving partner can help the 8 overcome.

If you want to make your 8 Life Path happy, do take care of your body, and make that extra effort to look your best when you get together. Even if they do not mention it, *it really matters* to them. And trust me, if you make that special effort, they will proudly show you off as their partner.

It is a trait of the 8 Life Path to care about their personal appearance, and if they gain a lot of weight or the 8 woman stops wearing makeup, this will definitely mess with their self-esteem. They can be very opinionated, and it is this trait they must overcome in order to be happy in a relationship.

If you let them know why you love them, and point out all the things that you love about them, your praise will go a long way in making them appreciate and value you. And when an 8 Life Path sees you as their ally, you will feel their love completely.

NATURAL MATCH NUMBERS: *2, 4, and 8*

COMPATIBLE NUMBERS: *6*

CHALLENGE NUMBERS: *3, 7, and 9*

NEUTRAL NUMBERS: *1 and 5*

The 9 Life Path in Love

One word frees us of all the weight and pain of life: That word
is love.

—SOPHOCLES

The first thing I would say about the 9 is that they generally have a lot of charisma. Their wisdom draws people to them. But at the same time, these same people can feel subconsciously that the 9s are somehow superior to them. It is very important for a 9 in a relationship to make every effort to let their partners know they see them as an equal. What is also interesting is that the 9 appears to be completely self-contained in every way and always seems to be doing well. Yet inside they often feel that the weight of the world is on their shoulders and that they have too much responsibility. It is incredibly difficult for the 9 Life Path to ask for anyone's help.

In a relationship, the 9 Life Path must learn to let their partner know what their needs and desires are, so that the partner can actually help. If they don't share their thoughts with their partner, there may come a day when the 9 will say, "I'm done here; I just can't do it anymore." Their partner will look at them in shock and say, "You never told me that there was a problem. You never even told me what you needed from me, and now you are leaving?"

If the 9 Life Path you love has emotional scars from their childhood, be a sympathetic ear and help them work through their pain. If you find they will not let it go, find ways to be in the moment together like catching a comedic movie or playing a fun game together. Put on some silly music and dance in your living room! If you help them to get back in the moment and let go of the past, they will be very grateful to you. The 9 Life Path will try to be the world's best parent and to avoid anything their parents did wrong. The 9 must learn that their sincere effort combined with love is more than enough, and that there really is no such thing as the "very best" parent.

On the opposite end of the spectrum, this lack of honest and open discussion is especially serious for a 9 Life Path, because they actually have abandonment issues. They so fear and dread the pain of abandonment that sometimes they won't allow themselves to connect completely with a partner, and eventually the partner leaves in frustration. It's a self-fulfilling prophecy: *That which I have feared most has come upon me.* So the 9 must confront and deal with this part of their personality.

The 9 is a loving energy, and if you have a thriving relationship with one of them, you will want to pinch yourself to make sure you are not dreaming, because you have found such a wonderful human being. This is someone who is hardworking and creative and willing to do whatever they can to help their fellow man.

NATURAL MATCH NUMBERS: *3, 6, and 9*
COMPATIBLE NUMBERS: *1, 2, and 5*
CHALLENGE NUMBERS: *4, 7, and 8*

CHAPTER 9

The Master Numbers 11 and 22

The best and most beautiful things in the world cannot be seen or even touched. They must be felt with the heart.

—HELEN KELLER

A Numerology book cannot be written about how to find gratifying love without discussing the Master Numbers 11 and 22. The Master Numbers apply to people who are born on the 11th or the 22nd. But the Master Numbers also apply to anyone whose Life Path Numbers add up to an 11 or 22 (before they are reduced to the numbers 2 and 4, respectively). Here are two examples:

Jennifer Aniston
Born 2/11/1969
$$2+1+1+1+9+6+9 = 29$$
$$2+9 = 11$$
$$1+1 = 2$$
The 11 is the Master Number.

Clint Eastwood
Born 5/31/1930
$$5+3+1+1+9+3+0 = 22$$
$$2+2 = 4$$
The 22 is the Master Number.

• THE MEANING OF MASTER NUMBERS •

You should definitely take notice if the person you are interested in is a Master Number. But also keep in mind that this 11 or 22 ultimately falls into the 2 Life Path Category or the 4 Life Path Category, respectively. You will recognize some of the traits of these Life Paths (as defined in Chapter 8).

When a person has a Master Number in their chart, that individual will have incredibly high standards. **Jennifer Aniston** is a great example of the Master Number 11, because not only does her entire birth date break down to the Master Number 11, but she was also born on the 11th. This tells me that Jennifer has tremendous tenacity and is very driven. It is as if she has a monkey on her back saying, "What are you doing with your life? What is the next step? What are you going to do to stay sensational?"

Master Number 11s often have issues with their bodies and work to perfect them. If you look at the early career shots of Jennifer Aniston, she was about 20 to 30 pounds heavier. She then dropped the weight and it was clear that mastering her body was part of her mission statement.

America became enamored with her when she first appeared on *Friends*. The show was originally created as a showcase for Courteney Cox, but in no time all eyes were on Jennifer Aniston, who played the character Rachel. Everyone wanted to emulate her, and her haircut became a phenomenon. People told their hairdresser, "I want the Rachel haircut." Then when she let her hair grow long, her fans wanted their hair to grow long, too.

To this day she cannot go anyplace without being photographed and her body discussed. If she is on David Letterman or any of the talk shows, she always makes sure we see her legs, and they all talk about how great her legs are. She has those Master Numbers, so she puts herself under tremendous pressure to look forever young, knowing that she does not want to disappoint. Appearing nude on the cover of *GQ* magazine right before turning 40, and looking fantastic, was her way of showing she had mastered her body.

One of the things that Brad Pitt said about his break up with Jennifer is that he was ready for children, and she wanted to focus on expanding her movie career. Sadly, the Master Number 11 wants children and a loving partner with whom they can share their life. I know by the numbers how much she loved her husband at the time. I believe she needed Brad Pitt to give her a moment to focus on that part of her life, but he chose not to wait. We all know the story of what Brad Pitt did next, and the choices he made while still married to Jennifer. When he left her for Angelina Jolie, America mourned with her and felt her pain.

As of this writing, Jennifer has had several major hits—*The Break-Up, Marley & Me,* and *He's Just Not That Into You*—that each earned over $150 million worldwide. Her movie career is on track, and I think love is what she really wants to master next. It is clear from her Numerology Chart that she wants to get love right but has not mastered it yet.

Clint Eastwood is the Master Number 22, and he is an excellent example of this Master Number. His career has spanned more than 50 years. Interestingly, as a very young man, he was rejected as an actor because some producers in Hollywood felt his Adam's apple was too big.

While visiting a friend at CBS News studio, a casting director spotted him and cast him in the TV show *Rawhide* because, she said, "He looked like a cowboy." So that was the beginning of his TV career. Still he had to move to Europe to become a movie star. At one time, he was Europe's most famous American movie star and still almost unknown here. After the Italian spaghetti westerns he made became hits in the States, Clint Eastwood became known as the ultimate macho man and is now considered a legend.

Not only has he had an amazing career as an actor, he also has had a stellar career as a director. Hilary Swank, Morgan Freeman, and Clint himself all won Oscars for *Million Dollar Baby* in 2004. In 2003, Tim Robbins and Sean Penn both won Oscars under his direction in *Mystic River*.

Clint Eastwood is known for letting the actors be themselves, and instead of saying "cut" or "action," he just says, "okay." He is also known for getting actors to give their best performance in the first take. So it is legendary that he consistently finishes films he directs on schedule, and on budget, which is almost unheard of in Hollywood.

I am convinced that all this excellence comes from his Master Number 22. Not only did he master his own persona as an actor, but he has also mastered the ability to direct and bring out the best performance in other actors. It is a very cerebral thing that he is doing, which perfectly sums up the Master Number 22.

When it comes to his love life, he has seven kids, with five different women. It would seem that in mastering his career, he did not necessarily master his personal life until much later. He has been happily married since 1996 to Dina Ruiz, a news anchorwoman.

When you have the Master Number 22, it is all about being methodical and getting the job done. It is hard to perfect your career and your personal life at the same time. One part can suffer and, in the case of Jennifer Aniston and Clint Eastward, career has definitely been their first priority.

What both Master Numbers 11 and 22 have in common is that feeling of "what's next?"; it keeps them in perpetual motion and forever getting ready for the next project.

Jennifer Aniston is still young and the fact that she has the Double Master Number (born on the 11th and a birth date that reduces to 11, before it becomes a 2 Life Path), she has a lot more to offer the world. I think she will surprise us in her upcoming performances. Instead of being boxed in as America's Sweetheart, she will come up with something we have yet to see her do. That is how Master Numbers operate. Clint Eastwood is already a legend, and whatever he decides to do next, all eyes will be on him.

So again, if you are interested in a Master Number 11 or 22, these people care deeply, and take things to heart, and no matter how much success they have, there is always an anxious voice inside saying, "You are running out of time. You have not done enough."

I recommend that you help your Master Number find a spiritual base that they can believe in, and encourage them to learn to meditate. Physical exercise plays a very big role in the life of the Master Numbers 11 and 22. Yoga, which combines meditation with exercise, is a good thing for Master Numbers to practice because their stress can be extreme. They must be aware that if they hold all their anxiety inside without dealing with it mentally, they can become physically ill. It is not uncommon for a Master Number 11 or 22 to become sick because they are not dealing with all their mental turmoil. Keeping a journal is a wonderful idea for those with a Master Numbers 11 or 22 because they can release on paper all the negative thoughts that are troubling them, and then let it go.

If you are creating a Chart Comparison with a Master Number, you want to make a note that they are here to master their life. But the Life Path definition of a 2 in love (for the 11), and a Life Path definition of a 4 in love (for the 22) will give you the information you need to understand the person in question. This Master Number Rule applies if you are born on the 11th or the 22nd. It also applies when you are breaking down a name and find an 11 before it reduces to a 2, or a 22 before it reduces to a 4.

• FURTHER STUDY •

I also discuss the topic of the Master Numbers in Chapter 14, where I spend time interpreting the two numbers that come before a Life Path is reduced to one digit. The 11 and 22 are included, and I cover what some Numerologists call the Master Numbers 33 and 44, because it is important to understand what the repeating numbers mean before you reduce the Life Path to one digit. Be sure to read Chapter 14 to learn a little more about the Master Numbers.

CHAPTER 10

The Attitude Number: How's Your Attitude?

Listening is an attitude of the heart, a genuine desire to be with another which both attracts and heals.

—J. Isham

The **Attitude Number** is the outlook a person presents to the world. It can confuse you in your quest for the perfect mate. For instance, the person you are interested in might have a **3 Attitude Number** and seem to be extroverted and fun, someone who likes people and crowds. In reality, he or she might be a **7 Life Path** who requires sustained periods of solitude and silence just to stay sane. The Attitude Number can be the great deceiver; it can be the Vibration you fall in love with when the real person is different. Before you leap, look over all six Numbers that make up the Numerology Blueprint.

To find the Attitude Number, take the birth month and day and reduce them to one digit. As an example, we will compare the Natural Match Attitude Numbers of **Tim McGraw** and **Faith Hill**.

Tim McGraw

Tim McGraw was born on 5/1

$$5+1 = 6$$

Tim McGraw has a 6 Attitude.

Faith Hill

Faith Hill was born on 9/21

$$9+2+1 = 12$$
$$= 1+2 = 3$$

Faith Hill has a 3 Attitude.

The Natural Match Couple

You can't beat a Natural Match combination in a love affair, and the 3 and 6 Attitudes are a Natural Match. What is nice about a 6 Attitude in a man is that he will make the woman in his life feel cherished. If he has children, he should be a really good dad. Everyone who knows Tim McGraw says he is a wonderful father.

Faith Hill has a 3 Attitude, which means a skill in communicating, and it resonates strongly in her singing. Tim and Faith met in 1996 at a concert in which they were both performing. Faith was the opening act for Tim, and the tour was called *Spontaneous Combustion*. During the tour, Tim proposed one night, just before she performed. At the time, she did not have a chance to answer him. She wrote her response in a mirror. Shortly after the tour ended, Tim and Faith were married.

Their Attitude Numbers are compatible, and so are their Life Path Numbers. Faith and Tim have gone on the road together and broken records with the money they have made. The country audiences adore them. They are truly country music royalty. When I look at their

Attitude Numbers and the rest of their Charts, it seems to me that they will be together for the long haul. It is a true blessing that they met and, by the Numbers, they were absolutely meant to be.

A couple whose Attitude Numbers are a Challenge is **Madonna** and **Guy Ritchie.**

Madonna

Madonna was born on 8/16

$$8+1+6 = 15$$
$$= 1+5 = 6$$

Madonna has a 6 Attitude.

Guy Ritchie

Guy Ritchie was born on 9/10

$$9+1+0 = 10$$
$$= 1+0 = 1$$

Guy Ritchie has a 1 Attitude.

The Challenge Couple

The Attitude Numbers 1 and 6 are a Challenge to each other. This can become a real power struggle. The 1 Attitude wants to feel respected and listened to, and the 6 Attitude does not want to feel controlled by anyone.

As of this writing, Madonna and Guy Ritchie are getting divorced. I was concerned about this relationship from the beginning because, not only were their Attitude Numbers a Challenge, but also Madonna's Life Path 2 is a Challenge to Guy's Life Path 7. The more Challenge numbers in a chart comparison, the bigger the potential problem. The word is that Madonna, while in concert, told her audience that Guy is "emotionally retarded." I am sure this is not true about Guy, but when you have Numbers that are Toxic, you can easily misinterpret each other. That is why this relationship imploded.

The 6 Attitude also means that Madonna wanted to be a mom. They have a lovely daughter and son and had adopted another child. Insiders report that Guy did not support the adoption. This would not surprise me, because his numbers are not as geared towards parenting as Madonna's are. Madonna recently adopted again without having a partner in her life.

So, if you see these Challenges in your Attitude Numbers, it helps you realize what could possibly occur in the future. Or, when trouble does brew in a relationship you are in already, you can say, "Okay, this is where we are different," and get to work on it. You don't have to let things fester and destroy the relationship, as was the case with Madonna and Guy Ritchie.

• ATTITUDE NUMBER DESCRIPTIONS •

1 Attitude Number
If you are interested in someone with the 1 Attitude, know that this is a competitive Vibration. I don't care what they may tell you, these people like to win. If they present you with their ideas, they usually have plenty of backup evidence to prove their point. It's almost as though they are in a courtroom. If you praise and encourage the 1 Attitude Number, they will do anything to prove your faith in them. On the other hand, if you are too demanding, or try to control them—let's say you issue the command "Go to the right"—be advised that they will almost certainly go to the left. So be aware of that trait in a relationship with a 1 Attitude. Easy does it.

2 Attitude Number
If you are interested in someone with the 2 Attitude, know that this is a sensitive Vibration. They are very aware of the feelings of the

people around them. If you, their loved one, are in a bad mood, your mood will affect them. If someone is too critical of them, it can ruin their day. They are more sensitive than they want to be. The gift of a 2 Attitude is their undeniable psychic insight into life. When they first get an intuition about something, it tends to be correct. If they second-guess these insights too often, they will find doing so to be a mistake. This Attitude Number really welcomes love.

3 Attitude Number

If you are interested in someone with the 3 Attitude, know that they will be the one cracking jokes or laughing really hard at someone else's. They communicate some very important information with a one-liner. If things get too serious, they try to lighten things up. Sometimes they can make life a little more dramatic than it has to be; they are definitely given to overreacting. So if you want to pursue this relationship, you have to remember that the 3 is a natural performer, and they play to an enthusiastic audience. If that is you, you can have a lot of fun with them.

4 Attitude Number

If you are interested in someone with the 4 Attitude, this person likes to have instructions; he or she does not like surprises. This Vibration hesitates to act on an idea, even a good one, because they are afraid they cannot get it done well. They must move on their ideas, or they will surely regret it later. They are loyal. If a 4 Attitude loves you, they will be with you for a long time. They care about the person they love and are always trying to help you avoid any pitfalls. Sometimes they can come off as killjoys, but that is not their intention. For instance, it is a beautiful day and you want to be out in the sun. The 4 would bring up the danger of cancer, suggest you lather on lotion, containing a strong SPF, and then repeat the latest warnings on the ineffectiveness of SPF lotions. They are not trying to ruin your beautiful day, but are truly concerned about your health. If you keep this in mind, you've got it made.

5 Attitude Number

If you are interested in someone with the 5 Attitude, they are likely to be high energy, excited about life, and looking for the new and different. They appreciate when someone goes out of their way to throw a special party for them. The 5s love life, and the thing they must avoid is falling into the trap of too much of a good thing—i.e., drugs, sex, and booze. Usually, they are avid seekers of knowledge. They devour information, and often you will meet them at a seminar or a convention. Wherever there is a gathering of lots of people, from a political rally to a concert, you are bound to find more 5 Attitudes than any other Number in the Attitude Category. So if you also have lots of energy, what fun this will be!

6 Attitude Number

If you are interested in someone with the 6 Attitude, know that they are the nurturing number. If they choose not to marry and have children, they will often be found running a large company and treating their employees like family. They are natural leaders, and people are drawn to them. It is hard for the 6 to just relax and enjoy what they have. They do not know what to do with themselves if everything is running effortlessly. It is important for them to learn that once they get through this list of to-dos, it is okay to stop and take a deep breath and say, "I have earned this time to relax and enjoy myself with the loved ones in my life. And that is what I am going to do."

7 Attitude Number

If you are interested in someone with the 7 Attitude, you will be drawn to them—not necessarily because they are talking, as much as they are watching you. They catch your eye and you wonder who he or she might be. The 7 Attitude knows how to share their opinions, but they do not share them with just anybody. Instead, they study everyone. In the entertainment world it is not uncommon for the 7 Attitude to produce or direct others because they do see all the details. This is a Number that usually loves the ocean and often looks for a career that enables them to explore the world. Doing so makes them happy. If you have met someone with a 7 Attitude that has not found their brand of spirituality, they can be cynical. At first it may be amusing, but after a while it is exhausting.

8 Attitude Number

If you are interested in someone with the 8 Attitude, know that those with this Vibration always speak their mind. If you are oversensitive, this is not the match for you. They don't mean to, but they do not consider how they come off, and therefore can hurt you. If you are attractive, you will be sure to catch an 8 Attitude's eye. They have a great appreciation for beauty.

This Attitude Number enjoys hard work, but they want to make sure they are financially compensated. Also they must enjoy what they do. Just working for a paycheck is not going to be enough. They are best in charge, and if living on the Positive side of their Number, can run a business efficiently. Having authority figures telling them how to behave does not go over well with the 8 Attitude. They have to find a way to be comfortable with and enjoy the money they work so hard for. The 8 Attitude needs to find that perfect balance and develop a good relationship with money.

9 Attitude Number

If you are interested in someone with the 9 Attitude, know that others will look to these people for guidance and see them as leaders. The 9 Attitude is always seen as someone who knows where they are going, and as someone who can help others get there, too. As a natural leader, some people will feel a little intimidated by their presence. If a 9 makes you feel insecure, then this Attitude Number is not for you. The 9 Attitude is really here to help everyone with whom they come into contact. They need to embrace the present in order to have a great time in this moment.

Whether they were the baby or the eldest, they always feel a sense of responsibility for their original family and must find a balance to keep themselves healthy. When it comes to their present relationship, if they have kids, they will take pride in being emotionally available to them. The 9 Attitude is a creative Vibration and must express itself in some way.

CHAPTER 11

The Destiny Number: Are You Destined to be Together?

To love is to receive a glimpse of heaven.

—KAREN SUNDE

The **Destiny Number** can never be changed because it is derived from your Birth Certificate Name. It is a foreshadowing as to what direction you are headed in your lifetime. When you are looking for the Destiny Number of your partner, you take the full Birth Certificate Name and reduce it to one digit. We will use **Harrison Ford** and **Calista Flockhart** as our example.

Harrison Ford's Birth Certificate Name is Harrison Ford:
DOB: 7/13/1942

1   +9 +6   +6   = 22 = 2+2= **4 Soul Number**

HARRISON FORD

8   +9+9 +1   +5 +6   +9+4 = 51 = 5+1 = **6 Personality Number**

4 (Soul Number) + 6 (Personality Number) = 10 = 1 + 0 = 1 Destiny Number
Harrison Ford's Destiny Number is a 1.

Calista Flockhart's Birth Certificate's Name is Calista Kay Flockhart:
DOB: 11/11/1964

1 +9   +1   +1   +6   +1 =   19 = 1+9 = 10 = 1+0 = 1 Soul Number

CALISTA KAY FLOCKHART

3 +3 +1+2   +2   +7+6+3   +3+2+8 +9+2 = 51 = 5+1 = **6 Personality Number**

1 (Soul Number) + 6 (Personality Number) = 7 Destiny Number

Calista Flockhart's Destiny Number is a 7.

The Natural Match Couple

Harrison Ford II is the name that appears on Ford's actual birth certificate. However, in Numerology, you do not break down suffixes such as II, Jr., etc. You only break down the purity of the name. Harrison Ford's Birth Name gives him a 1 Destiny Number, and when you break down Calista Flockhart's Birth Name, you get a 7 Destiny Number. The 1 and the 7 are a Natural Match in Numerology and helps explain why these two have had such an enduring relationship.

Knowing that Harrison Ford has a 1 Destiny helps us to understand his drive and determination to be the very best at what he does. With massive hits like *Star Wars* and the *Indiana Jones* movie series, he has had a solid film career, and many times has been chosen as the top box office draw by movie theater owners. His latest *Indiana Jones* film was also a box office hit, again proving that moviegoers adore him and will continue to support his career endeavors.

Calista Flockhart has a 7 Destiny Number, and the 7 Vibration explains her strong need for privacy. She has also had a solid career with her hit television series *Ally McBeal* and her more recent series, *Brothers and Sisters*. Yet for someone who has been around as long as she has, the public still knows very little about her, and that is just the way she likes it.

When these two first got together in 2002, I ran their Numerology Charts and saw that not only were their Destiny Numbers a Natural Match, but so were their Life Path Numbers 6 (Calista) and 9 (Harrison). At that time Calista had recently adopted a baby boy. Since she is a 6 Life Path, being a mother would help to fulfill her strong maternal instincts. Harrison Ford also has a 6 in his chart, and when they started dating, he immediately stepped in to help raise her son. Everyone who knows them as a couple says he treats her adopted son as his own.

Before their relationship, there was a lot of speculation that Calista might be suffering from an eating disorder because she was incredibly thin. Once they started dating, she gained some weight and looked much healthier.

Harrison Ford had just been through a difficult divorce after 18 years of marriage and looked emotionally drained. Yet, once he and Calista got together, he seemed rested and happily content. Since there is a 22-year age difference, many in the media thought the relationship was a part of a midlife crisis for Harrison Ford and would soon end.

I knew better just by studying their Numerology charts and felt confident that this was the real deal. In 2009, Harrison proposed to Calista on Valentine's weekend, and this is wonderful news for the two of them, their young son, and, I might add, for all of us who admire and wish them well. They have a very strong connection in Numerology, and their Destiny Numbers 1 and 7 are a Natural Match, which further confirms that their love was meant to be.

• DESTINY NUMBER DESCRIPTIONS •

Destiny Number 1

If the person you are interested in has a 1 Destiny Number:
These people are destined to be independent. They push themselves hard and never stop trying to be the very best at everything they do. The 1 Destiny Number can inspire others to be at their best as well.

It is important for the Number 1 to have goals, but it is equally important for them to rest between triumphs. People with this Vibration need to work on savoring the moment, as they always feel that they are running out of time. The 1 Destiny Number has to remember that, as human beings, we can only do what we can while we can, for as the poet Robert Browning wrote so long ago, "A man's reach must exceed his grasp, or what's a heaven for?"

It's okay to make mistakes on the way to achieving excellence. It would be wise for the 1 Destiny Number to center themselves with yoga or one of the other Eastern schools of exercise and meditation.

Destiny Number 2

If the person you are interested in has a 2 Destiny Number:
They are here to bring peace to the world. The 2 Destiny Number is all about bringing people together. They are the mediators and altruistic in their search for justice; you will often see 2s involved in civil rights and at the forefront of peace movements. It is important for them to stay strong within themselves, as they can become overwhelmed with sympathy for the less fortunate, and then find they are no longer effective in their work. They have the ability to love unconditionally and that is a real blessing to their mates and children. The 2 Vibration is a psychic Energy and they will find that some of their dreams come true or they have déjà vu when they meet someone. They must maintain a distance from those they help, or their emotions will get the better of them, and despair can cause them to retreat into themselves. This would be unfortunate for all of us, as their destiny is to stay in the world and help provide hope to those who have lost it.

Destiny Number 3

If the person you are interested in has a 3 Destiny Number:
They are here to express themselves in creative ways and motivate others. These individuals are here to encourage others to be the best they can be. The 3 Destiny Number will find a way to master some form of communication. They do so through writing, speaking, selling, etc. The 3s are here to bring happiness to others in various ways. They have a need to make life around them better, and how things look is important to them. They should pick partners who are

on healthy paths, not more dysfunctional people to heal, so as not to fall into depression. They are a joyous presence in the world, not just for others but for themselves as well.

Destiny Number 4

If the person you are interested in has a 4 Destiny Number:
They are here to provide stability and a solid foundation for themselves and the people in their lives. They are excellent teachers because they like to share what they have learned with all of us. A person with a 4 Destiny cares about their home. It is not uncommon for them to become architects, interior designers, or to work in construction. They enjoy communing with nature, whether by hiking or camping. The 4 Destiny is blessed with having inventive minds. They must have the courage to act on their own innovations.

Destiny Number 5

If the person you are interested in has a 5 Destiny Number:
They are here to live life to the fullest and get others to do the same. This Vibration is called to transform our daily lives. The 5 Vibration brings magic to everything they touch. This Vibration rejoices in each new adventure. If you have a quick wit, you will never have a better audience. It is the Destiny of the 5 to travel because each trip gives them knowledge that they will value for the rest of their life. Because of their passion for living, they have to be careful not to overindulge in food, sex, or drugs.

Destiny Number 6

If the person you are interested in has a 6 Destiny Number:
They are here to take charge and learn that no one can do it all. The 6 has great intuitive powers (think 6th sense). They feel things deeply and even have dreams that come true. They are hard workers, and

you can count on them to come through for you. If a Destiny Number 6 is a social worker, he or she can make a shelter, or a halfway house, seem like a real home. They bring a certain warmth with them wherever they go, and are fiercely loyal. Anyone lucky enough to know this person will feel very safe indeed.

Destiny Number 7

If the person you are interested in has a 7 Destiny Number:
They are here to discover the meaning of life and to find peace in the answer. To be fulfilled, they must ask these vital questions—always remembering that humans are finite, and it is not possible for us to know all. It is when these people are alone that answers come to them, but sooner or later they must reach out to share what they have gleaned. A good way for them to do so is through keeping a journal. Sometimes the answers they seek come slowly, and they can become skeptical and lack a belief system. That's the time they should find solace in the world of nature, and the beauty of the physical world. They must remember that their spiritual legacy is to live a spiritual life. The 7s influence on others is far greater than they can ever imagine.

Destiny Number 8

If the person you are interested in has an 8 Destiny Number:
They are here to manifest abundance in their life, and to share it with others. A great deal of this security is based on what they believe. They either believe they can be very successful, or that they can never catch a break. They need to find a balance.

When living on the Positive side of the 8 Destiny Number, the 8 can do very well helping others organize their finances. The 8 living on the Negative side of the Vibration may suffer from feeling victimized, and that can manifest into physical and mental pain. I recommend they do appropriate Affirmations in Chapter 22 to overcome these feelings. The key for the 8s is to keep their sense of humor and stay focused on their goals. If they do this, they will most certainly achieve the success for which they were destined.

Destiny Number 9

If the person you are interested in has a 9 Destiny Number:

They are here to share their wisdom. The 9 Destiny must impart their knowledge to others and help them achieve a state of higher consciousness. They are a formidable force and that is why people turn to them for leadership in a crisis. Their main test in life is forgiving and letting go of the past. Because they are so evolved (9 is the number of completion), people can sometimes misinterpret their words as dismissive and feel that they do not want them in their life. The 9 actually needs and welcomes love and friendship. They also know in their heart of hearts that they are not always that strong, and sometimes they could use a little help. They must learn to ask for it by name. As they achieve balance in their own path, it is their destiny to teach others how to do the same.

So these are the Destiny Numbers. If the Life Path Number is a Challenge to the Destiny Number, it will take a little more time to achieve our Destiny, but no matter what, *we are bound to get there*!

CHAPTER 12

The Maturity Number: Midlife is not Always a Crisis

Love is but the discovery of ourselves in others, and the delight in the recognition.

—ALEXANDER SMITH

The Maturity Number is not as well known in mainstream Numerology, but through my counseling I have come to see that the Maturity Number is especially relevant to couples. This Vibration will reveal itself in midlife, and this information gives you an idea of what you can expect at that time.

To recap what we've learned so far, there are six Numbers that make up a person's Numerology Blueprint: the three Numbers found in the name give us the Soul Number, the Personality Number, and the Power Name Number. The person's actual date of birth gives us the Birth Day Number, the Attitude Number, and the Life Path Number. These 6 Numbers are the basic blueprint of that person's identity. We have also covered the Destiny Number, which comes from the Birth

Certificate Name, and that is the Number that gives you a sense of what you can achieve. This is how you get your Maturity Number: take your **Destiny Number**, add it to your **Life Path Number**, and reduce it to one digit. When I discovered my Maturity Number, it was a special moment for me. My birth name is Glynis Kathleen McCants, which breaks down to the Destiny Number 1, and I have the Life Path Number 3.

Life Path Number (3) + Destiny Number (1) = 4 Maturity Number.

My husband's Birth Certificate Name is Charles St. Denny Youngblood, which breaks down to the Destiny Number 9, and he has the Life Path 4.

Life Path Number (4) + Destiny Number (9) = 13 = 1+3 = 4 Maturity Number.

Charlie's Maturity Number is a 4.

I was blown away to discover that my husband and I have the same Maturity Number! I didn't even know I had a 4 in my Numerology Chart until I learned about this number. So not only had I met the love of my life and we were planning to get married, but our Maturity Number 4 is all about finding a partner, settling down, and having a true commitment.

Meeting and marrying Charlie was a part of my Maturity Number, and the fact that it was the same for him proved a blessing for us. It means the things we want in life are very similar. I knew that sharing the 4 Maturity Number would only enhance our relationship.

Since we used Paul Newman and Joanne Woodward to help us find out about the Numerology Blueprint in Chapter 2, let's use them as our Maturity Number example as well. Paul Newman's birth certificate name is **Paul Leonard Newman:**

```
1 +3      +5+6  +1        +5      +1   = 22 = 2+2 = 4 Soul Number
 | |       | |   |         |       |
P A U L   L E O N A R D   N E W M A N
 |  |  |   |   |  | |  |   |  | |   |
 7  +3 +3  +5  +9+4 +5  +5 +4  +5 = 50 = 5+0 = 5 Personality Number
```

Soul Number (4) + Personality Number (5) = 9 Destiny Number
Paul Newman's Destiny Number is a 9.

Paul's Destiny Number is a 9. When you add it to his 8 Life Path Number:

Destiny Number (9) + Life Path Number (8) = 17 = 1+7 = 8.
Paul Newman's Maturity Number is an 8.

Since we used Paul Newman as an example on how to get the Maturity Number, we will cut right to it with Joanne Woodward. Her Birth Certificate Name is **Joanne Gignilliat Trimmier Woodward.**

When you break down her birth name, you get the Destiny Number 7. You then take her Destiny Number 7 and add it to her Life Path Number 6.

Destiny Number (7) + Life Path Number (6) = 13 = 1+3 = 4.
Joanne Woodward's Maturity Number is a 4.

Paul and Joanne's Maturity Numbers are the **4** and the **8**, which is a Natural Match in Numerology.

In the case of Paul Newman, you look at the 8 and say, 8s are here to master the art of establishing financial stability, which he certainly achieved.

In Joanne Woodward's case, with her 4 Maturity Number, not only was she taken care of financially, but she also went to Sarah Lawrence College to get a degree, along with her daughter, when she was in her 60s. Keep in mind, a 4 cannot get enough information and is always seeking knowledge. So Joanne doing this later in life is a good example of the influence of the 4 Maturity Number. Joanne and Paul's Maturity Numbers are the capstone of two very compatible Charts.

Maturity Number Descriptions

You may be in a marriage, getting older, and thinking to yourself, "Will I be with this person for the rest of my life?" Perhaps your children are grown and on their own, and it doesn't feel as though you and your partner have a connection. The Maturity Number can give you some insights as to how you might want to deal with that feeling.

The 1 Maturity Number

If the person you are interested in is a 1 Maturity Number:

A 1 Maturity Number consists of people who, as they have gotten older, feel the need to make a mark on the world that is uniquely their own. So if you are married to someone who is a 1 Maturity Number, and right now they seem not as disciplined as you'd like, just know that this will change as they get older.

They can't escape their Maturity Number. That 1 Vibration is going to show up, and it's going to help them make a difference in the latter part of their life. The 1 Maturity Number will become more passionate, more excited, and more determined to do something with their life. If they have other 1 Vibrations in their Numerology Blueprint, maybe a 1 Life Path, then you may have already seen some of this in their behavior, but as they mature this will intensify. So, that can be very good news for you. On the down side, their ambitions can make them appear overbearing. Encourage them to think before they speak to people, as it really isn't their intention to be offensive.

The 2 Maturity Number
If the person you are interested in is a 2 Maturity Number:
The 2 Maturity Number will be somebody who, if he or she has not already done so, will now find love. Perhaps earlier on they couldn't meet the right person, but as they get older, they come into a loving, healing relationship. It also means that the gift of intuition, that gut instinct of knowing what is true, will become much stronger.

Whatever those hard lessons were in the 2 Maturity Number's life, as they get older, they are just going to have a natural sense of what is the right thing to do. I think the 2 Maturity Number is a huge blessing, and ultimately, there will be more harmony in the life of this person. So if you are in love with someone with that Maturity Number, know that is where they are headed. You may not see this in your loved one right now, maybe they seem frustrated and angry, but all of that will calm down as they get older.

The 3 Maturity Number
If the person you are interested in is a 3 Maturity Number:
The 3 Maturity Number is a good Vibration, because it is about lightening up; it is about getting in touch with that inner child, having a lot more fun, and becoming more social. They have more time to spend listening to good music, going to nice parties, and getting to know people.

Let's say that their Life Path Number is a 4 or an 8, and that they have had some negative intensity in the earlier part of life. With this 3 Vibration, they are bound to get to a happier place. The 3 Maturity Number will make more friends as they get older. For someone who is in love with the 3 Maturity Number, if this person is too uptight right now, just know that they will loosen up.

They may also get in touch with their creative side, writing their memoirs or joining their church choir to sing their heart out. The 3 Vibration finds ways to express itself, as this Maturity Number comes into play.

The 4 Maturity Number

If the person you are interested in is a 4 Maturity Number:

The 4 Maturity Number does invite someone with whom you can share your life. If their Life Path is a 1, 5, or 7—high energy Vibrations—the 4 can calm that down. As they get older and come into their own, they just get more practical about knowing what they want. When they have an idea, they will follow through with it, instead of feeling as though they are always out of time. It is really a remarkable Vibration for establishing that nest egg for the future.

The 4 Maturity Number has to guard against becoming too narrow-minded or opinionated. They may give people a hard time for what they believe, especially if it is not in alignment with what the 4 believes.

The 5 Maturity Number

If the person you are interested in is a 5 Maturity Number:

A 5 Maturity Number means "fasten your seatbelts." As they get older, life will become more exciting. They will realize that they are free to do things they never had time to do before. I think of those mothers and fathers who raised their children and who were so responsible: it is finally their time to play.

The 5 Maturity Number will have time to experience the world. They will try foods they have never eaten before, change their hairdos, and look at life with childlike wonder. You'll hear them exclaiming, "Wow, I am so glad I did all this before my life was over."

The 5 must be careful not to overwhelm themselves with too many ideas. They could then be tempted to just throw up their arms and say, "The heck with it!" They should pick one thing, focus on it, and go for it. Then focus on one more, and so on. As they grow older, their life becomes an ever more exciting endeavor. The 5 Maturity Number is all about living life to the fullest.

The 6 Maturity Number
If the person you are interested in is a 6 Maturity Number:
This Number encourages these people in their later years to have a deeper connection with their friends, family, and even their community. They feel this nurturing need to make sure that others are taken care of, not just themselves. Financially, they will create a personal nest egg and will also be willing to give to charities and anything else they feel will make a difference in our world.

Maybe they were just too busy in their earlier years to form close relationships and find they have time now. By the time their life is over, there will be many people who love and value them. This is especially true if they didn't have 6s in the rest of their Chart, and a 6 showed up in their Maturity Number. They will find the 6 Maturity Number to be a real blessing in later years.

The 7 Maturity Number
If the person you are interested in is a 7 Maturity Number:
As these folks get older, they find themselves contemplating the big questions in life, and they will do whatever they can to get the answers they seek.

If the Maturity Number is the only 7 in their chart, it's all about finding their spiritual base. With the 7 Maturity Number, they will be asking, "Why do I exist?" Now, if they already have a 7 Vibration or two in those six Numbers that make up their Numerology Blueprint, they have to be careful not to become complete hermits, ditch their loved ones, and simply focus on the need to seek answers to all of those unanswered questions.

The 7 Maturity Number will encourage them to trust their intuition. They have a natural psychic ability to discern what is true and what isn't. They will not waste time putting up with someone who is not sincere. They have no time for it, and just want a partner who knows what he or she is talking about.

If you love someone with the 7 Maturity Number and it's not a Natural Match to yours, just know that solitude is a part of them. If you cannot have long periods of silence with your partner, you have to keep in mind how that will affect the long-term part of your relationship.

The 8 Maturity Number

If the person you are interested in is an 8 Maturity Number:
This time of life is about establishing financial success once and for all. They will come into that feeling of, "I'm alright, and I'm handled." One lesson for the 8 Maturity Number is to learn to disconnect with the money, and not to get caught up in how much more money they can make. It is about embracing the fact that they have enough for themselves and enough to help other people as well.

Their homes and their surroundings will matter to them. After working so hard to accomplish their financial goals, they can now relax and enjoy the freedom it provides. If they do this, they are going to be very happy with the Vibration of that 8 Maturity Number.

If they do have the 8 Vibration somewhere else in their Numerology Blueprint, you may have seen them struggling to establish financial security. This ease with money will show up later in their lives, as their 8 Maturity Number starts to kick in. So if you know one that is struggling right now, just be aware that in later life, there is a good chance that it won't be an issue.

The 9 Maturity Number

If the person you are interested in is a 9 Maturity Number:
The 9 Maturity Number feels called upon to leave the world a better place than when they found it. As they get older, this is going to be an even more important priority.

Think of a disaster like Hurricane Katrina or the tsunami of 2004, someone with a 9 Maturity Number would fly there to offer help, or at least contribute all their spare money to the victims if they couldn't get there. They will organize others for the task as well, and see that they carry through with the mission

If there are 9s elsewhere in their Numerology Blueprint, then this has already been part of their life purpose. One of the things they have to overcome, if they are a 9 Maturity Number, is any resentment of unfair treatment in their childhoods.

As they get older, they will realize that we are all connected and ask themselves what they can do to leave their mark in a positive way. If you love someone who has the 9 Maturity Number, but has a Personal Numerology Chart filled with more self-centered Energy, be aware that they will become more involved in unselfish service to others in their later years. Just be prepared to join them on their journey and be willing to abandon some of your own selfish desires for the greater good. If your Personal Numerology Charts are in sync, then this can be an exhilarating time for both of you.

CHAPTER 13

Every Life Path Love Combination: Have You Truly Met Your Match?

In the arithmetic of love, one plus one equals everything, and two minus one equals nothing.

—MIGNON MCLAUGHLIN

In this chapter, we are going to look at how every Life Path Number interacts with every other Life Path Number. Note that the order of the number in each combination does not matter. If you are a 2 Life Path in a relationship with a 1 Life Path, this means the same as a 1 Life Path in a relationship with a 2 Life Path (the combinations are not listed twice).

The 1 Life Path with the 1 Life Path

This relationship is considered a Natural Match in Numerology. When two 1 Life Path Numbers come together, it is so important that they pick a common goal. They must say, "We are in this together." They must not be competitive with each other; otherwise the relationship will sour. They must learn to say that whatever comes their way, they can talk it through, they can work it out, and no pointing fingers or playing the blame game.

The 1 Vibration strives to do the best that they can, and if they do it together, they are twice as strong. But I have found time and again that the 1 Life Path Number does not take criticism well, so nagging and nitpicking are out of the question. The most important advice I can give you, if you are both 1 Life Paths, is to treat each other with respect and find ways to compliment each other. If you start feeling judgmental toward your partner, it is best to and keep your negative feelings to yourself. When you do work together as a team, you make for fierce competition and then the sky is the limit!

The 1 Life Path with the 2 Life Path

This relationship is considered Compatible in Numerology. The 1 Life Path usually counts themselves as lucky because the 2 Life Path will go out of their way to make the 1 comfortable and happy, and they are affectionate and kind. The key to keep the love strong for the 1 is to be aware of how sensitive the 2 can be. Sometimes 1s are so caught up in their career—or whatever their goals are—that they just shoot off their mouths and say what they think and feel, and the 2 is crushed.

That is when the 2 will shut down, and when they do, they look so unhappy and wounded. To avoid that from happening, the 1 needs to thank the 2 for all the good that he or she does, and the 2 needs to continue praising the 1, because as strong as 1s appear, they actually have trouble with self-esteem. They have an inner prompt telling them, "I am never good enough."

I think that the 2 is a wonderful gift to the 1 in the way that they love to give praise. Keeping a close check on each other's feelings will keep this relationship healthy.

The 1 Life Path with the 3 Life Path

This relationship is considered a Natural Match in Numerology and can be loads of fun. The 3 Life Path has a sense of humor and can make the 1 Life Path laugh, so the 3 helps to lighten things up. They both can be very sexy and creative in the bedroom, coming up with ideas to keep that part of their life exciting and fun. The 1 Life Path, again, must learn the art of not being too judgmental with their partner, and the 3 has to remember that if things get too serious, they are very good at lightening things up with a great punch line.

The big thing is to get back in the moment by keeping the conversation going and enjoying each other's company. The 1 must be careful not to focus only on what matters to them each day. The 3 will listen and give good advice, but will eventually resent the 1 and start thinking that they only care about themselves. It makes me think of the line, "Well enough about me, let's talk about you; what do you think of me?" Be each other's best audience, and you can't go wrong!

The 1 Life Path with the 4 Life Path

This relationship is considered a Challenge in Numerology and can have a few difficulties. The 1 Life Path is high energy, the mover and the shaker, eager to get things done. The 4 Life Path, on the other hand, likes to know what the plan is, and where do we stand? Because you two operate differently, you must understand and respect your differences. The 4 Life Path likes to analyze things and talk it through, whereas the 1 is more spontaneous and can be frustrated and feel that the 4 is trying to slow them down. When it comes to sex in the relationship, again, the 4 wants to know what their partner desires, whereas the 1, again, thinks that if you just trust it is going to be good, the lovemaking will be great.

The biggest problem this relationship faces is the lack of understanding of what the other person is saying. They are a Challenge, and a Challenge can feel as though they are speaking two different languages.

The best thing these two Life Paths can do for each other is write down the problems and the potential solutions. Freed from the emotions of verbal expression, you can honestly share why you feel the way you do. Both the 1 and the 4 Vibrations will respond well to this, and it will keep the relationship on the right track.

The 1 Life Path with the 5 Life Path

This relationship is a Natural Match Combination. They are both cerebral Life Path Numbers, and that means they have a lot going on in their heads. I find that if they stay busy, this relationship will remain solid. It is not uncommon for these two to have a career in similar fields, such as writing, reporting, producing, or teaching at the university level. If they do, they do not invade each other's space. They just do their own thing and when they come back, they have a great time.

This couple has to work at keeping things interesting in the bedroom. Maybe it could be role-playing, such as pretending to have a secret affair with each other, just to keep things sexy and fun, because both the 1 and 5 enjoy that. It is important to watch out that this sort of activity doesn't degenerate into unwise behavior, such as too much drinking, or too much work, the kind that keeps you from family time, and so on. Travel is an excellent choice for the 1 and 5 couple. I believe the more trips you take together, the more satisfying the relationship will be.

The 1 Life Path with the 6 Life Path

This relationship is considered a Challenge in Numerology, and this couple has got to find a way to compromise. These are two powerhouses that have come together, and both want to be in charge. The only way to make it work is to have an agreement, something like, on one day, the 6 Life Path calls the shots, and the other day the 1 Life Path makes the decisions. They can't afford to butt heads daily, and that's a good way to solve the dilemma.

Usually chemistry is the reason the 1 and 6 get together. It is common for the 6 Life Path to think the 1 Life Path would be a great parent. So they get married quickly to have a baby, and then, all too often, they will end up in a lifetime power struggle. Nevertheless, I have seen 1 Life Paths and 6 Life Paths succeed as a couple. They did so by each being in charge of separate things in their lives. One would take care of the bills; the other would plan vacations for the family. Compromise is key. If they can find a way to work together, the relationship will last.

The 1 Life Path with the 7 Life Path

This pair is considered a Natural Match in Numerology, always a good thing; however, the paces for these two are a bit different. A 7 Life Path usually doesn't move as quickly as the 1. The 1 Vibration can be spontaneous and is an excellent multitasker. This can sometimes be overwhelming to a 7.

There are times a 7 needs to regroup by being alone, and the 1 Life Path should not take this personally. There is an anxious energy to a 1, and when they want an answer to a question, they want it right away. Sometimes a 7 can't respond as quickly as they have been asked to. The 1 needs to take a deep breath and understand that the 7 will come around when they are ready.

This is a wonderful configuration of Numbers for a couple that can take trips together. These Numbers call for movement and activities. They can explore the world together, a wonderful way to keep the romance in the partnership. In any marriage, it is important to date one another, to dress up, eat dinner by candlelight, to keep that romance going. The 1 and the 7 should intentionally make plans to keep their love alive. If the 7 does not have faith and is cynical, the 1 will tire of that unpleasant attitude pretty quickly.

The 1 Life Path with the 8 Life Path

This relationship is considered Neutral in Numerology. I have found that if they meet in some sort of business capacity, they can achieve big things together. The 8 likes to be with the best, and since the 1 strives to be number one, it is not too surprising when these two find each other, the fireworks begin! They can respect one another, and what both parties need to keep in mind is that 8s are direct and tell you what they think and feel. As I already noted, the 1 Life Path is not comfortable being criticized, because they take it to heart.

If you are an 8 Life Path with a 1 Life Path, you have to learn to choose your words carefully. Otherwise you will have trouble with this relationship. It is not uncommon for the 1 and 8 to get together and at first, the relationship is exciting, sexy, and passionate. Then suddenly it turns ugly and volatile. You have to decide if this relationship is worth it. And if it is, always think twice before you open your mouth to say something you might regret.

The 1 Life Path with the 9 Life Path

This relationship can be exciting, because the 1 Vibration is considered the beginning of the Numerology Numbers, and the 9 is the Number of completion. That means all the numbers are encompassed in this relationship: 1, 2, 3, 4, 5, 6, 7, 8, and 9. Let's look at this:

1 is ambition;

2 is love;

3 is communication;

4 is learning together;

5 is exploring life together;

6 is family, making a commitment and sharing your lives and home together;

7 is working on your faith together, finding something you can believe in;

8 is money matters, what can we do to make money and be successful as a couple;

9 is the caring Vibration, doing good works together.

So if you are 1 Life Path joined with a 9 Life Path or vice-versa, just look at the opportunities in this relationship! What you have to watch out for is whether the 9 has let go of the past. Have they been able to resolve whatever issues they have from their childhood? As for the 1, since the 9 is the old soul Number, the 1 subconsciously might feel the 9 knows more than they do and feel the need to prove themselves to the 9. Don't do that. Instead just enjoy all the possibilities in this relationship. It can be incredibly exciting and fulfilling for both of you.

The 2 Life Path with the 2 Life Path

This relationship is considered a Natural Match in Numerology and can be lovely, especially if the two people involved have been in bad relationships before. There is an appreciation of the kindness each shows the other. Since the 2 is a natural giver, they seem to compete in caring. It is nonstop and sexually it can be difficult to get out of that bedroom, because the chemistry is so fantastic.

The only thing that can get in the way of this perfect match occurs when the 2 feels angry or defensive and becomes the "Terrible 2," like a child having a temper tantrum, and the other 2 (when calm, that is) won't take well to that. Anger can cause some hard feelings. They have to be careful not to let their emotions get carried away, and realize that this fellow 2 supports them and wants them to be happy. They should take the time to relate their feelings to each other every day, to keep a wonderful union going smoothly.

The 2 Life Path with the 3 Life Path

This relationship tends to be very Compatible. The 3 is a communicator, usually has a great sense of humor, and the 2 makes a great audience. The 2 gets the biggest kick out of the 3, and the 3 is a natural performer, so you definitely have the complete attention of the 2 Life Path.

The 2, however, is affectionate and needs love, and the 3 can get caught up in their work. If they are not careful, that can be a problem. This is especially true if the 2 has a 5 somewhere in their chart, or another number that makes them look for love elsewhere, if they cannot find it at home. The 3s needs to keep in mind that the 2 Life Path is a loyal person, but don't take them or their kindness for granted. They need nurturing. Check on them, often, to see what they think and how they feel, and then the relationship will be magical.

The 2 Life Path with the 4 Life Path

This relationship is a Natural Match in Numerology, so there is natural rapport. The 2, again, is a loving person who welcomes the intelligence of the 4. The 4 usually likes to settle down and have a partner. In that way they are very compatible, but the 4 can become a workaholic and not always communicate what they think or feel. This is hard on the sensitive 2, and can result in an unhealthy partnership. I suggest, since the 4 is not always one to verbalize what they think, they make an effort to show their appreciation to the 2. Not just on the big holidays but unexpectedly, just to say how much they love and value this person in their life. Use your imagination, 4. The 2 will be so appreciative.

This is especially important if they do get married and have children. The 2 Life Path would be such an emotional support to the kids, and the 4 Life Path needs to really recognize this and communicate how grateful they are, and then this relationship can last forever. When the 2 Life Path and the 4 Life Path are living on the Positive side of the numbers, it is a beautiful thing to witness.

The 2 Life Path with the 5 Life Path

This relationship is considered a Challenge in Numerology and can be tricky. The first thing I would say is that they have chemistry, and that is what brought them together. It is the reason that at first they cannot keep their hands off each other. But the underlying truth is that a 5 must feel they can come and go and have the freedom to do whatever they feel needs to get done. The 2 Life Path can appear needy and say, "Where are you going? What time will you be back?" Words like these scare a 5 Life Path, and they can suddenly feel stifled.

My message to the 2 in this relationship is that you've got to let that 5 go off, do their thing, and trust they will come back. They really will. As a wise woman once said to me, "Hold on tight, with open hands."

The 5 also has to understand that when the 2 is feeling a little insecure, they shouldn't think that they are being controlled by the 2. Just let the 2 know that they are valued. It is all about checking in with the 2 Life Path to let them know what your plans are, so they are not surprised that you are not coming home for that amazing dinner they cooked for you. By keeping in touch throughout the day, the 2 will be understanding, which is what the 5 really wants. By making this effort of being considerate, you can help this relationship last and avoid what can become an inevitable breakup.

The 2 Life Path with the 6 Life Path

This relationship is considered Compatible in Numerology. A 2 Life Path and 6 Life Path can be terrific together, especially when they choose to have a family. If this couple doesn't have children, they might have pets or own a company in which both are passionately involved. Again, the 2 is the supportive one, and the 6 is a powerhouse that needs to be looked up to. They want to be valued and respected, and the 2 does that very well.

Still, the 6 needs to make sure the 2 is not feeling taken advantage of or used, because when they do, the 2 can become the "Terrible 2," and nobody wins when that happens. The 2 Life Path needs to keep in mind that the 6 Life Path has no problem working hard, but they are highly motivated by gratitude. The 2 might think that the day will come when the 6 knows exactly who they are and won't need their praise or feedback. Not *true*. The 2's job as cheerleader is safe for the duration of their time together. It shouldn't be too hard to do. The 6 Life Path can be a pretty terrific person!

These are champion parents so, if they have kids, it's important for them to make time to get romantic, to take off for a weekend of wonderful romance. It is not a good idea to be so involved with the children that you lose sight of why you got together in the first place. Remember, someday they will grow up and be gone. Keep your love alive.

The 2 Life Path with the 7 Life Path

This relationship is considered a Challenge, but I have seen these Vibrations work well together. The 7 Life Path and the 2 Life Path are very sensitive, but in different ways. If it is a man (the 2 or 7), they have the sensitivity of the woman. If it is a woman (the 2 or 7), she can be strong, and even a little tough, but there is still a vulnerability there.

There are times that the 7 Life Path needs their solitude; that can be difficult for the 2 Life Path to understand, because the 2 wants to have a solid partner. They want to be held by and connected with their mate all the time. It is just natural for them. Sometimes the 7 will reject that connection, and the 2 must learn not to take it personally.

The 7 Life Path knows that some of the biggest breakthroughs in their understanding of life occur when they are alone. So if the 2 Life Path can learn to give them that space, doing so can be a very healing to the relationship. Otherwise, the 2 will feel all alone: they can be in the same room as the 7, and they will feel no one is there. That is the difference between these numbers—one needs closeness and the other, plenty of space.

When the 7 Vibration finds a basic faith that they believe in, it is wonderful for the 2, but if they don't, they can become champion pessimists. The 2s are in tune with the emotional climate around them, and when they experience that emotion, they will feel vulnerable or depressed. So respecting each other's feelings, no matter how different they are from your own, is the best thing to do in a 2 Life Path/7 Life Path pairing.

The 2 Life Path with the 8 Life Path

This relationship is a Natural Match couple that can be very good together. If it is an 8 male that is attracted to the 2 female, the 2 must care about her appearance because the 8 male appreciates a woman who works on looking her best. As for an 8 female, she needs a sweet, gentle guy and will want the loving 2 Vibration male. However, the 2 male must also be strong, so the 8 female does not feel she can walk all over him. The 2 reminds the 8 to take the time to love life, because 8s can be workaholics and sometimes they forget to stop and really relax. The 2 can remind them to do that.

If they choose to get together, they should treat their love like a business. They can make time to be with each other by scheduling it. Also take the time to arrange date nights, because the romance in a long-term relationship has to be nourished by more romance. It is especially important for these two Vibrations to keep the affectionate part of their love alive and well.

The 2 Life Path with the 9 Life Path

This relationship is Compatible and can be a great connection in Numerology. The 9 is the lover of humanity and has a lot of wisdom. The 2 will respond beautifully. As I said earlier, the 2 loves a strong leader whom they can respect, so the 2 can look up to the 9 and say, "Wow, what can I learn from you? What insights do you have for me?" The 2 is sincerely intrigued and interested.

It is important the 9 let go of those occasions in the past that caused them pain, because if they cannot find a way to be in the moment, it will lead to unhappiness for the 2. The 2s are psychically in tune to their partners and can feel when they are not emotionally there for them.

That is the key to success here: if the 9 cannot let go of the past, it will really hurt this relationship, but if the 9 learns to be in the moment with the 2, this partnership can be terrific; a real love match in Numerology.

The 3 Life Path with the 3 Life Path

This relationship is considered a Natural Match and can be loads of fun. It can be very passionate and sexy. But someone has to do the dishes and take out the trash. This means that at least one of these starry-eyed 3s has to be responsible and stay grounded. They need to be paying the bills and making sure someone is bringing home the bacon. Sometimes these two enjoy each other so much they have a hard time being in real time. As a result, the relationship can fall apart.

Although the 3 is a giving person, if one 3 is comfortable taking too much and not reciprocating, that can also be a problem. When the two 3s get upset, it tends to be a pretty loud argument because 3s are all about expressing themselves. Chances are good that they will both say what they think and feel, very probably at the top of their lungs.

So, if you are both 3s, take care to work on the financial and practical side of your life. There will always be plenty of fun and passion, but if you neglect the nitty-gritty, the realities of life can suddenly overwhelm you. My advice to you lovebirds is simple: keep ahead of the daily grind, and remember your wonderful sense of humor saves you every time!

The 3 Life Path with the 4 Life Path

This relationship is considered a Challenge and will require some work on both sides. The 3, because they are usually creative, expressive, and outgoing, seeks to become a star on some level. They need to know that the 4 is that solid base that they can come back home to. The average 4 is responsible and very loyal. If they make a commitment to you, they stand by it. The 3 must learn to express their appreciation of the wonderful qualities the 4 brings to their relationship.

The 3 must not get into the habit of being critical of what they feel the 4 lacks. A deeply wounded 4 is someone no one wants to be around, especially the 3 who gets over things so quickly. The 4 does not. It is possible that the 4 isn't able to provide all the exciting conversation that the 3 might want. In that case the 3 should seek that trait in other friendships and just love and honor what the 4 does bring to the union. The stability the 4 brings to this relationship is a gift beyond compare to the electric energy of the 3.

The 3 Life Path with the 5 Life Path

This relationship is considered Compatible in Numerology. I call this pair the "lights of Numerology." People are very drawn to these Vibrations, so the 3 and the 5 have to be careful not to bring people into their lives that cause chaos and hurt their relationship. They need to find ways to spend quality time with each other. If the 5s go off on their own too often, if they have to travel a great deal in their work and they are not spending much time with the 3, the 3 will feel neglected. The 3s do need attention and must feel valued by their partner. If this does not happen, the 3s can end up feeling neglected and that can really hurt the relationship. The 3 and the 5 must develop creative ways to spend quality time together—joining each other on weekends even if it entails an 8-hour flight, for instance—and not let outside forces interfere with what can be an enduring, loving relationship. Every time I have witnessed a 3 Life Path/5 Life Path break up, it had to do with outside forces getting in the way of an otherwise positive love relationship.

The 3 Life Path with the 6 Life Path

This relationship is a Natural Match, which is always a good beginning. If this couple chooses to marry and have children, they will enjoy being parents. The 6 is the natural parent. So they have that nurturing side to them. The 3s can be playful, almost like another kid, with their children. Although they certainly know how to discipline, there is still a real playfulness to the 3, which works beautifully with the nurturing of the 6. The 3 and the 6 appreciate each other and let the other shine.

The 3s need to know that the 6s must be in charge and call the shots on many levels, and they should try to respect that. The 3 is very verbal and sometimes will say something without thinking about how it sounds, and they can hurt the feelings of their 6 partner. Occasionally, it is best for the 3s to keep their thoughts to themselves, and let the 6 Life Path do their thing without offering their unsolicited opinion. The 3 should know the 6 is usually striving to make the relationship more fulfilling for both of them. The 6 needs to also be aware of how sensitive the 3 is to their unsolicited comments as well. The 6 should encourage the humorous side of the 3, to keep both laughing and enjoying each other's company.

The 3 Life Path with the 7 Life Path

This relationship is considered a Challenge and serves as an interesting Number combination. The first thing I see when I look at the 3 and the 7 is their tremendous chemistry. I have counseled many people who are a 3 Life Path and 7 Life Path couple. They would always say it was the sexual fireworks in the beginning of the relationship that brought them together.

What can go wrong is the need the 3s have to explain and express themselves. Unhappily, the 7 Life Path can mentally tune them out. The 7 can look at the 3, and the 3 can tell they are not listening and are no longer involved in the conversation. That lack of response can be so hurtful to the 3 Life Path. The 3s need to understand that the 7 is not doing this to be cruel. Sometimes the 7s have to zone out or be by themselves and get back to their own thoughts, needs, and desires. I have seen this relationship work well when the 7 Life Path has a 3 in their Personal Numerology Blueprint or vice-versa. This helps them to relate well to their differences.

If the 3 can help the 7 find a spiritual base to believe in, that is extremely important in the relationship. Otherwise, the 7 can get bitter and upset the 3, because the 3 wants to look for the best in any situation. If the 3 is in a great mood and the 7 is feeling down, it can take the sun right out of the sky for the 3 Life Path. That is why this couple must be aware of each other's feelings.

The 3 Life Path with the 8 Life Path

This relationship is a Challenge and requires some compromise on both sides. The 8 Life Path cares about what things look like. The 3 Life Path is known for their bright eyes and beautiful smile. The 8 Life Path tends to love the special beauty of the 3. The 8 likes to be proud of their partner. The irony, of course, is that the 3 does not want to be judged for their looks. They want to be praised and want to be told, "You look beautiful" no matter what is going on. That is something the 8 must learn in order to make this relationship with a 3 Life Path long lasting. But if the 8 feels that the 3 comes up short and the 8 expresses that opinion, this can lead to a real problem in this relationship. That is why this pairing is considered a Challenge in Numerology.

It is best if these two numbers can just focus on their good traits. For instance, if the 8 is making money and providing, the 3 needs to understand that is the gift they bring to their relationship. However, if the 8 Vibration is having issues with money and becomes really comfortable spending the 3's money, this relationship will not work.

Again, the 3 and the 8 need to sit down and decide what it is they want from one another, and what they can do to keep it secure. It is all about the 8 expressing their thoughts too directly, and the 3 needing to consider what the 8 really meant before they go off on a tangent to verbally execute the 8. Both these Life Path Numbers need to choose their words carefully.

The 3 Life Path with the 9 Life Path

This relationship is a Natural Match, and can make for a lovely relationship. The 3s feel called upon to motivate and uplift others, and the 9s are the humanitarians. These two can actually partner and make the world a better place. They can volunteer for a charity, or any endeavor where they help other people.

On Thanksgiving Day, shelters invite people to serve dinners to the homeless. The 3 and the 9 would feel so good about such a mission. They celebrate life. They love to throw parties to bring their friends and families together, and make everyone feel loved and taken care of.

One caution for this relationship is that the 9s have to let go of the past. Any of those hang-ups from earlier periods of their life are unhealthy for the relationship. The 9 Vibration must learn to be in the moment. Otherwise, if the 3 feels like the 9 is not really emotionally there for them, it can damage the relationship.

Also, if this couple chooses to have children, the 9 must be living in the moment to enjoy their offspring. He or she must focus on the present and on the current family. That is something the 9 has to work on in order to keep this relationship thriving. When the 3 and the 9 are doing well and live on the Positive side of their numbers, this can be an enchanting relationship.

The 4 Life Path with the 4 Life Path

This relationship is a Natural Match. When a 4 Life Path gets together with another 4 Life Path, they tend to feel safe. The only concern I have here is that 4s are like turtles. They stick their heads out when they feel safe, and they pull their heads in when they do not. So, if you are both a 4 Life Path, are you sticking your heads out together, or are you staying stuck in your shells? In other words, two 4s can sometimes become imprisoned in their own environment and not want to deal with the rest of the world.

So I say, if you are a 4 who has joined with another 4, start a garden together, walk around your neighborhood, find a park, and experience nature's beauty, because it will make you feel so much better. By sharing experiences, your love will grow stronger. Also, I would suggest that you take classes together, since the pursuit of knowledge is such a big part of your Vibration. You will encourage each other and learn that much faster. Try studying finances. Find a way to make your security grow for your future.

The 4 Life Path with the 5 Life Path

This relationship is a Challenge in Numerology. There is a lot of sexual chemistry here, but you two are very different. The 4 would like to settle down and have a partner, get married, have kids. The 5 wants to explore the world, be spontaneous, and if they wake up one day and leave town, they do not want to feel tied down. The operative word is *feel*; just smile and let them go and they'll be back before you know it.

So if a 4 and a 5 get together and marry, they have to find a balance. The 4s need to understand that sometimes the 5 will have to be with friends or perhaps take a job that includes more traveling than the 4 would like. The 4 cannot take this need to be free as a form of rejection. It is actually a survival mode for the 5 Life Path.

The 4 is that solid person you can count on, and the 5 needs to know that trait is a blessing. If the 5 begins to feel bored in the relationship, they can't blame the 4. The 4 never pretended to be anything other than what he or she is—first and foremost, someone you can rely on.

Keeping the love alive in your union is all about continuing to talk honestly with one another. Remember that person you fell in love with. Don't make false accusations. Jealousy can end this relationship. Keep your discussion channels wide open.

The 4 Life Path with the 6 Life Path

This relationship is considered Compatible in Numerology. The 4 and the 6 Life Paths usually marry so that they can have children. They both believe in the beautiful home and the wonderful mate. They tend to have the same personal goals, which makes this combination work very well. The key to success here is to make sure that you don't get bored.

Demi Moore and Bruce Willis are good examples. Demi is a 4 Life Path and Bruce is a 6 Life Path. They have those beautiful children. They never said anything bad about each other in public. So when they broke up, it was a real shock. They are not only good friends to this very day, but Bruce bought a house across the street from Demi so that he could stay close to his kids. That is what the 4 and 6 Vibrations would do. If the relationship doesn't work out, they would both feel that it is a priority to be great parents and take care of the children. You remember when you were little and there was a special, warm, caring home you'd want to go to because there was food you loved, a fun back yard, and festivities for the holidays? That was probably a 4 Life Path/6 Life Path home. A home with a 4/6 Vibration can be a blessing for everyone. If you do not have children, or if you are a 4/6 couple that is just dating, then your home, friends, and family will still be a major priority for you as a couple.

The 4 Life Path with the 7 Life Path

This relationship is considered Compatible in Numerology and can be really comfortable. There is a good connection between the 4 and the 7. The 4 shares their factual information, and the 7 is fascinated. They are both intrigued with what the other has to say, and they also have a love of nature. If they can get away on vacations to a beautiful place, such as Greece, Tahiti, or Aruba, it is a good thing to do for this relationship. Their minds are so attuned that when they are hanging out in a room, without saying a word, they both are comfortable with the silence.

The concern I have is that a 4 and 7 get so comfortable they act like roommates, and romance simply fades away. Lovemaking becomes scheduled as physical exercise. It is no longer passionate, sexy, or creative. Unfortunately, when this happens, one of them may step out of the relationship. I have counseled many couples with this Number combination where one of the two had an affair, yet they came back to the 4/7 relationship because the 4 and the 7 feel safe with each other, and they enjoy the financial success they have created as a couple, or they come back for the family they love. They might step out for sexual excitement, but they will return. When this happens, a certain amount of trust is lost forever, and to avoid this unhappy chapter, it is really important this couple find a way to keep sex fun and to keep their love alive. Find ways to interact with each other every day and be as intimate as you can be. Don't lose the magic that brought you together in the first place.

The 4 Life Path with the 8 Life Path

This relationship is another Natural Match in Numerology, but this one has some difficult lessons attached to it. When things go wrong, the 4 and the 8 have to join forces and say to each other, "We're in this together and there is nothing we can't overcome." If in this economy, one of you loses a job, repeat, "We are a team." That way the relationship can remain solid.

The minute it becomes a blame game, when the 4 says it's the 8's fault and the 8 says the same thing about the 4, the relationship can become ugly very fast. I have seen this Number coupling get divorced and remain bitter with their ex-spouse for years afterwards.

Yet I've also had 4/8 couples who tell me, "Look, we have been through some tough times, but we weathered the storm. We are stronger now than before, and we love each other more than ever."

So if you are a 4 and 8 Life Path combination, just know that, by working as a team, you always can get it right. If you find yourselves heading down separate roads, just stop and say, "We are a Natural Match, and we have more things in common than not, and we can make this work."

The 4 Life Path with the 9 Life Path

This relationship is considered a Challenge in Numerology. The 9 Life Path is selfless and cares a lot about the world, and the 4 Life Path can definitely join with that sentiment. The biggest conflict in their personality is that the 4 can become very quiet, and the 9 really loves to share their thoughts with their partner, so they can feel frustrated with the 4. Also, the 4s, who are direct and just tell you what they think and feel, can seem unduly critical to the 9 still healing (no matter what age they are) from the emotional scars from their own original family. They will not hear any more criticism, even if it is constructive.

The 9 is not trying to talk down to the 4, and the 9 does not think that they are superior. It is just that they have a lot of intuitive information that they believe the 4 can benefit from. So keep an open mind about where each of you is coming from. Compliments go a long way in this relationship. If the 4 can remember to flirt and be playful with the 9, and vice-versa, this can really have a healing effect and make it possible for lasting love.

The 5 Life Path with the 5 Life Path

This relationship is considered a Natural Match in Numerology. These two will never have a boring moment. This is a passionate pairing, exciting and creative, but it can also be volatile. These two have to be careful not to move too fast.

These are obsessive people, but if they keep their obsessions in check, and pick something positive that they are passionate about, they can have a terrific relationship. When two 5 Life Paths get together, the excitement becomes nonstop. Please note it would be good for one of you to focus on the details and help ground the other, to avoid unnecessary chaos. It is also very easy for a 5 to start a project and then fail to finish it. This tendency is something you could both work on overcoming together.

I have found that things go well here as long as neither 5 lapses into feeling the partner doesn't understand them; as long as you keep discussing all the things that are going on in your life and listen raptly to the other 5, this can be an exciting relationship.

The 5 Life Path with the 6 Life Path

This relationship is considered a Challenge to each other, due to their different views on what makes a good life. I have seen the 5/6 Life Path couples make their relationships work by respecting each other's schedules and maintaining trust in the marriage. The key to this love relationship is you must stay busy. Both should have a career. It can be a career if the stay-at-home partner is totally involved with the home and kids. The 5s and 6s should be in charge of what each does. At your job you are using all your creative energy; when you return home, you should concentrate on quality time with each other.

The 5 has charisma, which the 6 will enjoy, but the 5 must be appreciative of the 6's animal magnetism. The 6 values being told why the 5 thinks they are so special. They also love a sincere "thank you." Say it often and there is nothing a 6 won't give you. Sometimes the 5 gets so busy they don't even think about verbal appreciation. They just get comfortable in the relationship, and that can cause a problem.

The other pitfall would be any kind of substance abuse. If the 5 Life Path or 6 Life Path is abusing, it is particularly bad for this relationship. Since they don't spend all their time together, they really want to count on their partner. When substance abuse is involved, there is no trust. Any kind of jealousy festering in this relationship must be dealt with immediately. Otherwise the union will end.

The 5 Life Path with the 7 Life Path

This relationship is considered a Natural Match in Numerology, and there is a strong rapport and connection. These two Life Paths need to understand that the 7 usually has a slower pace than a 5, unless the 7 Life Path has other high-energy Numbers in their Personal Chart such as a 1 or 5. There is usually a strong intellectual connection, where they can talk nonstop for hours about things that fascinate them, especially when they first meet.

There may be times that the 7 can have trouble keeping up with the 5, and it makes me think back to an article I read where Catherine Zeta-Jones was in a limo with Michael Douglas. She is a 5 Life Path, and he is a 7 Life Path. He fell asleep in the limo, and the limo driver said, "We're here." And Catherine looked at him and said, "Just let him take a nap, he needs it." To me, that was a classic example of the difference between the two vibrations.

Here Catherine is a nonstop 5 Life Path, "gotta go, gotta do." But sometimes the 7 needs to take a nap and regroup to restore the energy it takes to keep up with the 5. Also, 7s sometimes have a lethal tongue, and they say things they don't really mean. The 5s will have none of that. So be careful what you say to this Life Path or you might find your 5 looking for the nearest exit door. Taking trips together is always a good idea for the 5/7 combination. Pace yourselves and speak softly, and this Natural Match relationship can be a long and happy one.

The 5 Life Path with the 8 Life Path

I call the 8 Life Path a Neutral Number to the 5 Life Path because I have seen this relationship go both ways. This combination can be really good or bad—and trust me here, when it is bad, it is really bad.

This relationship can start out quickly, where the 8 is dazzled by the 5 and things can move a little too fast. It can be lusty and passionate, but then when it is time to confront the realities of life, this sexy flame can burn out. If you are in a 5/8 love relationship, try to keep your hands off of each other long enough to see what else you have in common. I have found that when a 5 and 8 go into business together, it can actually be very good for the relationship.

As for romance, sometimes the 5 Life Path doesn't quite know how to commit to the 8 Life Path. They may become restless while they are still dating the 8 and find they want to keep their options open. Now, the 8 wants to know where they stand and where the relationship is headed, and when they ask, the 5 can feel smothered by the 8. You both will have to look at your relationship early on and decide what it is you want from each other, in order to make this work.

To keep the 5 happy and in love, the 8 must give the 5 a lot of room in this relationship. The 5 must be aware that, although the 8 seems very strong, they are quite sensitive. You both appreciate beautiful things and exotic locations. Getting out of your regular environment is essential. If you make time to escape into each other's arms, you will return from a vacation rejuvenated and ready to take on the world again.

The 5 Life Path with the 9 Life Path
This relationship is considered Compatible in Numerology. The 5 Life Path enjoys the 9 Life Path because the 9 has insights that they don't have. The intellectual power that the 9 possesses is a trait the 5 will appreciate. The 5 gets easily bored if their partner doesn't stimulate them intellectually. It is extremely important for the 9 to let go of past hurts, whether a previous messy divorce or anger at the original family. Or if they are very close to the original family, make sure they treat their current relationship as the first priority. They have got to

stay in the moment with the 5. The 5 will keep them busy, so it should make it easier to do so.

The 5s look at their lives as an amazing journey; *This is great and what's next?* could be their mantra. As a couple, be spontaneous and go away for the weekend. Do things that keep you out of your regular environment because that is a lot of fun for both of you.

The 9 Life Path will be a good adviser to the 5 unless the 5 Life Path lives on the Negative side of the Number and spends too much time feeling sorry for themselves. The 9 will not tolerate that behavior, and if they do choose to stay, they will do so because they have children. Children are the first priority for a 9 Life Path. They may stay together, but the relationship can, nevertheless, shut down on an emotional level. So keep on reaching out, and really talking to each other every day, and then this combination will thrive.

The 6 Life Path with the 6 Life Path

This relationship is considered a Natural Match in Numerology because two strong individuals have come together to love each other, and when respect and appreciation are given, the sky is the limit! When these two get together, they focus on home and environment. When you are a 6 Life Path with a 6 Life Path, there is no way that the inside of your house is not attractive and beautifully decorated. I always say 6s are the natural interior decorators. If the house doesn't look good, it tells me something else is wrong in your life. It could be other numbers in your chart that deter you from your natural ability to make your surroundings lovely.

The 6s care about the quality of the food they eat and prepare for others. They like things that are aesthetically pleasing like plants and a fresh, beautiful bouquet of flowers in the house. As a matter of fact, 6s will not tolerate a bad smell. Both of you will go nuts as a couple until you find out what is causing the odor. There is a lot of love here, and your life together can be incredibly sweet. Usually when two 6s get together, it is about having children. If you do not have children, you may have pets that you treat as your children. The 6/6 couple might run a company where they treat their employees like family. This is a powerful, nurturing vibration and it is reciprocal in the double 6 Life Path relationship.

This couple must realize that they both deserve some smooth sailing in their life together. If they become competitive with each other, it is possible to destroy what could be a beautiful love relationship.

The 6 Life Path with the 7 Life Path

This relationship is considered a Challenge Number combination. What matters to a 6 Life Path may not necessarily matter to a 7 Life Path, which can cause a problem. The 7s care more about mental and spiritual breakthroughs and sometimes they need to be by themselves. The 6s are more social. The 6s like to be with their partners. They have their breakthroughs when they talk things through and it suddenly becomes, "Ah ha. Now I get it." Sometimes, however, a 7 just doesn't want to talk and that can turn this relationship sour because the 6 will feel rejected.

The term "I'm at sixes and sevens" means "I am confused and not sure." This would also be true for the 6 and the 7 when they get together. If you are a 6 who wants to love a 7, know that they will teach you things that you just don't know about. They look at life in a way that you do not, and instead of being judgmental, or asking them for the kind of attention that they cannot give you, it is more about honoring what is good and sweet about them.

I find that when the 6 Life Path hugs a 7 Life Path, they can feel the gentleness, it is almost a spiritual feeling. It is a goodness that comes from a 7, once they find their base in a faith that they believe in. The problem for a 6 is when the 7 does not have faith and becomes bitter and negative. This response can really do damage to the 6's love of life. Just know how different the two of you are, and learn to appreciate this fact so that you can find harmony and stay together.

The 6 Life Path with the 8 Life Path

This relationship is considered Compatible in Numerology. But if the 8 is trying to figure out ways to create financial security, the 6 needs to know those plans. They have to ask, "What is going on with the finances? Does the 8 have the ability to save money, or does he or she spend every penny they get?" If it is a 6 male with an 8 Life Path female, and she is out there spending his money, that can make him crazy. But let's say the 8 woman is the breadwinner and the 6 male is counting on her in a financial way. That can also be a problem, because 8 females need to feel that the man she picks is also financially stable.

I do believe that a 6 and an 8 can do very well together if the couple honors the need to take care of those things that need to get done each day. Then, this relationship can be pretty impressive. If the 6s and 8s are solid, they should have a beautiful home. When this couple throws a party, it is impeccably done. If they have kids, the children will be dressed nicely and have good manners. Again, when I think of a 6 and an 8 as a couple, it's all about the home and family. If not, it can also be about being number one in their chosen professions and finding ways to enjoy the vacations they so dearly deserve.

The 6 Life Path with the 9 Life Path

These two Numbers, the 6 Life Path with the 9 Life Path, are a Natural Match, and this can be a dynamic relationship. The 6 does respect the 9, because the 9 has a lot of fascinating insights that the 6 appreciates. The 6 is not easily impressed by people and they will not hide their boredom if someone tries to impress them with their knowledge, especially if it is not sound. They can call you out when what you are saying is bogus, and they will not pretend that your conversation is interesting.

The 9s have a lot of information and life experience that appeals to the 6. I've witnessed the 6 and the 9 Life Paths enjoy a delightful relationship. Again, family plays an important part in their lives. Make sure that the boundaries are there with the original family and that they are not invading the space of this couple. It is especially important for the 9 Life Path to not let any family members meddle in the dating relationship or marriage.

If this couple chooses to have children, the 6/9 relationship can make a good team for parenting. The 6 Life Path has natural instincts on how to do it. If it is a man, perhaps he is a provider working hard, and the 9 raises those children or vice-versa. The only thing that can get in the way is that the 9 Life Path will internalize their feelings and not confide in the 6 Life Path. That will surely distress the 6 Life Path.

The 6, for their part, must make an effort to view their partner realistically and not place such high expectations on that person. Overall, I think this relationship can be wonderful as long as these Vibrations avoid these common pitfalls. Study each other's complete Numerology Blueprint and embrace your differences.

The 7 Life Path with the 7 Life Path

This relationship is considered a Natural Match in Numerology. Usually this starts out as a friendship, and then the friendship grows into a relationship filled with love and kindness. The concern I have is that because the relationship is so intellectually stimulating, the physical part can be neglected. You may wake up one day and realize that you haven't even made love in years. Although you love each other, you suddenly feel you are in a brother-sister relationship, or you are just roommates.

Occasionally I will get a letter from someone who says, in effect, "Well my husband is a 7, he's got ED, and so we don't make love." And I think about that "little blue pill," Viagra. It's been a blessing to millions of people because it helps men be able to make love again, and I know that does wonders for their self-esteem. I think sex is very important in a relationship.

If the blue pill is not an option, then there are other creative things you can do to pleasure each other, and I do suggest you use your imagination. You'll have to communicate your real needs. The big thing is that 7s are cerebral and must make a special effort to keep the relationship physical and loving. I know that people can be happy in a marriage where sex is no longer the most important thing. But too often I have seen the physical love ignored, and one or the other seeking comfort somewhere else.

The love of wildlife and the environment also play a big part in a 7/7 relationship because they have such an appreciation for it. It is very good for you to be near a body of water, either on a trip or, ideally, near the place you live. And when you find that base of faith that you can both believe in, what a blessing that will be for you and everyone around you.

The 7 Life Path with the 8 Life Path

This relationship is considered a Challenge Number Combination because an 8 wants financial security and usually money is not a big issue or goal for a number 7 (unless the 7 has an 8 somewhere else in their Personal Chart). So their goals in life may be different, but remember, there are six numbers that make up a Numerology Chart, and there are probably other numbers in each other's chart that are drawing you to this relationship. If you are going to team up, just know that a healthy 8 Vibration will do well to plan your future financial goals. Read all about the 8 Life Path because they come in two flavors, and you, as a 7 Life Path, want to know which one you are dealing with.

The 7 will be more about intellectual conversation and appreciation for all the beauty of nature, such as plants, rivers, the ocean, trees, etc. If the 7/8 can travel as a couple, doing so can be beneficial to this relationship. Compromise is necessary for this couple. Trust can be an issue for both Vibrations. The absence of trust will force the relationship to fall apart. Again, the 8 has to trust that the 7 Vibration loves them, and wants to be with them, and vice-versa, to keep this union constantly evolving.

The 7 Life Path with the 9 Life Path

This relationship is considered a Challenge in Numerology. The 9 is a number that the 7 is automatically drawn to. It is a subconscious admiration, since the 9 is an evolved Vibration. The 9 has usually found their spirituality and the 7 can learn from them in that way. A well-adjusted 7 who has found their faith and has a sense of self will find it easy to love the 9 Life Path.

But if the 7 is drinking or doing any unhealthy forms of escaping, problems will arise in this relationship. The 9 often has issues of abandonment, and when the 7 does their thing without telling the 9 where they went, the 9 can get very upset. The 7 will not know what to say. The 7 might say something stupid like, "Get over it." The 7 Life Path can be insensitive to the feelings of the 9, and that will not be tolerated for long.

But if they are both on track, altruistic interests are a big part of this relationship. The 7 and the 9, when living on the positive side of the numbers, can really impact the world in a wonderful way.

The 8 Life Path with the 8 Life Path

This relationship is considered a Natural Match; however, two 8 Life Paths together is a tricky Number Combination. When two 8s get together, sometimes they feel like "crazy eights" as a couple. They find that whenever they get ahead, things turn upside down, and that they are right back where they started.

But remember, there are other numbers in a Numerology Blueprint that can alter this Vibration. When two 8s come together, let's hope that it is in some setting where they at least begin with the same expectations. Do they both believe it is possible to be successful, or does one of them think money is bad and the other one think it is great? These conflicting attitudes about money can be a problem.

When it comes to physical love, both can get caught up in doing things perfectly. The key here is to surrender and say, "There is no such thing as perfect. It is okay." There is a bumper sticker that says, "I'm not perfect, but I'm perfect for you." That is what two 8s have to start believing. They have to repeat, "Yes, I'm not perfect, but I'm perfect for you." Then surrender into each other's arms.

When they do finally come together and take time out for the kissing and the sensuality, they must make sure it's not just, "Let's make love, but hurry up because I've got to get back to work." It's really important that two 8s take time out to cherish each other as people, not just props in a "perfect" lifestyle.

The 8 female will usually go out of her way to make everything look nice, and the house will be beautifully decorated; that is something they will want to do. It's really important that the 8 male expresses his appreciation for her efforts. Doing so adds to the chemistry in this relationship. Because 8s are so direct, these two have got to learn how to say what they are thinking in a more pleasing tone. The one big concern I have for the two 8s is that sometimes life throws a hard ball, and if both feel victimized, one must help the other. It is important that they not fall into a pity pool together. They can't afford to be critical of one another, because there will be repercussions that can interfere in what could otherwise be a loving relationship.

The 8 Life Path with the 9 Life Path

In this pairing, the 9s have to figure out their life's purpose. Maybe you met them doing charity work, or at some other event where you were impressed with them. Perhaps you have seen the 9 speak in front of a group. The 8 will be drawn to this Vibration because 8s care about people who are doing something with their lives. They want a partner they can be proud to be with. The 8 loves to be impressed with their partners and say, "Look what I've got," because "having the best" is an important part of their life.

The 8s are into possessions, but are not materialistic. They really appreciate quality, and they love the best of things. A positive 9 is truly a catch for an 8 Life Path. Nevertheless, these two Vibrations are a Challenge Number to each other. If the 8 becomes too disapproving of the 9, it can destroy the intimacy that was once there. Think back to what brought you two together in the first place. The beginning can be passionate and great. But then, as time goes by, if the 9 feels under attack from the 8, they will pull back and get busy with their own thing. Because the 8s are so blunt, once they feel neglected by their partner, they will keep pushing and pushing to know why. They want an explanation, and they will be very in-your-face about it. Verbal expression is truly an art form, and this means that the 8 can tell the truth, but the 8 must realize there is still a way to say it, so as to not hurt the 9's feelings. This is something the 8 must work on if they want a lasting love with a 9 Life Path.

The 9 Life Path with the 9 Life Path

This relationship is considered a Natural Match in Numerology. When two 9 Life Paths get together, they are good at looking at life realistically, and they can't help at times becoming negative commentators because they are focusing too hard on the dark side of the larger picture.

The 9 must find a way to get their point across, but at the same time be protective of each other's feelings. Service is a big part of the 9/9 relationship. Both 9s feel called to help others, whether it is volunteering time at a shelter, or foster care for children. If two 9s come together and honor their need to selflessly care for others, they become a tremendous gift for anyone who knows them as a couple.

Privately, they can be a bit high-strung, and they can have self-doubts. One of the flaws in the 9 character is that they can come off as superior and belittling. Well, there is no way a fellow 9 is going to tolerate that. The 9/9 combination must find a way to speak to one another without inflicting hurt and anger. A 9/9 relationship helps them choose their words carefully. This couple should find ways to exercise together, maybe taking long walks together, jogging, or just being with and appreciating nature. The outdoors is very healing for the 9/9 relationship.

Spirituality is a big part of this pairing. It is fantastic if they share the same faith. Because then it means they both realize they are living on a higher plane and have learned to embrace their old soul Vibration. They have come through with a lot of insight and perception that they can share with others.

On the other hand, if these two allow themselves to dwell in the resentment of the unjust things that happened in their early life, then they are living on the Negative side of this Vibration, and it can ruin both of them. It's also really important that the two 9s never fall into unhealthy substance abuse, because that will interfere with the divine intuition they are both gifted with from birth.

The best thing the 9s can do is to stay in the moment and focus on today. That will keep their love alive. They have enormous passion and appreciation of each other, and when they hold each other, they just melt into each other's arms. This can be exquisite. When a 9 Life Path finds a 9 Life Path, and they embrace the Positive side of their Life Path completely, it is a true blessing, not just for them, but for all of us.

If your Life Path Number Combination is considered a Challenge to each other, the following chapter may give you some more helpful insights about understanding your particular relationship.

CHAPTER 14

Toxic Life Paths: Is There Any Hope?

Life has taught us that love does not consist in gazing at each other,
but in looking outward together in the same direction.

—ANTOINE DE SAINT-EXUPERY

If you do a chart comparison and find the Life Path Numbers are a Challenge, study this chapter. Even if your charts look great, but you are curious what is behind your Life Path Numbers, you will also enjoy this section of the book.

Through the years, I have received letters from people who share similar thoughts, like this letter from Mary Lou:

Hello Glynis,

My husband and I celebrated our 50th Wedding Anniversary last July 18th. My birth date is 10/23/1938 and his is 10/10/1932.

I think that I am a 9 Life Path and he is an 8 Life Path. I thought that this meant we were not very compatible? We have had our ups and downs, but we have been together a very long time, and have had a great life together.

I appreciate the fact that he always thinks of others first. I can't think of any big item that turns me off. I wish everyone could be as lucky as us.

When I read this letter, I wanted to know what the two Numbers are immediately before they break down to the final Life Path Number. In her case, she was born 10/23/1938 = 1+0+2+3+1+ 9+3+8 which equals 2$\underline{7}$. His birth date 10/10/1932 = 1+0+1+0+1+9+3+2 which equals 1$\underline{7}$. When you look at the two Numbers, before they become the one-digit Life Path Number, you will notice that they both share the 7 Vibration. The 7 Vibration is considered a spiritual number. Although she does not mention that they share a similar faith, I would venture to say that they do. They must have reached their agreement about having a higher power, and it is understood between the two of them. Also, they share their love of nature's beauty. I will bet in those 50 years, they have done plenty of traveling. It also means that there are times they find comfort in the silence. Nobody feels neglected when they are not talking, because they share the Number 7. I also see that she has a 2 Vibration, and he has a 1 Vibration, and those two Vibrations are also Compatible in Numerology. So the two Numbers that come right before their Life Path Numbers are considered Compatible (2,1), and a Natural Match (7,7). In this case, although their Life Path Numbers are still a Challenge, they have another layer of Numerology that is helpful to them.

You have to ask, "How can a couple survive 50 years of marriage if their Life Paths are Toxic?" Well, there is the answer to that question.

When you break down a full date of birth, right before you reduce it to one digit, there are two Numbers that are important. I have found that if those two Numbers, before arriving at the single digit, contain a Number that you share, the special connection can be explained.

Update

I decided to write Mary Lou and ask her about two specific questions that I was making assumptions about in Numerology. I asked her about what part religion and traveling played in their marriage. She wrote back and said:

> *When we married in 1958 I changed my faith. I embraced my husband's faith and became a Roman Catholic. We have attended church all of our married lives. We also financially support our church. We celebrated our 50th Anniversary with Mass and a blessing from our priest.*

That answered the spiritual question. In response to traveling:

> *We have done a lot of traveling through the years. My husband is originally from Holland. His family came to Canada in 1950 and settled in Alberta. He is the only one that came to Ontario, Canada. Most of his family moved to Vancouver Island. We have been back to Holland twice and visited other countries when we were there. England, Holland, Italy, France, Germany, and Switzerland.*
>
> *We have traveled most of the United States and Canada. Also an Alaskan Cruise for our 50th Anniversary. We have been to Hawaii. We even have a traveling trailer that we use as well.*

You can imagine the big grin on my face to read that not only did I find that hidden Number 7 that has kept their love alive when their Life Path Numbers are a Challenge, but her response could not have been any more validating to the science of Numerology!

• WHEN LIFE PATH NUMBERS • ARE A CHALLENGE

I pride myself on keeping Numerology as simple as possible, so that you can easily apply it to the relationship in your life. However, I felt compelled to discuss the two Numbers behind the Life Path Number because of my relationship with Charlie. When I first got his Birth Date Numbers and discovered he was a 4 Life Path, I thought, "Oh bummer," because it is a Challenge to my Life Path Number 3. Then, when I did the breakdown of his birth date, I saw that the two Numbers right before his Life Path were 31, and that made him a 31/4 Life Path.

That was good news because the two Numbers right before my 3 Life Path were 30, which makes me a 30/3 Life Path. We share the Number 3, which encourages a sense of humor, and keeping things light and fun. Charlie and I laugh every single day. I know it is because of the 3 that we have in common. Plus, the 1 shows the ambition that is inside him, which matches my Destiny Number 1. So we are both very independent, and we are trying to achieve success. We have an understanding of each other, and no one is upset or feeling neglected. We both need to have focus when it comes to our chosen professions and cheer each other on!

As is always true when I have employees, inevitably one will come up and ask about their own Numbers. One of my assistants mentioned the fact that she and her boyfriend had Challenge Life Path Numbers, which upset her at first, but then she started applying Numerology to her relationship, which really helped. We decided to take a look at their birth dates, to see the two Numbers behind their Life Path. She was born 5/6/1985, 5+6+1+9+8+5 = 34, and when you break down her birthdate, it becomes a <u>34</u>/7 Life Path. Her boyfriend's birth date was 8/27/1981, 8+2+7+1+9+8+1=<u>36</u>, and when you break his Birth Date, it becomes a <u>36</u>/9 Life Path.

What do they have in common? Again, they both share the Number 3, which reflects being playful and having fun together. They also have the 4 and 6, which represents the love of family. There are certain things they mutually care about that are the same, perhaps goals for their future or what they are trying to achieve as a couple. That information made her very happy, because it gave her another insight that she did not have when she looked at those final Life Path Numbers.

• DISCOVERING THE TWO NUMBERS • BEHIND THE LIFE PATH NUMBER

So to summarize, when breaking down a birth date to find the Life Path Number, you can look at the two numbers that come *right before* the Life Path Number to give you more understanding into your relationship. If you have a Challenge Life Path Number, this allows you to see if there is some other Number behind the Life Path that brings you together. I am now going to show you every Number pattern that can result in a Life Path Number, and we will examine what the two Numbers that come before the Life Path Number tell us about the person you are studying.

The 1 Life Path
10/1 Life Path
When you see the **10**, before it reduces to the **1 Life Path**, know that the 0 always means that person has divine intuition, that they

have a gift of understanding. If they trust their inner voice, they will not fail to make the right decisions. Since the 10 gives us the **1** and 0 Energy and there are many birth dates that break down to a **10** before becoming a **1**, I thought it would be helpful to study the two Numbers right before they become a **10/1**.

19/10/1 Life Path

In this case, there is a 9 Vibration as one of the two numbers before it becomes a 1 Life Path. The 1 is for their ambition and drive, which is normal for the 1 Vibration, and the 9 loves humanity. But the Negative side of the 9 Vibration can mean that there is some unresolved conflict with the original family.

28/10/1 Life Path

The 2 indicates great sensitivity and the need for love. The 8 tells you that this particular 1 Life Path cares about finances. Money is important to them and taking advice can be a difficult. If you are a 4 or 8 Life Path, this particular 1 Life Path could be good for you because the 2 and 8 are the Vibrations that make up this particular 1 Life Path and are a Natural Match to you.

37/10/1 Life Path

There is a 3 for sense of humor. He or she can be playful and has the ability to communicate. This person also has the 7, which is about having a little secrecy. You are not always going to know what's up with the 7 Vibration. When a 3 and a 7 appear in a Personal Chart, I see someone who has to learn to trust. In a partnership with such a person, you must work hard to build a trustworthy relationship in order for that person to fully open up to you. So it may take them a little time.

46/10/1 Life Path

The 4 is all about settling down into a lasting relationship. The 6 is the Family Number and is concerned about running their own business, if possible. Both these numbers like to be in charge, as indeed does the 1 Vibration. So again, normally a 6 Vibration or a 4 Vibration would be considered a Challenge to a 1 Life Path, but if there is a 4 or a 6 in your chart as well, that could be very helpful to your relationship if your Life Path is a Challenge to the 1 Life Path.

The 2 Life Path

Master Number 11

Here, we are dealing with the **Master Number 11**, which has a **double 1 Vibration**. They are determined to be creative and the best that they can be, which is a characteristic of the **1 Vibration**.

The 11 ultimately becomes a 2: 1+1 = 2.

We know that the **2 Vibration** can sometimes feel overly sensitive. When you see that double 1, in the Positive, the double 1 can encourage confidence. The **Master Number 11** will feel very motivated and usually holds strong opinions, and you should take a look at that as well.

As I stated in Chapter 9, which talked about the Master Numbers, the **Master Number 11** reduces to the **Number 2**. So in the following examples, it is the two Numbers before it becomes an **11/2** that you also need to study in order to see the subtle differences of each **Master Number 11/2**. This will help you gain a little more insight into the person you are studying.

29/11/2 Life Path

The 2 is the part of them that will need people, welcome friendships, and will want to feel connected to their partner. The 9 Vibration will exude independence, and will be sure not to be too dependent on their partner. This can cause confusion for the person who loves a 29/11.

The 29/11 needs to find a balance when it comes to work and play. If they are using all their creative juices for their work, it can deplete their stamina by the time they enter the bedroom to be intimate with their partner.

The other extreme is that they can be very sexual, and will embrace that part of the relationship, and have a harder time focusing on finding a career that uses all of the creative gifts that they naturally possess.

The thing to consider when you see a 2 and a 9 as the numbers before it becomes a 2 Life Path is the family stuff. Are they okay with their past? Have they worked through it? Are they in the moment with you so that you two can love each other completely?

38/11/2 Life Path

The 3 is about laughter and the ability to communicate. The 8 is about financial security and having a sound future. The 11, of course, becomes the 2 (11 = 1+1 = 2), which adds compassion to the mix.

47/11/2 Life Path

The 4 means that they strive to learn, and may feel that they come up short. This Vibration can be far too self-critical, and you should note that. The 7 Vibration is not an open book, but a love of what nature has to offer will play a big part in this person's life, and finding a belief system they can embrace is crucial.

20/2 Life Path

This Life Path gives a double 2 Vibration. The 20/2 hooking up with a Toxic Life Path Number really could be a problem—unless there is a 2 Vibration in your two Numbers before you get your Life Path Number as well. If a person is born a 23/5 Life Path or a 25/7 Life Path, the 2 in their chart would be helpful in this relationship. The 2 Vibration really likes to be connected to their mate, and if they feel rejected, they can hurt the relationship by shutting down emotionally and physically. It is important that you know the 20/2 is truly the purity of the Number 2 Vibration. The 0 from the 20 makes this person physically in tune to the truth. So do not waste your time trying to deceive them. They will see right through you. You may want to refer to Chapter 8 to obtain a better understanding of the 2 Life Path Number, and then know that it is doubly true for the 20/2.

The 3 Life Path

39/3 Life Path

In this case, the 39/3 Life Path contains another 3. This particular 3 Life Path will be extra playful and have an unquenchable need to express themselves. Then the 9 will be about family and selfless instincts of wanting to make a difference in a profound way.

48/3 Life Path

The 4 and the 8 in this 3 Life Path are both about financial prosperity. These are strong-minded Vibrations and very frank in verbal expression. If the 3 is considered a Challenge to you, and yet you share a 4 or 8 Vibration, this could be a good combination for you.

30/3 Life Path

Remember: every time you see a 0 (zero), divine intuition plays a part in that person's life. It means that there is also a 3 Vibration, and these people tend to be correct when they follow their hunches. If you are in a relationship with a 30/3, do not even think about lying to them. They will see right through you.

Because of the purity of the two 3 Vibrations, with no mitigating Numbers, if you are a 4, 7, or 8 Life Path, you may have trouble with the 30/3. However, if you have a 3 in the two Numbers before you reduce to your Life Path, that can help:

Examples: 31/4 Life Path; 34/7 Life Path; 35/8 Life Path

The 30/3 will not settle for less than what they want. They will communicate their needs to you in no uncertain terms, and it will not matter if you ask them to stop. So have a seat and listen up!

12/3 or 21/3 Life Path

You have the 2 for the sensitivity, and the 1 for ambition and drive. Then it becomes a 3, and we know that the 3s are the communicators.

The 4 Life Path
Master Number 22
22/4 Life Path

A 22/4 is the 22 Master Number. The Double 2 means this person is really in tune with the Vibrations of others. They are very intuitive. They feel things deeply even if they sometimes seem aloof or disconnected. There is a brutally honest element to a 22/4. These people will not spare your feelings, and they set high standards for themselves and for you.

The double 2 also means they are very sensitive. There could be times when you end up in a conflict with the 22/4 and they will come back to apologize because it was never their intention to distress you. They do need their friendships, and they do need to have love in their life.

13/4 or 31/4 Life Path

You are dealing with the 3, so this adds a lighter energy for this particular 4 Life Path. Many famous people have this pattern in their charts. **Nat King Cole** was a 31/4 and **Arnold Schwarzenegger** is a 31/4. The 3 would encourage humor, and the 1 fosters ambition. **Oprah Winfrey** is a 31/4 Life Path. The 3 Vibration is so apparent in her ability to express and share herself in a big way. We also see her 1 coming through because of her tremendous success. So that is how it works.

The 5 Life Path

23/5 or 32/5 Life Path

We know the 5 needs to feel uninhibited. If they are a 23/5 or a 32/5, the 2 means that friendships matter, and that their family does too. Having a special bond and a connection to someone is necessary. The 3 is about expression, having friends to compare notes with, having a partner to laugh and play with. These Numbers greatly diminish the 5's fear of being controlled or tied down in a relationship with someone in their life.

14/5 or 41/5 Life Path

Having the 4 in the two Numbers before it reduces to a 5 Life Path promotes a need for security. The 5s have so many different ideas about what they want to do with their lives that they get confused about narrowing it down to what they really desire. The 4 Vibration helps them to be more focused.

If they have that 41/5 or 14/5, then the 4 is saying, "I will find a way to establish security. I will find a way to settle down in an environment that makes me happy." The 1 is about ambition and drive. If you are a 4 Life Path who has hooked up with a 5 Life Path, it would be helpful if it were a 41/5 or a 14/5, otherwise it is difficult for the 4 Life Path to coexist with the 5 Life Path.

The 6 Life Path
33/6 Life Path
The 33/6 is also considered a Master Number in Numerology, as is the 11 for 2, the 22 for 4, and the 44 for 8. What it really comes down to is that there are two 3s, and the 3 is about expressing oneself fluently, and the need to be heard. Because this is a 6 Life Path, the 6 does have high standards, and they are perfectionists.

They are afraid of any kind of rejection, so they will put up a front by trying to look picture perfect: clothes, hair, makeup, every day, all the time, and that is not realistic. This can cause them to burn out and stop trying all together, if they are not careful. The lesson they must learn is to occasionally show who they really are, warts and all, because their partners will only love them more. They have to learn to trust that this is so. If the 33/6 is a male, and they do not use their creativity in some way, it can lead to depression.

The 6 also seeks perfection in those they love, and of course being human, the loved one is bound to fall short. I really see this trait strongly in the 33/6. Keep it in mind that the double 3s are about expressing themselves. There are many people in the entertainment industry who have the 33/6, as those numbers are very favorable for a performer. The one that immediately comes to mind is **Meryl Streep**. The 6 also feels called to take care of others, but this Vibration must learn to ask for help when they need it.

The 33/6 needs to love and accept themselves before they can feel love and acceptance from others. This is more true for the 33/6 than for any other Number Combinations.

15/6 Life Path
If you or your partner is a 15/6, then you have definite opinions on how things should be. The 5 Vibration can promote scattered energy, so sometimes it is hard for them to focus and know exactly what they want to do. They can get restless.

The 1 Vibration encourages incredibly high standards, and on the Negative side of the 1 Energy, one of two things can happen here: they will either become workaholics or escape through substances instead, such as drinking or recreational drugs.

When you see the 1 and the 5 before the 6, you are looking at someone who is intellectually stimulating. If you are a 1, 5, or 7 Life Path, ordinarily that group is considered a Challenge to the Number 6. However, in this case you could be quite compatible, because of the 1 and the 5 Vibrations that make up this particular 6 Life Path.

24/6 or 42/6 Life Path

When you are looking at the 24/6 or 42/6, these patterns reflect someone who very much wants a relationship. The 4, in any case, is almost always a solid, looking-for-a-commitment type of person. The 2 is also a partnership Vibration and the 6 Vibration is all about relationships: having a home and a partner with whom they can share their life. The 24/6 or 42/6 Numbers are great indications of a solid life partner.

These people do like to run things, and at the same time they are very caring of those under them. The 24/6 or 42/6 people are careful with money and try to save for the future. The 4 Vibration will help them do this, and the 2 Vibration will want a partner to share it with.

The 7 Life Path

16/7 Life Path

The 1 and the 6 modify the 7 Life Path, which quite often has a loner quality and a need for solitude. The 6 Vibration, on the other hand, can make sharing their life with someone a priority. This is good news for someone wanting this particular 7 Life Path.

The 1 Vibration coupled with their 7 Energy can make these people very cerebral and hypercritical of themselves and others. This 16/7 pattern must learn to trust their partners, as well as accept them and their failings unconditionally.

If they are willing to believe in their partner, and if they really surrender to love, they can love so strongly that the love and love-making is not only powerful, it actually becomes a healing force for them as well.

It is also common for this 16/7 to have a crush on someone who is unattainable. They will have a long-term fantasy about that individual instead of being involved with the actual person. They must make an effort to be realistic about it and not have illusions.

25/7 Life Path

This is an interesting combination because you have the 2, which is the ability to love deeply. Then you have the 5 Vibration, which does not want to be controlled or taken advantage of by anybody. So it is a delicate balance with this particular 7 Life Path. The 7 seeks a base of faith, so if the 25/7 can find that, it is a major breakthrough for them.

Here is something special about the 25/7: the 5 Vibration is always willing to welcome advice from others, but the 2 actually knows the answer from within. So when the 25/7 is living on the Positive side of their Numbers, they are comfortable, really enjoy people, and also have a spiritual understanding from which others can learn.

The 25/7 living on the Negative side of the Numbers can actually feel paranoid, and this is because one part of the combination wants to communicate, but the other part does not. That is why that base of faith for the 7 is so important. Until they can literally surrender and trust there is a Higher Power that supports them. Their partners can really feel the struggle in their personality, and this can interfere in their love life.

34/7 or 43/7 Life Path

You definitely want to take a look at that 3 and 4, because the 3 is the social part of this Number Combination. The 34/7 or 43/7 has a sense of humor that can be a biting wit, even sarcastic, which may not be to everyone's taste, but they are definitely clever. The 4 Vibration may be looking for ways to make a profit, but because the 7 Life Paths ultimately do not care too much about material things, the 4 in the two Numbers before it becomes a 7 will make this particular 7 Life Path keenly aware of finances.

The 34/7 or 43/7 needs to find a way to enjoy all the wonders that the world has to offer. The ocean is very good for them, and it is very good for them to be near water where they can meditate, which they should do. It is also good for them to experience other cultures. Their 3 gives them ease in conversing with others.

The 8 Life Path

17/8 Life Path

This is a powerful combination. First, there is the 1, which is the Number that makes a person strive to be successful. Then you have the 7, which encourages spirituality. This means when these people have faith in God, they know what really matters in life. They work hard and through the power of the 8 Vibration, it is clear that success is within their reach.

When 8 Life Paths find their way to stability, they feel good about themselves. On the other hand, if they are living on the Negative side of the 8 Vibration, they can become too comfortable living off others. They also get very good about "performing well" in the bedroom, but really connecting on an intimate level with their partner can be difficult. Here is what I always say about intimacy, it means *in-to-me-I-see*. Sometimes the 8 Life Path is not comfortable looking within, and especially the 17/8 will not let down their guard and be willing to reveal their deeper feelings with their partner. So if you love a 17/8, help him or her be more trusting and therefore much closer with you.

But again, if they are living on the Positive side, this can be a very dynamic, wonderful 8 Life Path.

26/8 Life Path

The 2 is sensitive and loving, so a relationship will matter to them. The Number 6 values family and friends above all things. The 8 is about success in this lifetime, so these two Vibrations together should make for a good dependable mate. And if living on the positive side of the Vibration, this is certainly true about the 26/8.

Some pitfalls can occur when this 26/8 has impossibly high standards, and once they feel disillusioned by their partner, it can become emotionally difficult for both of them. This particular 8 Life Path also has to find a way to have a healthy relationship with money. They should not be jealous of those who have more and understand that there is plenty for all of us. Once they find a satisfactory relationship with money, they are much happier.

People with this 26/8 number pattern feel deeply. The 8 Life Path can be tough and straightforward, but with the 2 and the 6 Vibrations part of that 8, they are devastated when their partners betray them. Also, the 26/8s are straightforward and tell you what they think, but they do not take blunt feedback at all. If you are in this relationship, be aware of how deep their feelings run.

They take pride at being "good in bed" and love to please their partner. Later they may resent that their own needs are not being met, even though they have not expressed what it is they wanted. So be sure to ask them what satisfies them sexually, and what makes them feel loved in an intimate relationship. All-important questions to ask the 26/8.

35/8 Life Path

First you have the 3, which is the Vibration that can light up any room when they are in a good mood. Then add the huge energy field surrounding the 5. This makes the 35/8 very dynamic indeed. But this 8 Vibration must learn to focus. There are just too many things they can do, and do well, and the result can promote a scattered energy, which leads to frustration for them and for their partners.

The 35/8 does feel called upon to be successful, and they do welcome the respect power can bring them. However, they must be careful how they obtain it. They have to be direct in declaring their goals, and they should write them down. If a 35/8 does not have a plan, they may be comfortable having their partners take care of them while they figure things out, which can lead to problems.

The 35/8s need a lot of attention. Often they become performers to obtain the attention they seek. That, of course, is the healthiest way. **Sandra Bullock** is a 35/8 and so is **Matt Damon.** They are using their creative energies and have found a way to increase their financial success by producing and directing, as well as acting.

So if you are interested in someone who is a 35/8, make sure they use their creative side in their work. Otherwise, they can become despondent. This is not good for anyone who is a part of this relationship. When the 35/8 is successful, they are extremely generous to their partners and everyone else. It is not uncommon for this particular 8 Life Path to marry later in life, because it takes them some time to pick the right person. Once they are happy with that person, the result can be a marriage of mutual love and respect.

It is also important that the 35/8 find ways to be friends with their lover, because not only is it about being physically compatible, but it is also about being mentally compatible. If the relationship is just physical, it will soon burn out for this Number 8. So if you are in love with the 35/8, you just need to realize that you need both emotional and physical compatibility to make a lasting relationship.

44/8 Life Path

This is also considered a Master Number. The double 4 Vibration needs to find stability. Family matters very much, and within the framework of that family, they must build for the whole picture. For the 8, the absence of financial stability and the lack of money to maintain a carefree lifestyle can blight what otherwise could be a healthy relationship.

If you are with a 44/8 and you have decided that your mate is a workaholic, you cannot take their total involvement with their livelihood personally. It is the natural way for 44/8. The good news is they will feel the need to share their success with everybody. Giving for them is incredibly healthy.

Your sexual relationship can be lusty, passionate, and fun, unless they are dealing with scars from childhood. So if you have a partner who is a 44/8 and has shut down sexually, find out what is troubling them. Encourage them to seek counseling, because if they are willing to do so, the result will be a breakthrough for them, and good for both of you.

Also keep in mind that a 44/8 is going to be direct. They will tell you exactly what they think, and you cannot take their comments personally. The 44/8s are attractive or certainly strive to be. They like quality things, and they have a thirst for knowledge.

The 9 Life Path

18/9 Life Path

Here you are dealing with the 1, which is a highly motivated Vibration. You also have the 8, which means business minded, always asking,

What can I do to be successful? When you combine the 1 and the 8 in a positive way, there is nothing that this particular 9 Life Path cannot achieve. They have so much to offer the world, and by combining the ambition and the ability to create success, they can make the world a better place.

Their spirituality is extremely important. If they do not have that true sense of self, then they can become insecure and critical of their own physical bodies and their partner's. Behaving this way can sabotage their love life to the point of the couple being unable to physically connect. Yet, if they stay healthy when they make love, it rejuvenates them on all levels, mental, physical, and spiritual.

27/9 Life Path

Both the Number 2 and the Number 7 are considered naturally psychic and very much in tune with the universe. This particular 9 Life Path should be able to cut through the bologna. When the 2 and the 7 offer wisdom or advice, they tend to be dead-on accurate.

By the same token, if they have not found the spiritual nourishment they seek, they can be distrustful and overly sensitive. If you do not choose your words carefully, they tend to misinterpret what you are saying, and then feelings will get hurt. When a 27/9 feels emotionally wounded by their partner or unloved, they can shut down physically. If the 27/9 completely opens themselves up to their partner and is in tune to that spiritual base, then when they make love, they experience a beautiful, all-encompassing feeling.

Again, when they are in tune with their spirituality, they are amazing. The great twentieth-century spiritual leaders **Gandhi, Yogananda,** and **Khalil Gibran** were 27/9s. Number 9 Life Paths living in the Positive aspect of the Number have so much to offer on a spiritual level that when they hug and hold you, you feel loved and protected.

36/9 Life Path

I think the 36/9 is pretty terrific, because the 3, 6, and 9 are a Natural Match in Numerology, and here is all that energy in one person. The 3 has the ability to laugh and communicate; the 6 is the nurturer, being in charge and taking care of others. The 9 is the Number of completion, loaded with wisdom and insight.

When the 36/9s are in love, they are very clear about it. You do not have to wonder, because they will shout their love from the rooftops. If they are living on the Negative side of 9, they can still be nursing hurts from their past. If that is the case, then this is something they have to work through to be in the moment.

I always suggest that this particular energy is best when performing: teaching, doing motivational speaking, or even running a little theatre group. If they do not use their creativity, the 36/9 will feel miserable.

When they have found the right love, they're able to freely express their needs and wants and can abandon their mask of supreme self-reliance. They finally give themselves permission to admit that they could use some help. That is the lesson that they must learn, and if they find the right partner, the sky's the limit for their sex and love life.

45/9 Life Path

You need to pay close attention to the duality in the Numbers 4 and 5 that make up this particular Life Path Number 9. The 4 is the Vibration that works very hard, and may also want to be a teacher on some level, where people listen to and value what they have to say. Then the 5 is all about exploration and having fun and the freedom to come and go as they please. Since the 4 and the 5 are such polar opposites in Vibrations, it makes it is a little more difficult for people to understand this particular 9 Life Path.

Usually there are unresolved issues from family when you are a 45/9. They have to find ways to make peace with this issue, so that they can be in the moment and enjoy their life. If this 9 Life Path attracts a partner who understands their duality, they will trust that home and family matters to the 4 Vibration. And that sometimes the 5 Vibration part of them will feel a desire to escape and go play. If you can embrace both parts of their character, then the 45/9 will love you forever.

As you have gathered by reading this chapter, although a Life Path breaks down to one Number, there is a little mystery behind it. The two Vibrations before it becomes the Life Path Number will give you invaluable insight into that person. This is especially true if your Life Path Numbers are a Challenge, and you really want to understand your differences to improve your relationship. Remember, if you share one of the two numbers before it reduces down to the Life Path Number, that will have a helpful effect on your relationship.

CHAPTER 15

Loving Your Partner's Life Path Number: Just the Way They Like It!

Love is that condition in which the happiness of another person is essential to your own.

—ROBERT HEINLEIN

I have an enthusiastic following, and I asked them to share their own Numerology stories when I did my research for this book. From the thousands of letters I received from my clients, I've included in this chapter those I feel best sum up the Life Path traits of each number. In the sections that follow, you'll find revealing examples of the specific likes and dislikes of each Life Path Number, so that you can gain more insight into truly loving a person "just the way they like it."

• NUMBERS ARE ASEXUAL •

Note that in general, most of the traits of each Life Path Number are interchangeable for a man or a woman. However, I have noticed some interesting gender patterns worth mentioning. A man who is a 2 Life Path or a 7 Life Path tends to be in tune with his feminine side; there is a gentleness there. The 7 Life Path male often has an androgynous face, which is quite beautiful, especially in his youth. **Leonardo DiCaprio, Mel Gibson,** and **John F. Kennedy Jr.** all come to mind.

I have also noted that a 4 or 7 Life Path woman tends to be in touch with her masculine side. You will often meet a 4 Life Path who embraces her feminine side by wearing makeup, dressing up—but, be very clear, she does not need a man to rescue her! These ladies are strong enough to take care of themselves. **Oprah Winfrey, Demi Moore,** and **Helen Hunt** are all 4 Life Paths, and they are very good examples of this kind of woman.

Then there is the 6 Life Path female. This is the nurturing Number. These women know in their hearts that if they had to do it alone, they could. By believing that, it is not uncommon for them to divorce, if they think it is for the best, especially if they have children. Their children are their first priority, and if their partner is not a good role model, they may prefer to raise their children as a single parent. They have to be careful not to lose their lives to their children, thinking "When the kids are grown, I will do things for me." Too much time will pass, and when it finally is their turn, they are at a loss of what to do with themselves.

So with the exceptions I have just shared with you here, remember that most of the traits of each Life Path Number can belong to a man or a woman. Be sure to read all of the turn-ons and turn offs on the following pages to learn more about loving and understanding each Life Path Number.

• TURN-ONS AND TURNOFFS •

Turn-Ons and Turnoffs for the 1 Life Path

Aileen, a 1 Life Path, writes:

Turn-ons:

What I like in a partner is someone who takes good care of himself and sees his health as a priority. He should be loyal. Someone who enjoys helping with the things that need to get done, such as making dinner. I look for a partner with a strong intellect who is respectful of me and others.

Turnoffs:

What I do not like is laziness, dishonesty, stinginess of any kind (for instance, someone who is physically stingy, as well as financially stingy). Also, I have no time for a pessimist.

Verda, a 1 Life Path, writes:

Turn-ons:

What I appreciate in a man is his ability to give me a sense of what he is feeling, like, "I am happy, I am frustrated, or I am discouraged." Whatever it is, sharing that little bit of emotional information is important so that I don't feel I'm in the dark. Also, when they want to talk openly by saying, "Look, I am feeling vulnerable, and this is hard for me," so that I'm prepared to listen and not be on the attack or defensive.

Turnoffs:

What completely exasperates me about a partner is when they want to know exactly what I am doing, where I'm going, or what I did for the day. That kind of controlling behavior does not work for me at all!

Note from Glynis:

Verda brings up a valid point for any 1 Life Path. I have witnessed, time and again, that if somebody is in a relationship with a 1 Life Path, and wants to know about every move they make in the day, the 1 Life Path will feel smothered and want out of the relationship almost immediately. They may stay because they are married and have children, yet they will be angry and frustrated and become even more secretive.

So, if you love a 1 Life Path, let them do their own thing. You must realize that they have high energy and like to be busy. They will be the first to share whatever it is about their day that they really want to go over with you. As a matter of fact, if you don't push, the 1 Life Path will be much more open to sharing everything with you.

Paul, a 1 Life Path, writes:

Turn-ons:

A partnership should be encouraging, supportive, and nonjudgmental. Gender does not determine willingness to share, to be trusting, and to remain open to communication. It is shared like the sea in the tide, a partnership that ebbs and flows. Although it may sound easy, it actually takes a lot of work.

Turnoffs:

What I cannot stand is someone who has trust issues, is jealous; someone who is passive-aggressive, and someone who hangs onto their old pain from the past and will not let it go.

Daniel, a 1 Life Path, writes:

Turn-ons:

I like a woman who is secure and knows exactly who she is. Who can take charge in her life and does not need someone else to give her direction. Someone who is intelligent, enjoys adventure, and is nurturing with children. I like a woman who has a curious mind and is constantly looking for new knowledge. A woman who has goals and an actual plan on how to attain them really turns me on!

Turnoffs:

A woman that constantly looks to me for everything we do. Whether it is which restaurant to go to, and has no idea in her head, or what our next trip should be. I want a woman who thinks for herself. I do not like a woman who whines about her life or doesn't do anything to make it better. Or a woman who is comfortable sitting on the couch, saying she is going to find a job, and does nothing to make it happen. A woman who feels she is lacking an education, yet she is doing nothing to educate herself. This turns me off big time.

Note from Glynis:

As Daniel's letter makes clear, The 1 Life Path, if anything, wants you to achieve success in your life, just as they want it for themselves. So, if you are the type of person who says you want to improve yourself and then does nothing to make it happen, it is going to turn off the 1 Life Path. They will become more critical of you because your behavior is draining to them. You should think of the 1 Life Path as a vibration that enjoys being in constant motion. The more you accomplish in your day, the more in love the 1 Life Path will be with you, because they will appreciate that you are making the most of each day—just as they try to do.

Lisa, a 1 Life Path, writes:

Turn-ons:

I love the quiet strength of a man, a man who tells you he loves you and follows through by showing it in every way. That he is truly sensitive, yet he has a total sense of who he is, so he is still a man's man.

Turnoffs:

What I don't like is arrogance. Nothing makes me walk away faster from a man who thinks he is better than I am. Men with that superior attitude turn me off. They act as though women are second-class citizens. I will not tolerate it. Also, when they are completely self-centered and it's all about them.

Theresa, a 1 Life Path, writes:

Turn-ons:

What I most appreciate in a partner is a deep sense of stability, providing me with the security that I need to know we have a solid partnership, and I have the freedom to explore the world around me.

Turnoffs:

What turns me off is when my partner is not grateful, and does not appreciate what I do. If he cannot be strong and will not take charge of the situation, that is also a turnoff.

Note from Glynis:

The 1 Life Path does not mind doing a lot to keep their relationship healthy. But if their partner does not express gratitude, and begins to take their kindnesses for granted, that could end the relationship. The 1 Life Path needs you to contribute fully to the relationship as well. Find a way to compromise, so that the 1 Life Path doesn't feel that he or she is carrying too much of the load.

Turn-Ons and Turnoffs for the 2 Life Path

Shelly, a 2 Life Path, writes:

Turn-ons:

What I like in a partner is a really great sense of humor and strong intellect. He should be supportive, secure financially, and in touch with his feminine side. If he can cook, that is great. If there is something he cannot do, it is important that he is open to learning. If he has all these attributes, I am definitely going to fall in love.

Turnoffs:

What I do not like in a partner is indifference to other people, someone who has no sense of humor. I do not want advice on how to decorate, cook, or what to buy. In other words, do not try to control me. I need my independence.

Phyllis, a 2 Life Path, writes:

Turn-ons:

When a man has a gentle, soothing voice, yet is still tough, that turns me on big time! When a man is kind and considerate, it makes me very happy, and certainly he can get a lot more from me just because of his pleasant disposition. Of course a man with that kind of voice who also knows how to touch a woman and massage her and care about her instead of just moving in for the kill. Wow!

Turnoffs:

A man who does not care about his personal hygiene is positively my number one turnoff, but anger is a close second.

Note from Glynis:

I found it interesting how many of the Life Path Numbers mentioned a person's hygiene, or taking care of the body, as being so important. Certainly if a person does not care about keeping up the basics with their own body, how much are they going to care about their partner? I have also found that certain numbers are very sensitive to odor, such as the 2 Life Path, the 4 Life Path, and the 6 Life Path. A bad smell can make them crazy until they can get rid of it. So if you love one of these scent sensitive vibrations, do what it takes to stay fresh!

Dan, a 2 Life Path, writes:

Turn-ons:

I love a woman who gives meaningful hugs and who likes to receive them as well. I am turned on by someone who is smart enough to have a lively conversation and discuss things like politics and other things that are going on in the world. Someone who can be spontaneous and who has that gentle touch.

Turnoffs:

I am turned off by games of any sort. I cannot be with a needy person, the kind that needs too much help and support. It is not even about a reciprocal relationship. They are looking for someone to rescue them. I will never stay with someone who enjoys fighting and thinks that it is actually some sort of sport.

Note from Glynis:

Dan wrote, "I will never stay with someone who enjoys fighting and thinks that it is actually some sort of sport." This is so true for the 2 Life Path. I have found that a 2 will argue if they feel pushed up against the wall and feel they have to defend themselves. But when it is over, it completely drains them. It is the worst thing they could possibly do. Some Life Path Numbers can fight and consider it somewhat fun. A 2 cannot handle this kind of conflict. If you are looking to love a 2 Life Path or are already in a relationship with them, know that arguing is not the way to their heart.

John, a 2 Life Path, writes:

Turn-ons:

What I appreciate is a woman who makes an effort with her looks. I appreciate a woman who takes care of her body, is intelligent, has a great sense of humor, a wonderful laugh, is kind and gentle, optimistic, and spiritual.

Turnoffs:

What I cannot handle is someone who is ignorant or who chooses not to educate themselves. I do not respect women who do not take care of themselves on an emotional level. Selfish women, and those who are obsessed with their own beliefs as "the only way," are also turnoffs for me.

Elizabeth, a 2 Life Path, writes:

Turn-ons:

As a 2 Life Path, I am into cuddling and quiet time with my partner. I just like being with my partner and, in addition, doing things with him. I like an easy, nonargumentative partner, someone who is moderate and who trusts me completely—no jealous scenes, please.

Turnoffs:

I do not like being pressured by someone I am dating. I do not enjoy rough sex or anything like pornography. In fact, it turns me off completely.

Note from Glynis:

Elizabeth's thoughts on turnoffs make perfect sense for the 2. The 2 Life Path is a very sensual vibration. They want to really make love with their partner, not just go through the motions. Being intimate is very important to them. To reduce lovemaking to talking dirty or watching pornography is not a good idea. If you know a 2 Life Path who does enjoys that, I can assure you that there are other numbers in their Numerology Blueprint that are open to exploring unusual and even kinky avenues regarding sex. However, that is not the norm for the 2 Life Path.

Sarah, a 2 Life Path, writes:

Turn-ons:

I love honesty and lots of communication, someone who makes me feel special, not so much by words, but by actions. This person should be my intellectual equal, tender, passionate, and loving. There should be physical and mental time together, and we can be doing nothing or doing something. Creativity is important, the willingness to grow together, and to work on our spirituality together.

Turnoffs:

What I do not like is harshness, someone who is mean or abrasive. Dishonesty is not acceptable, and someone with a large ego who is unfaithful with their body, as well as their mind and spirit. A lack of communication makes me nuts because I feel like something is missing. Also a stagnant spirit with no interest in art, spiritual endeavors, or mental and physical exploration.

Note from Glynis:

Again, more than any other vibration, the 2 Life Path has a deep-seated need for physical love and being treated well. When they feel like they are just being used, they can physically and emotionally shut down.

Turn-Ons and Turnoffs for the 3 Life Path

Margaret, a 3 Life Path, writes:
Turn-ons:
I really appreciate a partner who makes me feel cherished. In my marriage, I feel that was what was missing. I also appreciate a man with a sense of humor who is good at expressing himself, who tells me what he thinks and what he feels, so I don't have to wonder what is on his mind.

Turnoffs:
My turnoff is being neglected and ignored. Or having to feel that what I say and think does not matter.

Mary Anne, a 3 Life Path, writes:
Turn-ons:
What I enjoy most is a man who makes me feel secure and loved. I do not want to wonder if I matter to him. I enjoy feeling that I am being listened to by someone who is open to real communication.

Turnoffs:
What I dislike is a bad temper, jealousy, and men who shut down emotionally; a man who does not want to talk about it, has secrets, and feels aloof—I cannot handle that.

Note from Glynis:
Both Margaret and Mary Anne are great examples of a 3 Life Path's needs and desires. The 3 Life Path must express what they feel, and they do need a partner who can respond and tell them what is going on with them as well. If there is no communication in the relationship,

it can lead to great unhappiness for the 3 Life Path. You must speak up and tell them your thoughts. If they cannot get any kind of response from you, they will just keep talking and talking and they will keep pushing for interaction. If they still cannot get it, they will seek a new relationship with someone else.

Wes, a 3 Life Path, writes:

Turn-ons:

I am turned on by someone who is open mentally, spiritually, physically, and sexually.

Turnoffs:

I cannot put up with a woman who is unfair, demanding, manipulative, controlling, and just generally hard to live with. What really turns me off is a woman who will shut down sexually and use it as some sort of bargaining chip. This behavior has caused me great frustration and caused me to step outside of my marriage, which is not something anyone would want to do. Now that I am out of that relationship, I know I cannot let it happen again with a woman. It is just not worth it.

Norman, a 3 Life Path, writes:

Turn-ons:

I am turned on by a woman who has beauty, charm, class, intelligence, and who knows how to have a nice conversation and speaks eloquently. Someone who dresses well and can make you feel special when you are not feeling that way. One thing most men appreciate is a woman that can teach you something that you do not know how to do. And a woman who acts like she is interested in the things that interest you, such as golfing, fishing, etc.

Turnoffs:

I do not like women who are pushy and unfaithful, or women who are comfortable spending your money, and then when you do not have money, leave you for someone who does. I do not like a woman who drinks in excess, and who cannot conduct herself like a lady.

Note from Glynis:

If you have noticed, both Wes and Norman talk about what they want from a woman on a sexual level. When it comes to love, they both desire someone who is sexually faithful, and who also does not use sex as a form of manipulation. A 3 Life Path is a great conversationalist, but they are also very passionate people. If they want to be spontaneous and make love to their mate, it is incredibly painful for them if they are rejected.

A healthy 3 Life Path is one that opens their heart completely. So, it is a great shock for them to find out their partner is unfaithful. It is better for them to move on because their level of trust has been violated. It is always hard for the 3 Life Path to open their heart again to someone who has hurt them so deeply.

Leslie, a 3 Life Path, writes:

Turn-ons:

What I enjoy most is a sweet nickname. Also special little things, like a guy who takes the time to recognize a romantic song and says that it is our song. I am drawn to a man who calls me on the phone "just because" so that I know how special I am to him.

Turnoffs:

I cannot stand a man who lies to me, and I just can't get past it once they do. There is no need to stay in the relationship. For me, it is the ultimate betrayal.

Nicolette, a 3 Life Path, writes:

Turn-ons:

I like a guy who calls just to say "hello" in the middle of the day, for no reason. He may have just left, but he just reaches out to say, "I miss you," just to make me feel special.

Turnoffs:

I am turned off by anybody who has too many secrets. You cannot ask too many questions without having them feel like you are invading their privacy. It is just not worth it.

Note from Glynis:

I was tickled by the fact that both Leslie and Nicolette talked about how much it means that the person they love picks up the phone and calls them out of the blue, just to check in, or tell them they love them. I am a 3 Life Path, and when my husband Charlie calls me in the day just to check in to say he is thinking of me, it always makes me very happy. It does matter a great deal to a 3 Life Path to know that they are loved and that their partner is thinking of them. It is all about keeping the lines of communication wide open to each other. Doing so is crucial if you are going to be in relationship with a 3 Life Path.

Turn-Ons and Turnoffs for the 4 Life Path

Sharon, a 4 Life Path, writes:
Turn-ons:
I appreciate it when my partner sends me flowers and makes sure we share a meal together, whether it is breakfast, lunch, or dinner. It matters so much to me that we take the time to really connect each day.

Turnoffs:
What I dislike is having to repeat myself because my partner is not listening. When someone lies to me, it is a big deal. If he smells funny, like a bad food odor, I'm unhappy.

Alicia, a 4 Life Path, writes:
Turn-ons:
What I love in my partner is that he writes me love notes. It touches my heart to know he would take the time to do this for me. I also enjoy the fact that when I have had a hard day at work, he rubs my feet and cooks dinner when I cannot get home in time to do it.

Turnoffs:
What drives me crazy, and is a turnoff, is when he does not always keep a promise. Even little stuff, like doing the dishes or not paying a utilities bill on time. It really gets under my skin.

Note from Glynis:
This letter made me think of my friend Karen who is a 4 Life Path, and who was married to a 3 Life Path. She said that when she would work and get achy, she would get in the bathtub and relax. Her

husband would sit beside her and read different kinds of books, like *Chicken Soup for the Soul*—just wonderful words for her to listen to while decompressing.

When I read about Alicia, I thought how true that is about my friend, too. So if you are a man reading this, and you are involved with or interested in a 4 Life Path woman, keep this pampering in mind; it will really do wonders.

Tom, a 4 Life Path, writes:
Turn-ons:
What I appreciate most in a woman is that she is a good listener, and I also like her to be health conscious and self-motivated.

Turnoffs:
I am turned off by a woman who is negative about her own life, critical of others, and is too judgmental about everything. That will not work for me. I need to believe there is some good news, and I expect to get a lot of that from a partner.

Jeff, a 4 Life Path, writes:
Turn-ons:
My wife and I have been married for almost twenty years. It has been the most wonderful time of my life. She is kind, considerate, and understanding. We have no secrets and talk about everything. She is a wonderful mother to our two children. I could not have asked for more. She is and always will be the woman of my dreams.

Note from Glynis:
I put Jeff's note in here because his thoughts regarding his 20-year marriage are what most women would want to have. I believe his

insights about why he is so in love with his wife are helpful hints to anyone interested in a 4 Life Path male.

Pam, a 4 Life Path, writes:
Turn-ons:
The first thing I'd say about a man that matters is that he is well groomed. He doesn't have to be pretty; I kind of like a rugged man. If he can make me laugh, it goes a long way for me in a relationship. He does not need to be a wise guy, just someone who is witty. I like to be a little challenged by someone who knows more than I do, so that I can learn from him.

Turnoffs:
If he has no sense of humor, it is a waste of time. And if he talks down to a woman, I will not tolerate that either. It is so important that a man be honest in the relationship. Cheating in the relationship is completely unacceptable.

Note from Glynis:
What I get a kick out of here is that Pam is a perfect example of a 4 Life Path female. It is clear that she knows exactly what she wants and does not want. She will not tolerate someone who complains or whines, or a man who is too clingy. It is all too exhausting for a 4 Life Path female to put up with.

Ingrid, a 4 Life Path, writes:
Turn-ons:
I want a man who is intelligent, spiritual, and who cares about the environment. I admire a man with a social conscience, someone who is strong both physically, and in his spirit. If a man has children, he

should give his kids their fair share of his time but still have time for me.

Turnoffs:
I am turned off by someone who does not smell good or who doesn't take pride in his appearance or someone who is inconsiderate and insensitive.

Note From Glynis:
I told you that "smell thing" is a big issue for the 4 Life Path. So keep it in mind if you want to make this Vibration happy!

Turn-Ons and Turnoffs for the 5 Life Path

Linda, a 5 Life Path, writes:
Turn-ons:
What I love is generosity. I actually have a man in my life who is incredibly generous. He spoils not just me but everyone in my life, and it is so refreshing.

Turnoffs:
What makes me crazy is when a man will not express himself when it is time that we really need to talk, because he does not know what to say. So he just shuts down, and it is really uncomfortable. I then find myself talking more and more to fill the empty air, and then I resent it.

Note from Glynis:
What turns Linda off as a 5 Life Path is very typical for this Vibration. The 5 Life Path women and men I have counseled are spontaneous and fast-thinking people. If there is a problem, they just want to talk it out and get it over with. If they have a partner who does not want to discuss the matter, who shuts down, it will make them feel anxious. So, if you are someone who is considering loving a 5 Life Path, and yet you know when things are uncomfortable your response is to stop speaking, you might want to reconsider. If you are also spontaneous, like to talk, say what you think, and feel in the moment, then you can't do better than picking a 5 Life Path as your life partner.

Debbie, a 5 Life Path, writes:
Turn-ons:
What I value most from a partner is being appreciated. When my partner thanks me and compliments me, I really feel happy and loved.

Turnoffs:

I am turned off by a partner who talks about himself all the time. These people are exhausting. It turns me off if my partner is only concerned about making himself happy sexually—that he only cares about his needs and does not even consider mine.

Note from Glynis:

To all who try to love a 5 Life Path: the 5 may be exciting and have that aura of the unobtainable that makes you desire them; however, the 5 is not a conquest and nothing upsets a 5 Life Path more than someone who does not care about them as a person. The 5 Life Path may not verbalize their displeasure but will shut down sexually. You must take the time to make them feel special and loved. Do things that actually tantalize and excite them. Then the 5 Life Path will be all yours!

Dari, a 5 Life Path, writes:

Turn-ons:

Making an effort to look attractive and having a strong mind are my two greatest turn-ons. I want a woman who is caring, but I don't want to be trapped or smothered. I want her to be outspoken, but at the same time I will not be controlled.

Turnoffs:

Henpecking is a definite turnoff for me. I want a woman who is a passionate friend, confidant, and fellow explorer.

Note from Glynis:

A special message to the ladies who want to love a 5 Life Path male: do not try to control them. Dari expressed his opinion beautifully when he says he can't handle a woman who "henpecks." A lot of women hate that phrase, but it really means asking questions like "Where are you? What are you doing? What time will you be back? What are you thinking? What do you feel?" Don't do that to a 5 Life Path. They will be out of that door so fast that your head will spin! Before that happens, let them do their thing, and know that they will come back. I have seen 5 Life Path males faithful to and happy with women who have their own busy lives as well. So, if you want them to be loyal, loosen those reins a bit!

Mark, a 5 Life Path, writes:

Turn-ons:

I want a woman who likes to travel and who is a great conversationalist. She should be generous in mind and spirit, but not someone who will put me in the poorhouse.

Turnoffs:

I dislike women who are boring, and what I count as boring are women who talk only about their own thing and actually don't care about me or my interests. Women with no real interest in what goes on in the bedroom, someone with no real passion—that's not for me.

Nina, a 5 Life Path, writes:

Turn-ons:

I value most a partner who is willing to watch the kids for the day, so that I have some freedom. I definitely have to have some time for myself when I am in a relationship. A partner who is aware of that is a real blessing.

Turnoffs:

What is not acceptable is, if we have children and my partner has to travel, he comes back and disrupts the whole pattern I have set up in his absence. The kids know what all the rules are, and suddenly they start to manipulate the parent who has been away and play the two against each other. That is a huge turnoff for me.

Note from Glynis:

Nina is someone who can accept a man who has a life of his own. But if they have children, he cannot come back and suddenly change the rules. If one partner is the main caretaker, the partner who has to be away must understand the rules both partners have accepted and agreed to. One of the leading causes of divorce occurs when the children decide to manipulate the parents. So, both of you must be determined not to let that happen to you.

Deanna, a 5 Life Path, writes:

Turn-ons:

I welcome a man who communicates clearly what he is thinking, enjoys taking trips, and also enjoys having company in our home. He also needs to know when I need time to regroup. He doesn't wonder what I am up to or what I am thinking or feeling. And he just trusts that I need a time-out.

Turnoffs:

A man who doesn't enjoy family and doesn't welcome the children, grandchildren, and all those people who are in our lives. A man who doesn't like holidays, gifts, or get-togethers; if they just want to be with me, and nobody else, that is not comfortable for me.

Turn-Ons and Turnoffs for the 6 Life Path

Gina, a 6 Life Path, writes:
Turn-ons:
I want him to be a leader. I like a man who likes to be in charge. He has to take command of the situation, and I can count on him to come through for me. I like it when he has a nurturing quality, and he is someone I feel I can lean on. If he is loving, compassionate, understanding, and has tenderness, especially sexually, that means a great deal to me. Chemistry is very important.

Turnoffs:
A man who does not know what he thinks and feels about important things is a turnoff. I do not want a person who just stares at me with a blank expression instead of answering my question. I want someone who is not comfortable having me take care of all the important things. I do not mind doing things for the home. I want to keep our home beautiful, but I don't want someone who expects me to do it all and is comfortable with that. And then not contributing to making things better for us—he is not doing his fair share, and that turns me off.

Note from Glynis:
Gina brings up a valid point as a 6 Life Path. The truth is 6s can and will do everything. They are multitaskers. Their fear is if they don't do it, it won't get done. Yet, at the same time, they do wish for a partner who volunteers to help and actually tries to make their lives a little easier. Helping with the chores goes a long way with the 6 Life Path. You will see the gratitude in their faces, and a happy 6 makes everyone around them happy.

Dawn, a 6 Life Path, writes:

Turn-ons:

A man whom I care about gives me a nickname and makes me feel like I am the one that really makes him happy. Surprise flowers, not necessarily for a special occasion, but for "just because." Sharing a sunset, romantic dinners cooked together, and laughing hysterically while making love. Knowing there are times when no words need to be spoken and just being together, because love is conveyed through the heart.

Turnoffs:

I am turned off by a man who is rude. The need to always be right, not giving up, fighting for no particular reason, with a big ego, and constantly bragging about themselves turns me off.

Paul, a 6 Life Path, writes:

Turn-ons:

I want a woman who is independent, confident, and trusting. I look for a woman who is on good terms with her family. She should have a kind and trusting heart.

Turnoffs:

I am turned off by a woman who has any kind of substance addiction. Jealousy and distrust are also not okay. Most of all I want someone who believes in me, as I would believe in her.

Note from Glynis:

Paul brings up a good point. When a woman tells a 6 Life Path male that she believes in him, then there is nothing he cannot achieve. The 6 male can be the knight in shining armor who rescues the damsel in distress. She is grateful and holds him in high regard. A woman who is critical and does not offer praise should not be with a 6 Life Path male. The relationship can quickly sour under those circumstances.

Mike, a 6 Life Path, writes:

Turn-ons:

I like women who are affectionate, intelligent, and have a sense of humor.

Turnoffs:

I am turned off by women who are bossy, pushy, and overbearing. Good manners are a must.

Carol, a 6 Life Path, writes:

Turn-ons:

Someone who loves me completely and is comfortable saying that they feel you are their soul mate. They are not afraid to abandon themselves in the love that you share. I am turned on by a man who is sexy, loveable, sharp, and clean-cut in his appearance. A man who is generous and actually goes out of his way to make the woman of his life feel like she is queen in his world.

Turnoffs:

I am turned off by a man who drinks too much; it is insulting, and he does not even notice how rude he is. I am really turned off by a guy who does not care what he looks like, is sloppy, and thinks that is acceptable. It means so much when a man takes care of himself physically, spiritually, mentally—on all levels. It certainly is my mission to do the same. It makes me a better woman when I meet a great man.

Note from Glynis:

When Carol used the actual phrase that she welcomes a man who makes her feel like she is the "queen of the world," it made me smile because there is something about the 6 Vibration that has an air of royalty about them. The 6s are like kings and queens. We are drawn to and automatically look up to them, show them instant respect. So, if you are going to love a 6 Life Path, know that they need to feel valued, adored, and uniquely special in your life.

Loretta, a 6 Life Path, writes:

Turn-ons:

I really like it when someone pays enough attention to anticipate my needs. For example, if I am not feeling well, I would not have to tell them, they would know that, and then they would buy me my favorite ice cream or chocolate bar just to try to make me feel better. Efforts like these make me feel warm and fuzzy and certainly help later on when we are being intimate. I like a man who wants to please me in bed, and when he does, you can bet that I will reciprocate!

Turnoffs:

I don't like it when they act like they are doing me a favor by making love, or they are doing all the taking and none of the giving. Or they have a foul mouth and call me names as part of a sex act. I am not a hooker, and that makes me feel like one.

Turn-Ons and Turnoffs for the 7 Life Path

Kathy, a 7 Life Path, writes:
Turn-ons:
I appreciate someone who is spiritual, and who wants to help the world or people in some way. He should be sensitive and caring and enjoy others and love to spend time alone as well as be with me. He should be a good listener and emotionally mature. I like a man who has the ability to sit in silence and is comfortable doing that. A man who loves children and animals, has confidence, and good self-esteem.

Turnoffs:
I do not like aggressiveness, especially passive-aggressive behavior. I also dislike rudeness, narrow-mindedness, a lack of faith, and one who does not read or learn and nevertheless tries to dominate others, especially me.

Alison, a 7 Life Path, writes:
Turn-ons:
What attracts me to a partner is someone who respects my space and quiet time. What is also important to me is that they are loyal and trustworthy. I want someone who is spiritually minded, and who understands and respects my creativity. The need for strong affection also means a great deal to me.

Turnoffs:
A partner who is dishonest, likes to manipulate, or is disloyal is a turnoff. I am not comfortable with someone who is too dependent on me, demanding, and immature. I need a lot of romance, but I do not like to have to ask for it. I want him to be aware.

Terry, a 7 Life Path, writes:

Turn-ons:

I enjoy a woman who is aware of her own sexuality, who is smart and has a good sense of humor. I appreciate a woman who takes care of her body and knows how to use it. I love warmth and intelligence. When it comes to politics, I don't want them to shove their opinions down my throat. They should listen openly to both sides. I love intelligent women; I enjoy a good laugh and a woman who enjoys good food but does not let herself go.

I like a woman who is trusting, knows that I am there for her and knows that I love her. If I am quiet, she does not question what I am thinking or what I am feeling; and if I choose to be quiet, she honors that. She knows that I love her, and she keeps herself busy while I am doing whatever it is I need to get done. I really value that understanding in a woman, and it makes me love her all the more.

Turnoffs:

I cannot stand a woman who nags. A woman who is so critical of her own body that I find myself telling her, over and over, how good she looks; that is extremely exhausting. I like a woman who is self-aware. I don't like a woman who needs me to validate her and make her feel special, or when she counts on me too much. If I am busy working, that is exactly what I am doing. It turns me off if a woman questions me, as if I am not at work because of her own insecurities.

Note from Glynis:

Terry, a 7 Life Path, is like most 7 Life Paths. When they are busy working, or spending time with friends, they do not want to be questioned. They want a partner who has faith in what they tell them. They need trust in their relationship, because they want to believe that they can trust the person in their life. A 7 Life Path has no time for someone else's insecurity. A 7 is very honest and straightforward. They are going to tell you what they think, so you don't have to wonder and worry if they are telling you the truth. There may be times when a 7 Life Path is quiet, but when they speak, they will always speak their truth.

Kurt, a 7 Life Path, writes:

Turn-ons:

I like a woman who has a lot of confidence. That gives her an extra sparkle that I find very appealing. I really love it when a woman makes an effort to keep in good shape, because I like to stay busy and need her to keep up with me. A woman who is selfless, who actually puts others first and sees it as a priority. It is not that she neglects herself, but that she knows when someone needs a helping hand. She is more than willing to be that person.

Turnoffs:

When a woman is neurotic—but I have found that if she has all those categories that I put before this, I could live with her neurosis!

Gloria, a 7 Life Path, writes:

Turn-ons:

I am happily married, and what I really appreciate in my husband, and feel that a 7 Life Path woman would appreciate in a man, is loyalty, honesty, and that he will go out of his way to make me feel special. My husband writes me little notes to let me know why I matter to him, and he keeps an eye on me to know what I like and do not like. He always makes sure I am taken care of.

Note from Glynis:

Gloria did not tell us what her turnoffs are, but what would turn her off is obviously the opposite of what she has written above. A man who is disloyal, or a man who does not consider her needs and does not go out of his way to make her feel special. This would be very true for a 7 Life Path.

Laura, a 7 Life Path, writes:

Turn-ons:

I am turned on by spending time with a man who is a great conversationalist. I love a man who knows a little more than I do, and believe me, they have been hard to come by! I also enjoy a man who lets me do my own thing, and if I am running a little late, does not give me the third degree when I get home. Nature really is a big part of my life, so a man who likes to sail, fly, or is a little adventurous makes me very happy!

Turnoffs:

I am turned off by a man who abuses alcohol or any substance, because then I never really get to know the real person. A man who is lazy, and not trying to get ahead in their life, yet wants me to support him is not okay! He must be willing to at least match me and if not, I am not interested.

Note from Glynis:

Time and again, I have counseled women and men who are 7 Life Paths who really appreciate a great mind more than any other attribute. They embrace the insights of someone who possesses knowledge and wisdom they do not.

If you consider loving a 7 Life Path or being with one, and feel you are limited in what you know, take classes, read books, educate yourself, because your 7 Life Path partner will appreciate your efforts. The intellect matters a great deal when you are involved with a 7 Life Path.

Turn-Ons and Turnoffs for the 8 Life Path

Mary, an 8 Life Path, writes:

Turn-ons:

I really appreciate a man who takes care of his body because appearance does matter, and I promise to do the same. I work out every day, keep up my hair and makeup to make sure I am presentable on any given day. I feel that is not too much to ask for with the man in my life.

It means so much to me that a man be trustworthy, honest, and faithful. I like a man who can cook up a wonderful meal once in a while. If he does not cook, he can take me to a restaurant with ambiance and be flirtatious no matter how long we have been together.

Turnoffs:

I am turned off by a man who is moody, does not think about what he says before he says it, and is insensitive to my feelings. If I go out of my way to make a beautiful dinner and decorate the house a certain way, I want some gratitude, praise, and positive feedback. I am turned off if he takes advantage of my caring or acts like it is no big deal.

When it comes to sex, I'm turned off by a man who has needs and wants to fulfill them and does not want to play. Foreplay means a lot, and when the man makes the effort to be romantic and sexy, I am raring to go when it is time.

Note from Glynis:

As is true for Mary, every 8 Life Path male and female I have ever talked to has said that appearance does matter to them. When they first meet you, you might have an excellent build, or a beautiful face and you take good care of yourself. But when you get married, you might drop the ball and let yourself go. This can hurt your relationship with an 8 Life

Path. They like to be proud of their partners. They want to show you off. So if you choose to love an 8 Life Path, know that every time they see you, there is appreciation for the effort you make to be your best self. They may not always tell you this, but believe me, it is so true!

Carrie, an 8 Life Path, writes:
Turn-ons:
I am turned on by a loving, kind, sharing man, who is trusting, understanding, and loves me unconditionally.

Turnoffs:
I am turned off by a man who likes to belittle women. He thinks it is funny, making smart remarks, and expects you to get the joke when it just feels as though he is diminishing you as a person. A man who feels the need to put you down, and tries to make you feel that you are not worthy of him, that somehow he is better than you, is a complete turnoff.

Note from Glynis:
Carrie would also be turned off by a man who does not value her opinion. An 8 Life Path does want you to listen to what they say, and a man who is not willing to do that would turn her off, as would be true for any 8 Life Path women.

Guy, an 8 Life Path, writes:
Turn-ons:
I really appreciate a woman who respects, and is not wasteful of, money. I also appreciate a woman who is considerate about us as a couple, and if we were to ever have children, that she would know I would want to participate in any of the big decisions.

When I come home from work, I want a woman who respects that I have been working all day and gives me a moment to relax before we compare notes about the day.

Turnoffs:

It is a real turnoff to be attacked the minute I am done working, because I am one of those people who works very hard and I have a stressful job. I really welcome a partner that understands that about me and who is loving and patient.

Rick, an 8 Life Path, writes:

Turn-ons:

I am turned on by a woman who is a team player, someone who wants to work with her spouse for a common goal, including finances. A good communicator and is enjoyable to be with. Someone who cares about her appearance, has a common interest, believes in a higher power, and is unselfish. Someone who enjoys intimacy/sex, and if she initiates it, it is a double plus.

That she acts like a woman, not a man trapped in a woman's body. I will say I love a woman who is willing to get along with others and is actually willing to say "I was wrong" when she is. I like a woman who is kind, understanding, and a good listener.

Turnoffs:

When a woman acts immature and has a hissy fit because she cannot have what she wants. When she gets loud and obnoxious on a regular basis—tone does matter! A woman who sounds insincere, does nothing to take care of herself, and then acts defensive when you mention it, or gets insecure because you are working hard to stay in shape.

I have trouble with a woman who holds a grudge, or a woman

who is not willing to work when the money is tight in the family and the money is needed to help the family, including the children; a woman who is stubborn, or is a pack rat who will not throw things away, or is high maintenance and expects everything to be her way or no way.

Note from Glynis:

Both Guy and Rick talk about how important it is that a partner is willing to help when it comes to the finances. With very few exceptions, we live in a society where both people in a relationship need to work. If the man cannot make ends meet, and the woman isn't helping out financially, it can cause a great amount of frustration in this relationship. So, if you are looking to love an 8 Life Path, you need to find out exactly what he expects from you.

He may want you as a wife who stays home to take care of the family. Or he may want you to contribute financially as well. Be sure to have this discussion before you commit to an 8 Life Path.

Lorain, an 8 Life Path, writes:

Turn-ons:

My husband passed away about a year ago, and what I just love in a man, and certainly loved about him, was his intelligence. This was a man who had profound conversations, and I was always intrigued with what he had to say, and I would welcome that with any man. He also had a great sense of humor, and I would be looking for that. What turns me on is someone who makes the effort to wear trousers as opposed to jeans. I welcome a man who actually wants to spruce himself up when we go out for romance, to a restaurant where you have to dress nicely. That extra effort just means so much to me.

Turnoffs:

A man who smokes, curses, or has an addiction to watching and betting on sports—none of that is appealing. It makes me feel a little dirty just being around it.

Note from Glynis:

Lorain's thoughts make a lot of sense for an 8 Life Path, because as I said earlier, they do care about what things look like, and how things appear. Someone who is an intellectual and who can teach them something new is also very appealing to an 8 Life Path.

Robin, an 8 Life Path, writes:

Turn-ons:

What I love about a man is when he has handyman abilities—a guy who has the ability to improve the home or fix the car. Any skill that I don't have, and I find in a man, rings my bell.

Turnoffs:

When a man makes promises he does not keep. Simple things like he will fix the heater and then doesn't. Or the electricity goes out, and he says he is going to get on it and does not. These are things I would normally do when I was single, but now I'm counting on him because we're in a relationship, and if he doesn't come through as promised, that is a major turnoff!

Turn-Ons and Turnoffs for the 9 Life Path

Judy, a 9 Life Path, writes:

Turn-ons:

I love intimate dinners and cozy nights and someone who is crazy about me and actually takes pride in finding the perfect gift. I love to be surprised, and I enjoy someone who's spontaneous, who wants to take me out for a fun night in the city, with dinner and tickets to a show, perhaps. It makes my heart sing.

Turnoffs:

What I don't like in a relationship is when a man is inconsiderate to my feelings and does not have any spontaneity and expects me to come up with all the ideas of what we can do with our time. A man who lacks imagination is a huge turnoff.

Rita, a 9 Life Path, writes:

Turn-ons:

What appeals to me most is truthfulness and honesty. With these traits, I know that I will be able to trust my partner. And for me, if there is no trust in a relationship, then it is built on shifting sands. Humor and optimism also mean a great deal to me, because no matter how hard life can get, no matter what life throws at you, if you have humor and optimism, it is going to be okay.

Turnoffs:

A man who is comfortable lying, doesn't quite tell the truth, does not want to talk about what he feels or what his needs are and expects me to read his mind. I like to know where I stand with my partner so that we can bring out the best in each other, and I certainly welcome a partner who expects the best in me, but who also asks me what I want in the relationship and does what he can to help make that happen. And a man who does not care about that and just wants me to satisfy his needs, especially sexually, turns me off.

Note from Glynis:

Rita brings up some great points that would be true for any 9 Life Path. A 9 Life Path will go out of their way to handle the day-to-day tasks at hand. They will get the job done, but like the 6 Life Path, they may secretly wish their partner would care enough to ask them if they are okay and what they can do to ease their life.

So, if you love someone who is a 9 Life Path, don't just assume that because they can get so much done, that they are always happy doing it all by themselves. They are not. That kind of insensitivity can turn them off and build resentment. Suddenly, they don't want to be with you, and they certainly don't want to be physically intimate because emotionally they have shut down. You can avoid the deterioration of your relationship with a 9 Life Path just by helping out!

Aaron, a 9 Life Path, writes:

Turn-ons:

I am attracted to women with fiery personalities. I don't want a 1950s housewife: "Yes, dear, anything you say, dear." Or a submissive woman: "How may I serve you?" I want a confident woman who will speak her mind. When we go out on a date, I would like her to call the shots at least half the time. In the bedroom I appreciate it if the woman will tell me if I'm getting it right. If she wants it "an inch to the left," just tell me, please.

Turnoffs:

I am turned off by mind games and any dishonesty concerning my role in her life. I do not want to be used.

Jay, a 9 Life Path, writes:

Turn-ons:

What I would be looking for in a woman are good communication skills. I would want someone who shares my interests and values, who looks at life realistically but with optimism. Sexual intimacy is very important, and I would want her to be warm and loving.

Turnoffs:

A woman lacking the attributes listed above.

Note from Glynis:

You will notice that both Aaron and Jay talk about what they want in the bedroom. They don't like surprises. They want their partner to tell them what it is they appreciate sexually so that they can satisfy them. I believe that is true for both the 9 Life Path male and female. Make a note; they do seek to satisfy your every need. Make sure you ask them what they want from you, too.

Beverly, a 9 Life Path, writes:

Turn-ons:

What I love about a partner is a mirror image of what I love about myself. That is, an enthusiasm for life, the ability to laugh at himself and the world, compassion for people, and deep love and respect for the earth and all aspects of nature. I want someone who loves who he is and the path that he has chosen.

Turnoffs:

The things that really turn me off are also the things I will not tolerate in myself. I will not put up with a man who plays the victim and just hides in the darkness of life. I cannot even be around the kind of person who is very needy, paranoid, or angry about the world. That kind of behavior brings out the worst in me so no thank you!

Note from Glynis:

Beverly brings up a compelling point that applies to all the 9 Life Paths I have ever counseled. They believe they are here to improve the world and to help the less fortunate. So, it is important for their partners to have the same level of compassion and respect for everything in life, and that includes nature.

If you are someone who has a lot of negative thoughts, or just feels that life has been unfair to you, it is best that you not get together with a 9 Life Path. At first, they will play counselor and will do whatever they can to cheer you up. Then the next thing you know, they will be depressed and unhappy as well.

If you are already in a relationship with the 9 Life Path, and that is what is happening to you as a couple, then I strongly suggest you get counseling and use your Personal Numerology Chart information to help find your way back to a love relationship that is good for both of you.

Nancy, a 9 Life Path, writes:

Turn-ons:

I am turned on by a man who actually checks to make sure I am doing okay, and if I am not, finds a way to help ease the stress in my life. I am a people pleaser, and I do get drained. So when I come home, I want a man who asks about my day and wants to cuddle and be affectionate. I am also turned on when we do things together and share a lot of common interests.

Turnoffs:

Nothing makes my blood run cold faster than a man who takes advantage of my kindness and wants me to run all his errands for him, such as taking his clothes to the dry cleaner, making dinner reservations, planning a vacation, etc....I will do it on automatic pilot, but subconsciously I will start to resent him, and then when he wants to make love, I am so not interested! I also do not like it when my partner asks me how my day was, and then while I am answering wanders off to go do something else. That is a real turnoff!

I recommend you take notes on the various suggestions that each Life Path Number has made in this chapter. I believe it will help you to love the Life Path Number you care about "just the way they like it." And if your partner is not making you happy, be sure to have him or her read all about the insights on your Life Path Number as well.

CHAPTER 16

Sex and Numerology: Is It in the Numbers?

Love is an irresistible desire to be irresistibly desired.

—ROBERT FROST

In Chapter 3, I wrote about how some Numbers can be a Challenge to each other. The Challenge Number relationship often starts out passionately, full of lust and nonstop excitement. But this kind of "love" can quickly burn itself out, as in the words of the old Cole Porter song, "Our love affair was too hot not to cool down." That is why being in a relationship with someone who has a lot of Challenge Numbers with you can feel *very toxic*.

So that brings us to this question: When we look at sex in Numerology, is it really in the Numbers? My answer is an emphatic *yes*. There are certain Vibrations that go together beautifully, and others that take some effort. In this Chapter, I will share some of the things I know that work in love relationships, including advice to each Life Path

Number 1 through 9. If you are a Master Number 11 or 22, refer to the notes for the 2 and 4 respectively.

• REPEATING NUMBERS •

It is very important to pay attention to a repeating number in your chart, especially if this number is not your Life Path Number. This number will have a major influence on who you are.

For example, let's say your chart looks like this:

59554*/5 Attitude

In this case, although you are a **4 Life Path,** you must also pay attention to all of those 5s in the Chart. If you are researching this chart, you would also look carefully at the information on both the **5 Life Path** and the **4 Life Path,** because both would apply.

• NATURAL MATCH COMBINATIONS •

Let's talk about the Natural Match combinations first, and how they influence our sex lives. As discussed in Chapter 3, there are three sets of numbers that are naturally matched: the mind Numbers, the business-minded Numbers, and the creative minded Numbers. The 1, 5, and 7 Life Paths are the mind numbers, which means they live in their heads. The 2, 4, and 8 Life Paths are the business-minded Numbers, and the 3, 6, and 9 Life Path Numbers are the creative-minded Vibrations. You may have several of these numbers in your chart, but we'll be focusing on only the Life Path Numbers in this chapter. Because the Life Path is ultimately the key to a person, it is the most revealing number for examining the sex life.

The 1, 5, and 7 Life Path

Since the 1, 5 and 7 Life Paths are very cerebral, fantasy plays a big part in their sex lives. Of course, you might read this and say, "Well gosh, I'm a 3 and fantasy plays a part in my sex life too," or "I am a 4 Life Path, and I care about fantasy." But remember that you may very well have a 1, 5, or 7 somewhere else in your Chart, so this will ring true for you.

If you are a 1, 5, or 7 Life Path, your imagination plays a big part in sex with your partner. If your partner whispers a little sex talk, this could add to the fantasy. The 5s like to put on a bit of a show when they make love. They may enjoy wearing special outfits such as a sexy negligee that makes them feel attractive and puts them in the mood. If it is a guy, at the very least he will apply cologne he knows women love. The 5 woman wants to look "performance ready" and ready for love.

The 5 Life Path is in tune to all 5 senses. They have a strong sense of touch, smell, taste, sight, and hearing—all equally important to the 5 Life Path. So taking them to a fine restaurant that has a lovely ambiance and outstanding food covers all the bases and gives them great pleasure.

If you love a 7, let the 7 do whatever they need to do in their life, and come back to you when they are ready. Hang on too tight and while they will be there physically, they will not be there for you emotionally, or mentally. They will be far more amorous when they return, because they appreciate the fact that you understand their deep need for freedom.

The 1, 5, and 7 category is spontaneous, and the best sex for them occurs when they are in the moment. You need to understand that, and if your Life Path Number is a Challenge to them—maybe you are a 2 Life Path with a 5 Life Path—you must take the time to tell them what your own needs are. Be very specific, they will listen, but you can not expect them to automatically know what your needs are.

The 2, 4, and 8 Life Path

The 2 Vibration is a sensual person. If you give back rubs to the Number 2, 4, or 8, it will feel like heaven on earth to them. Of course, I'm not saying that the rest of us wouldn't welcome it too! But the 2, 4, and 8 Life Path Numbers really need physical attention. It's most important for a 2 to be physically loved and cuddled. Foreplay is really important to the 2 Life Path. If there isn't any, and sex, for the partner, is more about jumping on and jumping off, it can actually shut them down physically and emotionally to the point where they don't even want to have sex anymore. If you are the partner, you have to keep that intimacy going on all levels.

The 8 Life Path is very affected by appearance. If an 8 thinks you have dressed a certain way or made an effort to create a romantic atmosphere, such as lighting candles in the room and picking an incense that you know they like, those efforts make a difference for setting the mood for this 8 Life Path. If you are a woman with an 8 Life Path man, taking great care of your body and having the latest style with your hair and makeup will surely be noticed by the 8 male. This would also be true for the 4 Life Path male. The 4 appreciates the effort that you make to stay physically fit and looking your best for them.

A Special Message for the 4 and 8 Life Path Male:

After doing several thousand readings, I cannot tell you how many women who try to improve their appearance for these two Life Path Numbers tell me that they never receive verbal appreciation. It is as if you 4s and 8s figure these women can read your minds or see the appreciation in your eyes and that should be plenty. *Well, it is not.* You 4 and 8 Life Path males can improve your relationships immensely just by verbally acknowledging the romantic efforts the women in your lives have made for you. It matters. If you are a male reading this, and you have a 4 or 8 somewhere in your chart and this applies to you, please take my advice. It can transform your relationship overnight.

The 3, 6, and 9 Life Path

Acknowledging the effort that these Numbers make for their partners will go a long way. If you are in love with a 3 Life Path, you might say something like, "I love your smile! You look so beautiful, you look so sexy, you smell so good, you feel so good." This will put the 3 woman in the mood for lovemaking. The 3 woman usually knows how to pump up the male ego, so my only advice is "just do it, ladies." Foreplay is important, but if you really spend your time praising them in the bedroom before you get started, that could be all the foreplay your 3 Life Path needs.

Because the 6 is a nurturing energy, it will be a natural for them to cater to your every need and make sure that you are taken care of and sexually satisfied. However, if you get in the habit of not reciprocating, you will build resentment with the 6 Life Path. Remember, the 6 Life Path puts the ones they love on a pedestal, but people on a pedestal tend to fall off, so beware of that. No matter how good it may feel with your 6 Life Path partner taking care of you and all your needs and desires in the bedroom, you must take care to consider them as well.

As for the 9 Life Paths, if something is troubling them, they find it difficult to make love. You must find ways to relieve their minds. You might want to whisper sweet nothings in their ear, or get some lotion or nice oils to massage their back and legs with and pull them into the moment. If your 9 Life Path partner does have unresolved issues that trouble him or her, then it's a good idea to talk it through before you go into the bedroom. You should also have a rule that by bedtime, you must release the stresses of the day, and forgive each other for anything that is bothering you. It's old advice, but still good: *Never go to bed angry.*

• EVERY LIFE PATH: ADVICE FOR • KEEPING THE LOVE ALIVE

Date Night Is a Must If You Are Married!

I do not care who you are, or no matter how great the relationship was when you first got together, and no matter how much lovemaking took place when you married, you can get caught up in your busy schedule and your sex life can suffer. If you have kids, you are going to worry about them and by the time you hit the bedroom, you are just so tired you've got nothing to give. That is definitely the formula to destroy a marriage. This is the case when one person who has needs and feels rejected may look elsewhere. If you want to keep the marriage alive, have a weekly date night.

When my husband and I go out, it's usually on a Wednesday or a Thursday night when it is not so crowded. We go to dinner, and we pick a romantic, sexy kind of place where we can be flirtatious again instead of talking and worrying so much about our careers, future, and whatever it is that troubles us. We try to remind ourselves why we are so in love and why we enjoy each other's company so much. I know this is one major reason our marriage is thriving.

If you are married or in a relationship and you haven't made love in several years, that is not an active marriage, that is like being room-mates. If you want to get back to being truly married, you have to confront your partner and say, "It is time for us to find our way back into each other's arms." I suggest you take a little trip to a local hotel for the weekend. You might want to just start out with intimate conversations, massaging each other, kissing, and being romantic. Then get back to actually making love again.

Life is too short to be married and yet feel all alone in your marriage. When you choose to marry someone, you want to make sure that person loves you and cares about your needs. Women and men become too critical of themselves. Obviously when a woman has children and gains some weight she judges herself harshly, and when a man's hair starts to thin, he doesn't like that much either. No matter what the situation may be, you should find a way to make your partner feel better. This will create a loving relationship that is alive and vibrant. Make an appointment to be romantic and intimate with each other and you will find it is a wise thing to do.

Making It Good Again

In all my years of Numerology counseling, women often say that men are insensitive and just don't get it, and I disagree with them. The men who have reached out to me have hearts as big as any woman's. They have so much love to give and they want so much to share their life with somebody. If you are married or dating someone right now and the sex has stopped, there are ways to bring it back to life. You just have to be willing to make the effort.

First rekindle the spirit, and the body will follow its lead. There has been something there that has snuffed out desire. Bring it back with subtle changes—the jackhammer approach will not make it happen. One suggestion I have is to give your partner a handwritten, thoughtful card. There is power in giving each other little notes. Sometimes I will take Charlie's name and I will write out each letter and say what is amazing about him. You know, something like C for charming, H for happy or harmonious, A for absolutely adorable, R for reliable, L for loving, I for intelligent, and E for endearing. It will always make him laugh because he never expects it. It puts him in a great mood and makes him feel good about himself. I don't care what your numbers are, everybody needs to be praised. Everyone needs to feel confident, and your mate can make or break you in that department.

A Day without Criticism

Pick a day and give your partner nothing but unconditional love and keep any negativity to yourself. There will, goodness knows, always be another time to bring up what is bothering you; after all, no relationship is perfect. But there are things you can do to make it better and this is one of them.

Don't Complain, Just Do It!

When I was single, if there was a problem—let's say some lights were not working in the house and needed an electrician, or the faucet in the bathtub had a leak, and I needed a plumber—I would automatically call someone to fix it. Once I married, my husband would offer, "I'll take care of it," which men tend to say whether or not they will ever have the time to fix it. When it didn't get done, I started to resent it.

Here is how I solved the problem. I realized that I did not need to count on my husband, and I could make that call just like I used to. The beauty of it was that by getting the problem fixed the resentment went away. As a Numerology Counselor, I know how many women resent their husbands for making promises they do not keep.

So, ladies, I say to you gently: if your finger is not broken, pick up the phone and handle it yourself. You will feel so much better, and it will not become a sore spot that can start to destroy the relationship.

Give Praise

Whether you are dating or married to someone, always give very loud applause when they do something special for you. Tell them how much you appreciate whatever positive quality he or she may have. If there is something great about your partner, always let them know how much you value it and love that quality. Doing so will help keep the relationship thriving, so that even in times of discord your partner can think of some of the wonderful things you've said about him or her.

• ADDICTIONS •

If your partner drinks, does drugs, or is sexually addicted, a compulsive gambler, or a workaholic, all of these things can interfere with what can normally be a healthy, loving relationship—regardless of what the numbers look like. You have to lay down the law, and even if you love your partner with all your heart, you should separate until he or she gets real help.

Staying in an unhealthy marriage only for the sake of the children is certainly not doing your kids any favors. If your spouse is an alcoholic, it is very common for children to imitate the habits that they see. Physical abuse is unacceptable. If you have a spouse who thinks it's okay to hit you when they get angry, you need to respond with an unconditional NO and remove yourself from an unsafe situation. Physical abuse is never acceptable.

Numerology can help you understand why you are in an unhealthy relationship and consistently make bad choices in love. You can only attract what you expect to attract. The Love Affirmations in Chapter 21 can also help you make better choices. You might have to do more work on yourself, but it is always possible to change your relationship. I have seen married couples that have lost their way, became roommates, and found their way back to an active, loving, nurturing relationship. If you are willing to invest the time, you can make your partnership work in a really positive way.

• HEAVEN IN BED, TOXIC ALL DAY •

Toxic Numbers are lusty numbers. When you have Challenge Numbers in your Numerology Chart Comparisons, it can be amazing in bed because your lovemaking is so passionate. But you don't really communicate. It's more like, "Whatever, just shut up, and let's have sex." The mind-blowing sex can mislead you into thinking, "Oh gee, this guy is so mean to me, but I am crazy about him." Or "All she does is yell at me, but her body is so hot."

You may be physically crazy about this person, but the lust alone will not sustain the long-term relationship you want so badly. One day, after you marry and you have children, you realize you are stuck in something you don't want at all. Now, whether you stay or go, everyone loses, especially the kids.

He's Just Not That Into You

I cannot count how many women start dating a guy and they think he is the one, but he only keeps in touch through text messages. He does not take the time to call or even email, and then maybe when he feels like it, finally makes a date. To the ladies out there who are stuck in an unrewarding relationship like that, I do recommend the book He's Just Not That Into You, written by Greg Behrendt and Liz Tuccillo.

Learning your Numerology Blueprint and looking at your potential compatibility with someone else is a remarkable tool. But since every Number has a Positive and Negative side attached to it, sometimes the potential mate you meet *is just not that into you*. It really does not matter why because, after all, it is his loss, right ladies?!

I did not come across this book until after I married Charlie, but I so wished that I had read it while I was still dating. There are so many men that I would have kicked to the curb, had I known the author's advice. If you are married, or in a healthy love relationship, then text messaging is fine. But if that's all you're getting, don't settle for those crumbs. You deserve the whole cookie.

For readers who are just dating, you have a wonderful opportunity to get love right from the start. When you first meet someone you're attracted to, you can move ahead with your eyes wide open. For those of you who are already married and your relationship has gone off course, please use the suggestions in this chapter and refer to the Affirmations in Chapters 21 and 22 to do some much needed healing.

Now here is a wonderful example of what love should be:

Missy Levy
DOB: 2/9/1961 14591*/2

Allen Carrol
DOB: 12/5/1952 48357*/8

Missy's Story:
Allen and I have been together five years. We keep romance alive by buying each other little gifts. He buys me flowers; I buy him clothes, food, personal gifts. We go on dates. We cook together; he does most of the cooking and I just assist. We take classes together. He opens the car door for me and helps with the housework. We kiss and hold hands daily when we are together. He gives me massages and lets me

sit in his lap. We just do little things, but we do them daily. We feel so blessed that we are together.

Glynis' Response:

As you read this beautiful description of Missy's relationship with Allen, it makes perfect sense. First of all, their Life Path Numbers are a Natural Match: she is a 1 Life Path, and he is a 7 Life Path, which is great. Their Attitude Numbers are also a Natural Match. Missy's Attitude Number is a 2, and Allen's is an 8 Life Path. The Attitude and Life Path Numbers are extremely significant in Numerology.

Technically, if your Birth Date Numbers are Natural Matches or Compatible, that is also a great thing for your relationship. You might have a Challenge in your Name Numbers, but that doesn't matter as much because a name is an accent of who you are, and since those Numbers come from the name you go by, they can always be changed. It's interesting that Missy and Allen take classes together, because they both have a 4 Vibration, which gives them strong need to know and learn. They are both romantic and considerate of each other and buy each other little gifts. The 7 in him explains his sensitivity and the gentle spirit to be not only a cook but, I would gather, a very good cook. If Missy and Allen choose to get married, I would suggest that she keep the name she has. After all, if it ain't broke, don't fix it! This is a great relationship and could potentially last for years.

Note that Missy doesn't mention any frustration concerning the fact that she and Allen are not married and that they are just dating. The Life Path Numbers 1, 5, and 7 don't feel as upset about that. They like the idea of a commitment, but they don't need to have that ring on their finger. Read again what she has written about their relationship. It's as if they were already married. It sounds exactly like that kind of loving, committed couple. Good for both of them.

• SPECIAL ADVICE FOR WOMEN •

Dr. Patricia Allen's *Getting to "I Do"* describes the all too familiar scenario of the modern woman, who meets someone who seems just right, and the chemistry is overwhelming, and she has a few too many drinks—and, well hey, the next thing she knows she's in bed with him. Then the guy leaves, and there she is dizzy with joy and thinking that was the best night she ever had, and then—he never calls. She's devastated. Dr. Allen covers this topic perfectly; it is a wise book and it talks about the fact that we all have male and female traits inside us. Even if your Numerology Charts are very compatible, moving too quickly to the bedroom can ruin the chances of what could have been a long-term relationship.

The confusion comes about, in modern times, because with women and men both earning paychecks, the male has become confused as to what his role should be. That's why no matter how painful it may be to wait for that phone to ring, it is important that a man reach out to you. You should not call him. For at least 48 hours, you are under the spell of the hormone oxytocin, which is released through the joy of sex, and your reasoning powers will not help you at all.

That's why you don't want to get physically intimate too quickly. You really need to get to know each other first. Yes, it's the old-fashioned way, but trust me, if you are a woman, it's the best way. If the chemistry is there, know that the relationship will grow, and by restraining yourself physically, it will only grow stronger. Then when that wonderful sex happens, it will be part of a larger picture and the chances of your love lasting will be so much greater. That is worth waiting for.

CHAPTER 17

Picking the Perfect Wedding Date

A happy marriage is a long conversation which always seems too short.

—ANDRE MAUROIS

Your wedding date may be the most important day of your life that you get to pick, so why not choose it by the Numbers? Knowing what Vibrations are coming from the numbers that surround a potential wedding date gives you an enormous amount of information that can help you determine the most ideal date for you and your mate.

In this chapter we will look at examples of wedding day dreams that came true, and at a few dates that turned into wedding day disasters. I will teach you the Numerology that explains why.

This first example will be a wedding date that I helped select:
My friend Michelle called me and told me that she was trying to pick the perfect wedding date for her daughter, Laurel. Laurel was born

on 5/6/1978, which makes her a 9 Life Path, and her fiancé Jared was born on 5/10/1980 and that makes him a 6 Life Path. So, the first thing I wanted to make sure of is that their special day was compatible to their Life Path Numbers 9 and 6. She gave me a couple of options, but one date stood out clearly. That date was 9/20/2008, and knowing Laurel and her fiancé's Birth Numbers, I was positive they could not beat this particular date.

I will use 9/20/2008 as the example on how to find the three Numbers that make up an actual date, and explain exactly why this was the perfect wedding day for this young couple.

First you take the month and day, and reduce it to one digit:

Date: 9/20
$$9+2+0 = 11$$
$$= 1+1 = 2$$
Then reduce the actual day to one digit:
Date: 9/20
$$= 2+0 = 2$$
Then reduce the whole date to one digit:
Date: 9/20/2008
$$= 9+2+0+2+0+0+8 = 21$$
$$= 2+1 = 3$$

So the three Numbers that make up 9/20/2008 are 2/2/3.

Here is what this date means in Numerology: the actual day reduces to a 2, which is love and romance. The Attitude of the day was a 2, which encourages even more love and more romance; and finally the whole date reduced to a 3, which is about laughter, communication, and celebration.

As we learned in Chapter 3, the 3, 6, and 9 Vibrations are in the same Natural Match Category. Laurel, the bride, is a 9 Life Path and Jared, the groom, is a 6 Life Path. Their Life Path Numbers are a Natural Match, and they picked a date that reduced down to a 3, the remaining number in their Natural Match Category. This is great news for them as a couple.

The other thing is that Laurel also has a 2 Attitude, so she is a romantic; having that day with the double 2 really brought out that part of her personality. She is a beautiful blond, and her wedding dress was stunning. In fact, everyone was gorgeous. The wedding was a black-tie affair and the festive occasion brought tears of joy and laughter to all. The guests danced through the night, and I've never seen a happier couple. So it is this kind of wedding date that brings tears of joy to my eyes, and yes, picking the perfect wedding date *does matter*.

• HOW TO PICK YOUR WEDDING DATE •

First, look at you and your partner's Numerology Blueprints. Let's assume your partner is a 5 Life Path and you are a 7 Life Path. You would want to complete the Natural Match Category 1, 5, and 7. So, if possible, you should pick a day that reduces to a 1 Day, or at least a day that has a 1 in the three Numbers that make up a day.

If you are a 2 Life Path and an 8 Life Path, you want to complete the Natural Match category of 2, 4, and 8. You should look for a date that has a 4 in it, and so on.

But sometimes your Life Path Numbers are a Challenge, as was the case with my husband and me. In that case, you need to be a little more creative. As I mentioned in the beginning of this book, I am a 3 Life Path and we married on the 30th (3+0 = 3) so that was my day. The

Attitude Number of the day was October 30, 1+0+3+0 = 4, which is the same Vibration as his Life Path 4. When we break down the entire date, our wedding was October 30, 2004, (1+0+3+0+2+0+0+4 = 10 = 1+0 = 1) it became a 1. So I happily said to myself: "10/30/2004 is the day that the 3 and the 4 became 1."

• THE DAY'S NUMBERS AND • THEIR MEANINGS

The 1 is about Independence, but because you also become "one," it does not hurt to have that in the wedding date.

The 2 is about Love.

The 3 is about Laughter.

The 4 is about Security, and since you are making a commitment to be together, it is a good number to use as one of your three numbers.

The 5 is about Celebration, and with this Vibration, there is never a dull moment.

The 6 is about Nurturing, and if having children is important to you, it helps to have a 6.

The 7 is about Spirituality; if the bride and groom have a strong religious base, the spiritual number 7 is wonderful for a wedding day.

The 8 is about Success in Money Matters, and it is an excellent Vibration if you want a stylish wedding, because the 8 is also about appearance. Make sure the 8 Vibration is not a Challenge to either of your Life Path Numbers if you want to use it.

The 9 is about Family, so if you want a lot of family there, the 9 is a great Number to have in the three Numbers that make up your wedding day.

• FINDING THE THREE NUMBERS •
IN EACH DATE

The wedding day numbers should be as compatible to you and your partner as possible. The key to finding a compatible wedding date is to first consider your six numbers and your partner's six numbers. Then you have to find some Numbers that make up the actual day that are Compatible to both of you. If you have a few Numbers in your chart that you share, you will want a date that contains those numbers.

• WEDDING DAY EXAMPLES: •
THE GOOD AND THE BAD

Gat's Story

		Their Personal Chart Numbers:
Gat Slor	8/23/1959	74251*/4 Attitude
Eddie Warner	5/23/1952	79759*/1 Attitude
Wedding Date:	9/7/2003 breaks down to 7/7/3	
	Month and day:	9/7
		=9+7 = 16
		=1+6 = **7**
	Actual day:	9/7
		=**7**
	Whole date:	9/7/2003
		=9+7+2+0+0+3 = 21
		=2+1 = **3**

The three Numbers that make up **9/7/2003** are **7/7/3**.

Gat writes:

Hello Glynis,

We had the most magical, spiritual, moving wedding! The ceremony started at about 4:30 PM in a beautiful park with a large pond and fountain. The weather was perfect. We had about 200 guests, and after the ceremony we had a potluck dinner outside. A friend flew in from New York and took pictures of our wedding and reception, and all of them came out beautifully.

My immediate family live all over the world, and to my joy, all of them were able to make it to our wedding. We were on a shoestring budget, and my family and friends helped us with the food, decorations, and even the cost of the wedding itself.

We had our reception at the club where we met for the first time on 10/11/1997. The band that played on the night we met also played at our reception. Everyone had a great time celebrating our marriage, and many people have told us that ours was the best wedding they had ever been to. Even more than five years later, people still talk about our wedding.

Glynis' response:

The right wedding date is personal for each couple. For example, your chosen day would not be successful for everyone, yet when I look at the Numerology of the two of you, I can see why it worked for you as a couple. Let's take another look at the numbers.

		Their Personal Chart Numbers:
Gat Slor	8/23/1959	74251*/4 Attitude
Eddie Warner	5/23/1952	79759*/1 Attitude
Wedding Date:	9/7/2003 breaks down to **7/7/3.**	

First of all, the Number 7 plays a big part in your relationship. Your husband has a 7 Personality Number in his name, and you both have a 7 as your Soul Number, so look at it this way: in 9/7/2003, the actual day is a 7; the Attitude of the day is a 7. So there was a double 7 in that day, and 7 is about God and spirituality.

Judging by your story about the wedding, it sounds as though you were both very much in tune to the spirituality of this wonderful occasion. On that particular day your souls were fulfilled, because the Soul Number for both of you is a 7. And then the day itself reduces to a 3 Vibration. When I look at the Number for the day, I want to know if it is Compatible to your Life Paths. Sure enough, your husband is a 9 Life Path, and 3 is a Natural Match to the 9, and the 3 is also a Compatible to your 1 Life Path. That is why the date proved so successful for you. Thank you for sharing your story.

Intuitively these two picked the right date. The 7s were in their Charts, double 7s in his, a 7 in hers, and there is the double 7 in the actual day they picked. Judging from Gat's letter, the day was a spiritual high for everyone involved. The fact that it was a joyous occasion with dancing, music, and laughter could be attributed to the 3 Vibration of the day. The 3 would encourage that absolute celebration of life, and of each other.

Vanessa's Story

Their Personal Chart Numbers:

Vanessa Hamm:	1/12/1978	89832*/4 Attitude
Michael Hamm:	4/7/1973	77574*/2 Attitude
Wedding Date:	**5/4/2002** breaks down to **9/4/4**	

Month and day: 5/4

=5+4 = **9**

Actual day: 5/4

=**4**

Whole date: 5/4/2002

=5+4+2+0+0+2 = 13

=1+3 = **4**

The three Numbers that make up **5/4/2002** are **9/4/4**.

Vanessa writes:

I planned an outside wedding in my parent's apple orchard, which is out in the country. I had no Plan B for bad weather. I just hoped for the best. Mind you, it had snowed very badly a month prior. No worries: on the day of my wedding the sun was shining and there was a lovely breeze. Good weather for early May.

My husband and I reside in Illinois and everyone from his family drove the nine-plus hours to get to our wedding. The bridesmaids wore apple colors: Red Delicious for my twin sister; Golden Delicious, Winesap, and Hunter Green dresses as well to represent the leaves on the trees. The guys were in their black tuxedos and black shirts with ties to match the girls' dresses.

The flower girls (twin cousins) wore white dresses with apple orchard embroidered aprons. The ring bearer carried our rings on apple cushions, and white doves were released as we said our vows. Once we were pronounced husband and wife, we had fireworks burst into the air. Everything went flawlessly. I think it was perfect planning on my part.

Glynis' response:

		Their Personal Chart Numbers:
Vanessa Hamm:	1/12/1978	89832*/4 Attitude
Michael Hamm:	4/7/1973	77574*/2 Attitude
Wedding Date:	**5/4/2002** breaks down to **9/4/4**	

Vanessa, your wedding date brings a big smile to my face. The 9 Vibration, which was the Attitude Number of the day, is all about family, and it sounds as though your entire family gathered, and maybe they were all praying for that good weather.

It is interesting that the day is a Natural Match to you and your husband. Your 2 Life Path and his 4 Life Path are completely compatible to that day because the actual day was a 4, and when you reduce the full date to one digit, it became a 4 as well. His Attitude Number is a 2 and your Attitude Number is a 4. If your Attitude Number is the same as your partner's Life Path Number, you have a very special connection. You have a 2 Life Path, he has a 2 Attitude; he has a 4 Life Path, you have a 4 Attitude. A wonderful combination for you as a couple. Congratulations!

Sandy's Story

		Their Personal Chart Numbers:
Sandy Shaw:	7/27/1954	96698*/7 Attitude
Jimmy England:	10/8/1949	46185*/9 Attitude
Wedding Date:	**12/14/1996** breaks down to **8/5/6**	
	Month and day: 12/14	
	=1+2+1+4 = 8	

Then reduce the actual day to one digit:

Actual day: 12/14

= 1+4 = 5

Then reduce the whole date to one digit:

Whole date: 12/14/1996

=1+2+1+4+1+9+9+6 = 33

=3+3 = 6

The three Numbers that make up **12/14/1996** are **8/5/6**.

Sandy writes:

The day I married I had cold feet, but I decided not to back out because my mom had gone through so much trouble to hold the wedding at her house. The preacher was almost 30 minutes late, and there were only a few very close friends of mine present, along with my immediate family and my future hubby's grown son. Suddenly something didn't sound right. The preacher had turned an extra page and was suddenly preaching for a funeral!

The preacher realized his error, apologized, and got back on track, but the mood was broken. I was so stunned I wanted to say, "NO WAY!" and run. It was like an omen that I didn't pay attention to. As soon as the preacher said, "You may now kiss the bride," my husband did something he'd never done before. He grabbed me and held me too tight. It felt like it was a kiss of ownership. I kept trying to pull away and he kept holding me tighter, until I almost couldn't breathe. I was shocked.

Later, we went out to eat and then came back home for some alone time. The phone rang and it was my husband's oldest son wanting to know if he could come over and visit. His dad said, "Sure, come on over." So there I sat with his son, who was eating fast food out of a bag while my husband fell asleep on the couch, leaving me to entertain my new stepson. I was livid!

I finally looked over at hubby and said, "Well, I'm tired. I'm going to bed." His son left and he woke up just long enough to go off to bed. I couldn't believe this had happened on my wedding day, and hubby spent most of the night alone in bed because I was up fuming until the early morning hours.

The next day, my new husband lay in bed all day long, making sure not to wake me as he watched the video of our wedding that he'd been recording all day long. I was so angry at him when I woke up that I could have killed him, and yes, I did let him have it then for ruining our wedding night.

Glynis' response:

		Their Personal Chart Numbers:
Sandy Shaw:	7/27/1954	96698*/7 Attitude
Jimmy England:	10/8/1949	46185*/9 Attitude
Wedding Date:	**12/14/1996** breaks down to **8/5/6**	

Yikes! Sandy, 12/14/1996 was definitely not a good day for you two to get married. That date is a 5 Day with an 8 Attitude Number and the whole day reduces to a 6. It's interesting to note Jimmy's Birth Numbers: he was born on an 8 Day and is a 5 Life Path, so technically, that day was more about him than it was about you. When a man with an 8

Vibration lives on the Negative side of the number, it is not uncommon that he feels his significant other is something he can possess. An 8 Vibration man wants to know he has a wife and is proud of her, so when he kissed you, that is why it felt so controlling.

You are an 8 Life Path. When you said you felt he owned you when he kissed you, to him he was uniting with the woman he loves very much and he felt that all was well. This was an ideal day for him. The biggest message we can take from your numbers is that an 8 Life Path must be careful not to blame others when things go wrong, or internalize the blame and feel like a martyr.

The 9 in your chart tells me you are someone who feels overly responsible for your original family, and you did say that you didn't want to let your mother down. You had cold feet, but you chose to go through with it anyway. Because you let this happen, here you are in a marriage that started out on the wrong foot.

The 6 Vibration, the third number that your wedding date breaks down to, represents family. That could explain why your husband thought nothing of his son coming over to visit on your wedding night. Not a good beginning, but picking the right date could have helped avoid much of this travail.

I can't tell from your letter if things are going better now, but the actual wedding date was part of the problem. You could have picked a date that was more compatible to you—the Number 2 should have been somewhere in there, because the 2 Energy would have brought some love and harmony to it. A 3 Vibration would have been good for some humor, because it doesn't sound like there was much lightness there. The preacher getting on the wrong page and reading words that you would say at funeral was macabre to say the least, and yes, I would have seen that as a bad omen as well.

A breakdown of the numbers in the names Jimmy England and Sandy

Shaw produces five Toxic numbers out of six, so it seems to me that your wedding date sums up exactly what Toxic Numbers feel like! I'm sorry about that wedding day; just know that this relationship will always require compromise, and I suggest you look at each number in your Name and Birth Charts and see what you can do to coexist more amicably. Good luck and thank you for sharing your story.

Taren's Story

                                        Their Personal Chart Numbers:

Taren Gubman: 8/5/1956   17857*/4 Attitude

Larree Baglor: 12/3/1946   96638*/6 Attitude

Wedding Date: **9/6/2002** breaks down to **6/6/1**

Month and day: 9/6

$$=9+6=15$$

$$=1+5=6$$

Actual day: 9/6

$$=6$$

Whole date: 9/6/2002

$$=9+6+2+0+0+2=19$$

$$=1+9=10$$

$$=1+0=1$$

The three Numbers that make up **9/6/2002** are **6/6/1**.

Taren writes:

When we got married, I did not take my husband's last name nor did I hyphenate it, and it has been a thorn in his side ever since. I had planned on taking his name and hyphenating it, but with my surname at the end. When they asked us to sign the marriage license, I didn't say anything and I just signed.

This happened after a caravan of four cars brought us to the place where we were supposed to get married. My husband was in another car with his daughter. He took off driving very fast and went the wrong way—the "scenic" route. I tried to catch up with him to tell him he was going the wrong way and I couldn't.

I also could not get a signal on his cell phone. As it was, we were almost an hour late, and I called the office of the justice of the peace and told them why we were running late. They agreed to stay open until we got there. Needless to say, I was very upset and frantic.

Glynis' Response:

		Their Personal Chart Numbers:
Taren Gubman:	8/5/1956	17857*/4 Attitude
Larree Baglor:	12/3/1946	96638*/6 Attitude
Wedding Date:	**9/6/2002** breaks down to **6/6/1**	

Hi Taren, thank you for sharing your story with me. The actual date did not help you or your husband. If anything, it brought out the flaw in your relationship, which can turn into a power struggle. Your husband has a double 6 in his chart. Your actual wedding date, 9/6/2002, is a 6/6/1. The 6 and the 1 Vibrations don't get along well together, especially when there is a double 6. The numbers battle themselves, and in this case it heightened the power struggle.

An ideal day would have been a 4 day, or a date that reduces down to a 4, because a 4 is considered compatible to the 7 Life Path and the 8 Life Path. You have 3 Challenges out of 6 Numbers right now, and you were wise not to take his name. Doing so would not help your relationship.

The name Taren Baglor breaks down to 4, 1, 5—Numbers completely Toxic to your husband's Name Numbers 9, 6, 6—so taking his name is not a good idea. This relationship requires a willingness to compromise. What you do have in common is the Number 8, which is the need for financial security.

You have a 1 in your Soul, and by the time you got to the location, you were furious and felt sabotaged. Yet you were still willing to say, "I do." Just as it did on your wedding day, your relationship will call for a lot of work. You also have a double 7, so you need to work on that spiritual side. *Let go and let God* is something you should adopt as your personal mantra. Say it over and over again. Your husband also needs to feel respected by you, so be aware of your verbal delivery when you talk to him. It will make a positive difference in your relationship and I am sure you would welcome that.

CHAPTER 18

Should You Take His Name?

Two souls with but a single thought, two hearts that beat as one.

—JOHN KEATS

The name you take in your marriage has the potential to alter your Numerology Blueprint. While the numbers that come from your actual birth date are permanent and you will live with them your whole life, you *can* change the three Numbers that make up the Energy of the name you use. The key is changing your name to improve, not hurt, your life.

In this chapter, we will look at some people who got married and took on their partner's name, only to see the relationship take a turn for the worse. We will also include an example in which taking on the fiancé's name turned out for the better.

Let's say you are dating somebody, and then you construct Numerology Charts, and you make a lovely discovery: you have a

Soul Mate Connection. Then, you decide to get married and you want to change your last name. Not so fast! If you don't know what you are doing, you can lose that strong Number connection you had when you were dating, or you can even create some Challenges with each other by the altered Vibrations of the new name. If that happens when you take on the married name, don't do it!

The good news is we live in a time where it is not necessary for the woman to take the man's name. As a matter of fact, my sister's husband took on her last name. He dropped his own last name because it was his stepfather's name and because he was very proud to be married to my sister and he really loved our family. The point here is we have choices. Some couples even make up a new surname by combining parts of both their last names.

It's important to choose a name that has the right Energy for both of you as a couple. You may be engaged or thinking about getting married, and wondering, "Should I change my name?" Or if you are married, took the new name, and the relationship went bad, you may be wondering if you should take back your maiden name. "When I married her, she totally changed." That can be literally true, and now you know why. This chapter will show you how to break down your maiden name and see if a name change will help or hurt your relationship.

Some Case Studies:

This chapter will illustrate the power of a name change and how it will affect your love lives. You can use these examples to help you decide whether you should take on your partner's name, or if you have kept a name from a previous marriage, to decide whether you should return to your maiden name.

Pamela Anderson and Tommy Lee

Maiden Name:	Pamela Anderson	12314*/8 Attitude
Married Name:	Pamela Anderson Lee	25714*/8 Attitude
Pamela's birth date:	7/1/1967	
Ex-husband's Name:	Tommy Lee	54934*/4 Attitude
Tommy's birth date:	10/3/1962	

Number Comparison Chart using Pam's Maiden Name,
Pamela Anderson:

CHART COMPARISON	Pam's Numbers	Tommy's Numbers	Number Connection
SOUL NUMBER	1	5	**Natural Match**
PERSONALITY NUMBER	2	4	**Natural Match**
POWER NAME NUMBER	3	9	**Natural Match**
BIRTH DAY	1	3	Compatible
LIFE PATH	4	4	**Natural Match**
ATTITUDE NUMBER	8	4	**Natural Match**

Number Comparison Chart using Pam's Married Name,
Pamela Anderson Lee:

CHART COMPARISON	Pam's Numbers	Tommy's Numbers	Number Connection
SOUL NUMBER	2	5	**Challenge**
PERSONALITY NUMBER	5	4	Challenge
POWER NAME NUMBER	7	9	Challenge
BIRTH DAY	1	3	Compatible
LIFE PATH	4	4	Natural Match
ATTITUDE NUMBER	8	4	Natural Match

Pamela Anderson is one of my favorite examples of someone who changed her name with poor results. She married Tommy Lee and became Pamela Anderson Lee. The name Pamela Anderson breaks down to 1, 2, and 3, a wonderful Number Combination that can prove to be very positive. The 1 is the Soul Number, and that Vibration is about ambition and helps you strive to be the best you can be. The 2 is the Personality Number, and it is about wanting love and romance. The 2 is a loving energy. Then the 3 is for expression, big smiles, bright eyes, laughter, communication, all the good stuff.

When Pamela took on Tommy's last name, Lee, it was as if she were the sun and a black cloud showed up to hide her. She took on a 2 Soul Number, 5 Personality Number, and 7 Power Name Number, which were all Challenge Numbers to Tommy Lee's name, and therefore bad for the marriage. The Negative side of the 5 and 7 Vibration is to escape through unhealthy addictions. Pamela has said that when she married Tommy Lee, she began drinking and partying more than she had ever before. The 5 Vibration can bring drama to your life, and the following scenario is the kind of drama no one wants. The story is that when they were getting tattoos, and the tattoo artist asked, "No one has Hepatitis C or anything, do they?" And Tommy Lee said "No" because he was too embarrassed to admit he had it, and he didn't want Pamela to know. As a result, she contracted Hepatitis C through their shared needle, and it was a long time before she regained even a part of her former good health.

There was also physical violence in their marriage, violence that, at one point, put him in jail. You can bet that with the sensitive 2 Vibration as her Soul Number, she shed many a tear in this marriage. When Pamela decided she had had enough, and divorced him, she took back her original name.

When she did this, her charisma emerged again. This is a stellar example of how Personal Name Numbers truly make a difference in a person's life. By taking back her original name, all of those Natural Match Numbers they shared while dating returned. This explains why no matter how many other loves come into their lives, they return to each other.

Another reason they do that is because they are both a 4 Life Path, and the 4 Life Paths are the soldiers of love. If they make a commitment, they want it to last forever. When children are involved, this need to commit is even truer for them. They still deal with each other, but Pamela Anderson is back to being herself. I believe she will always love Tommy Lee, but no matter what happens, she should never use the name Pamela Anderson Lee again.

A Client's Story

Jan writes:

Hi Glynis,

I just got engaged to Dan. We have been seeing each other for a couple of years, and we are ready to take the big step. But I am not sure if I should keep my maiden name, or adopt his. Please let me know what you think.

I would be willing to hyphenate my name, or just drop it, depending on what you think.

Maiden Name:	Jan Thommas	87664*/6	Attitude
Potential married name:	Jan Smith	13464*/6	Attitude
Jan's birth date:	9/24/1978		
Fiance's Name:	Dan Smith	16764*/8	Attitude
Dan's birth date:	2/6/1976		

Number Comparison Chart if Jan keeps her maiden name:

CHART COMPARISON	Jan's Numbers	Dan's Numbers	Number Connection
SOUL NUMBER	8	1	**Neutral**
PERSONALITY NUMBER	7	6	Challenge
POWER NAME NUMBER	6	7	Challenge
BIRTH DAY	6	6	Natural Match
LIFE PATH	4	4	Natural Match
ATTITUDE NUMBER	6	8	Compatible

Number Comparison Chart if Jan changes her name to Jan Smith:

CHART COMPARISON	Jan's Numbers	Dan's Numbers	Number Connection
SOUL NUMBER	1	1	**Natural Match**
PERSONALITY NUMBER	3	6	**Natural Match**
POWER NAME NUMBER	4	7	**Compatible**
BIRTH DAY	6	6	Natural Match
LIFE PATH	4	4	Natural Match
ATTITUDE NUMBER	6	8	Compatible

Glynis' Response

Hi Jan,

I was so excited when I saw your chart. You two are a very impressive couple. You were born 9/24/1978, which gives you a 6 Birth Day Number, a 4 Life Path, and a 6 Attitude. Dan was born 2/6/1976, which gives him a 6 Birth Day Number, a 4 Life Path, and an 8 Attitude. Those three numbers are considered Compatible, Natural Match, and Natural Match. So I am already thrilled with your Birth Numbers because those numbers have the strongest influence on you as a couple and cannot be changed.

I am concerned that your maiden name, Jan Thommas, has one Neutral Number and two Challenge Numbers when compared to the name Dan Smith. However, if you take his name and drop yours and become Jan Smith, your three Name Numbers will be a Natural Match, Natural Match, and Compatible. Doing so allows you to discard everything that is Toxic in your relationship! How exciting is that? You are a great example of why someone should change their name.

You also share the Number 6. The 6 is the parent number, so if you two decide to become parents, what lucky children they will be.

Your mutual 4 Life Path means you have an understanding of what you each want for your future, and what a wonderful future it will be!

I am now going to give you an example of a name change that would *not* be beneficial.

Colleen's Story

Colleen writes:

I am back to my earlier maiden name, Colleen Thompson. When I got married a couple of years ago, I changed my name to Colleen Stansel, and our lives fell apart. I felt such a huge stress in my life that I almost had a nervous breakdown! We divorced recently and my life is marvelous again. The stress is gone, and my ex and I are getting along now. Not that I'm going to marry him again, or anything crazy like that. Was my married name really the cause of all this turmoil?

Maiden Name:	Colleen Thompson	15631*/6 Attitude
Married Name:	Colleen Stansel	48331*/6 Attitude
Colleen's birth date:	12/21/1966	
Ex-husband's name:	Jerry Stansel	94494*/1 Attitude
Jerry's birth date:	1/9/1947	

Number Comparison Chart with Colleen's maiden name:

CHART COMPARISON	Colleen's Numbers	Jerry's Numbers	Number Connection
SOUL NUMBER	1	9	Compatible
PERSONALITY NUMBER	5	4	Challenge
POWER NAME NUMBER	6	4	Compatible
BIRTH DAY	3	9	Natural Match
LIFE PATH	1	4	Challenge
ATTITUDE NUMBER	6	1	Challenge

Number Comparison Chart with Colleen taking Jerry's name:

CHART COMPARISON	Colleen's Numbers	Jerry's Numbers	Number Connection
SOUL NUMBER	4	9	**Challenge**
PERSONALITY NUMBER	8	4	**Natural Match**
POWER NAME NUMBER	3	4	**Challenge**
BIRTH DAY	3	9	Natural Match
LIFE PATH	1	4	Challenge
ATTITUDE NUMBER	6	1	Challenge

Glynis' response

Colleen,

Had you called me before you got married, I would have looked at your Numbers and said, "Do not take his name." Even with your maiden name, Colleen Thompson, you have three Challenges in your chart comparison, which means you would always have to work on the relationship. But you could still weather the storm. When you took Jerry's last name, you took on four Challenge Numbers. As I have explained in Chapter 3, when you have four or more Challenges, you have to ask yourself, "Is it even worth it?" The relationship can be incredibly difficult, which is exactly what your brief note made clear to me.

One of the reasons you encountered so much difficulty was the result of your lighter energy. You have a 1 in your Soul, which is compatible to your Life Path 1. It kept you moving. You have a 5 for excitement and 6 for nurturing. You did not mention if you had children, but judging by the double 6, perhaps you do. Maybe that is one of the reasons you got together with Jerry.

When I look at his numbers, I notice all the 4s in his chart and think he should be a "steady eddy," a consistent guy—not necessarily one that can keep up with your energy or know how to have fun the way you do. When you took on his name, you took on the 4 and the 8, which are intense Vibrations in Numerology and where money can be a problem. So maybe finances got weird for you as a couple.

The bottom line is, I never would have suggested that you take on his last name. Now that you have divorced him and have gone back to the name you used previously, I am not surprised that you two get along again, just like when you were dating.

You are actually challenged twice by your Birth Numbers, the numbers that come from the birth date and can never be changed. There is only one Natural Match, which is the day you were born. It is not an ideal relationship for marriage. Interestingly you write, "We got divorced, and now my life is marvelous again." You were very happy before you married, and those 1s and 5s in your chart tell me that feeling controlled, or not having the freedom you normally have, could make you feel suffocated. I do not believe that was Jerry's intent, but I would not be surprised if that is how it felt in the marriage. You are a great example of not only being in a relationship that was not ideal, but getting married and taking on the last name, made it even worse.

• TAKING ON A NUMBER •

Taking on someone's name is all about the Vibrations. So, the question is, by taking on the name, will it make things better or worse? And are you ready to take on the changes the Vibrations will bring to you as a person?

For instance, if you take on your husband's name and suddenly you have a 6 in your chart that you did not have before, what will that do? The 6 might encourage you to have a family, so you have to ask yourself, "Do I want a family? Am I getting married to have a child?" If you are, by all means take the name that gives you a 6. If you aren't, think hard about the decision to take his name!

Let's now look at each potential Vibration that you could take on if you change your name due to a relationship. The general rule is that if the new name gives you more Challenge numbers with your mate than you had with your previous name, then it is best to not change your name.

Taking on a 1 Vibration

You might find that before the marriage you did not feel very motivated, and now you do. This is because there is a 1 in your chart. If having more energy would be a good thing for your marriage, go for it.

Taking on a 2 Vibration

The 2 is about love and connection, and that could be great for a couple. If you already have a 2 Vibration in your chart, taking on another one might make you feel too dependent on your partner.

Taking on a 3 Vibration

This vibration will add fun and an ease in conversation. The 3 is a very good Vibration for understanding each other. However, if your partner is a 4 or 7 and welcomes the quiet, taking on the 3 could cause frustration in the relationship because the 3 always has something to say.

Taking on a 4 Vibration

A 4 Vibration means settling down and having a solid base together. This is generally good for the relationship. The downside of the 4 is being quite opinionated.

Taking on a 5 Vibration

The 5 means there is going to be adventure and more excitement. If you have a mellow relationship right now, and like it that way, you may not want to add this Vibration.

Taking on a 6 Vibration

The 6 is the parent Vibration. If having children is a big part of why you are getting married, then this is a good Number for helping you in becoming a responsible parent. If the person you are marrying already has children, taking on the 6 could be about you helping to parent the children.

Taking on a 7 Vibration

The 7 is the number that embraces spirituality. Would you work on your faith with this person you are marrying? The 7 also likes time to be alone. Ask yourself if this would be helpful to the relationship you are in, especially if you are a couple that likes to always be together.

Taking on an 8 Vibration

An 8 pertains to money. Is money a major concern for you? If you are not good with finances, you may not want to take on the 8 Vibration because that is one of its lessons. The 8 can also have some other difficult lessons attached to it. So unless it gives you a Natural Match or a Compatible Number connection to your partner, do not take it on.

Taking on a 9 Vibration

The 9 is all about leading others to make a positive difference. But if you take on a 9 that you did not have in your name before, it may make you suddenly really delve back into your past, and it could cause some old emotional scars to resurface that you will have to work to resolve. So only take on the 9 if it is a Natural Match or Compatible Number to your husband-to-be's name.

CHAPTER 19

Homes, Apartments, and Hotels: Can the Number on a Door Ruin a Relationship?

Where we love is home, home that our feet may leave, but not our hearts.

—OLIVER WENDELL HOLMES

It's amazing how the Vibration of the Number on a door can make a difference in your life. It has happened to me in my travels. One hotel I booked offered me a room that added up to a 5. The room number was 509 = 5+0+9 = 14 = 1+4 = 5. I thought to myself, "Well, even though a 5 can promote drama and excitement, I can handle it." So they brought me to my room, and as God as my witness, there was a pool of dried blood on the carpet! Needless to say, I told them to give me a different room.

Another time I was offered a hotel room that added up to the Number 8. The 8 can be a Challenge to my Life Path 3, so I was a little concerned, but I decided to take the room. Traffic roared throughout the night, and I couldn't sleep. I just laughed to myself thinking,

"Here we go again." The next morning I moved to a room that had a Compatible Number on the door for me, and all was well.

When you travel with your partner, you definitely want to make sure the number on the door is good for you as a couple. Consider the purpose of your trip and decide how the Number on the door can help you achieve that goal. When my husband and I vacation, I make sure that the hotel room adds up to a Number 2. The 2 represents love and intimacy, both physical and romantic. Two other numbers that encourage that loving feeling are the Numbers 6 and 9. I have found that if we stay in a room that is a Challenge Number, we end up not relating as well to each other and will end up having some sort of silly argument. It has happened often enough for me to know—*the Number on the door makes a difference.*

• ROOM NUMBER DESCRIPTIONS •

If you go on a trip together, just make sure the Numbers for your room will lead to a happy and joyous stay for both of you. Here are the basic breakdowns:

Room Number 1

If you are on a business trip together, and each of you has separate meetings and goals, the Number 1 will reinforce your independence. If you are going on a trip together and you each have to do your own separate thing—let's say, you're going to a meeting; he or she is going to an art show—then the 1 could be just fine. You can safely stay in the room, because the 1 is not about romance.

Room Number 2

The Number 2 is about being physical and connected. It's the perfect number for the honeymoon, or second honeymoon, or just a romantic weekend away from the kids or work.

Room Number 3

This is the room to party in. It's about being social, having fun, sharing laughter and your playful side—a good escape number for the entire family. If you and your partner have not been communicating, this Vibration will help you to start talking again.

Room Number 4

The Number 4 is about learning. Perhaps you are exploring museums and attending lectures. Or maybe this trip is family related. The Number 4 is also about family, so this is a fine number if the family is with you. If you need to attend a convention to learn a skill, the 4 Room is a perfect place to study the material.

Room Number 5

The Number 5 means never a dull moment and staying very busy. Decide if this is what you want. The 5 can also bring unwanted chaos. However, if you and your partner are bored and want to spice up your sex life, then the 5 Room could help do the trick.

Room Number 6

The Number 6 Room should have a comfortable feeling. If you have been trying to get pregnant, staying in a 6 room could turn out to be your lucky number for conceiving. The 6 is also a strong Vibration for business meetings where you are in charge.

Room Number 7

The Room Number 7 is conducive to a peaceful time, a place to reflect on your life. So maybe you two are going to get together and just relax, because when you are at home, you push yourselves too hard. Now you finally get to go on a trip and you can rest peacefully and rest in each other's arms. Perhaps you will make a list of what you can do to improve your life together. And get in tune with each other once again.

Room Number 8

The Room Number 8 is all about business. Sometimes you may have to go on a business trip and want your mate to come along. It is not easy to combine business and pleasure, and you have to decide which it will be. If the 8 is a compatible Vibration to your Life Path Numbers, then it could be the perfect room for you as a couple.

Room Number 9

The 9 is the Number where everyone feels welcome. A great Number for a family reunion. Also, if you are experiencing family problems, spending time in a 9 room could actually help to resolve the conflict.

• CHOOSING THE PERFECT ROOM •

You want to make sure that the hotel number you choose is compatible or naturally matched to one or both of your Life Paths.

My husband is a Life Path 4, and I am a Life Path 3, which is a challenge for us as a couple. As it happens, the two Numbers that are considered compatible to both of us are the Number 2 and the Number 6. So I often pick a room that has either of those Numbers when we are together as a couple. If your Life Path Numbers are a Challenge, try to find a Vibration that is Compatible to both of you. Just keep in mind those basic definitions.

You might find yourself in a situation where you really can't change the room. Let's assume that your company has booked you into a hotel and you have the last room in the hotel. All is not lost. A client's mother was in a hospital room that added up to 8. I was concerned because I know the downside of 8 can result in someone becoming a victim. She was so worried about her mother not recovering.

My client put the Number 3 on the inside of her mother's hospital door. The room's Vibration was now a 2 (8+3 = 11 = 1+1 = 2). Within a week and a half, her mother had recovered much sooner than expected. So carry a few numbers with you; they can be magnetic or even made out of tape; you might pick up a magnetic number or just have some tape you can use to create a number. Some people even use clear nail polish to write the Number on the door. Whatever you do, altering the Energy can bring about very positive results.

• HOME AND APARTMENT ENERGY •

It stands to reason the Vibration you choose for your home, or permanent apartment, is of particular importance.

Here are the Vibrations:

Keep the basic meaning of the Numbers in mind when you choose the number for your home.

The **1** fosters independence.

The **2** encourages love.

The **3** promotes communication.

The **4** is the house of study and creating security.

The **5** can be chaotic, but brings nonstop excitement

The **6** is a home-loving Energy that welcomes family.

The **7** is for spirituality and a house of study.

The **8** is for money management, and learning to listen to what others have to say.

The **9** is where all are welcome, and where you learn to forgive the past transgressions of family members.

If you are married, the home Number 1 can be a problem, because it encourages you to do your own thing and not work together as a team. I have noticed that when women get divorced, they often subconsciously move into a Number 1 home or apartment, so they can be by themselves and assert their independence.

When they are ready for love again, I counsel them to alter the Number on the door to one that adds up to the Vibration they are now ready for. You always have the option. You may check your home address right now and realize your house is a 7, the home of a loner, as well as a house of study and spirituality. You may have not found someone to be part of your life while living there. In this case, you can just change the number. Review the list of Compatible, Natural Match, or Challenge numbers for your Life Path as described in Chapter 3 and make the right decision for yourself.

• IMPROVING YOUR HOME VIBRATION •

In my research, I have noticed the addresses of those big apartment complexes for mostly single people often add up to a 5. Assume the street number is 500, which reduces to a 5 (5+0+0 = 5). The 5 is fun and games, which seems to be a big part of that lifestyle and is not a problem. But maybe you're a husband and wife with children and you live in a house of 5. Your world feels crazy, chaotic, and out of control. Here's how you can calm down that Vibration. Pick up the Number 6 and put it on the inside of your door (5+6 = 11 = 1+1 = 2). The harmonious and loving 2 Vibration should do the trick.

One of my brothers had a house that was overwhelming for him. The street address was 800, which reduces to an 8 (8+0+0 = 8). He seemed to have continuous issues with money, so he altered the Vibration by putting the Number 4 on the inside of the door, and it became a house of 3 (8+4 = 12 = 1+2 = 3). The Vibration of the house immediately felt lighter, and he was able to find some work that had eluded him before. Everyone who came into the house could feel the difference.

Another client lived in a small house in the back of her property that also added up to an 8 Vibration. Money was not an issue (remember the Positive side of that Vibration invites financial security). This was a 2 Life Path, which is compatible to the 8, but she always felt completely alone the minute she walked in the front door. I told her to put up a 3 (8+3 = 11 = 1+1 = 2) on the inside of the door, which changed the house to a 2 Vibration. Almost immediately the lonely feeling disappeared. She was so excited that she called me a few days later to tell me about it. Incidentally, the Positive side of the 8 Vibration is not negated; remember, Numerology is like an onion—it has many layers—so she now has the advantage of both Vibrations.

Whether it's the Vibration of a home, apartment, or hotel, whatever number is on the door, it will in some way affect your life. You need to decide what you want to do with that Energy. Ask yourself, "Am I really happy here?" If you are alone and live in a House of 1, 5, or 7, those are numbers encouraging you to be by yourself; so if you wish, you can alter the number. It is all about doing that simple math.

> You can pick up a number for your home at Home Depot or any hardware store in your area. Put the number on the inside of your door and you will change the Vibration. Some people feel the new atmosphere right away; others experience the change a few weeks later.

When Charlie and I moved into our new home, our address was 556, which adds up to 7 (5+5+6 = 16 = 1+6 = 7). The reason I was drawn to it is that I was born at 421 Jade Cove Way (4+2+1 = 7). So that Vibration felt like home to me. Also, 7 is considered the Spiritual Number, so I was drawn for that reason as well. Earlier in my life, when I moved out of my parents' home, I lived in a Number 7 apartment. My next apartment was also a 7. I thought, "How interesting; no matter where I go, I end up in a House of 7." I know and love the energy, but now that I'm married, I want to feel as connected to my husband as possible.

My new house with Charlie was quite large and I felt separated from him. So I placed the Numbers 3 and 1 on the inside of the door. I chose those Numbers because they add up to 4 (I did not want the actual Number 4 on the door because that number is a Challenge to me). With the 3 and the 1 on the inside of the door, these numbers added to the 7 that was already present: (1+3+7 = 11 = 1+1 = 2). My house of 7 became a house of 2. The House of 2 represents love and harmony, having someone to bond with. Suddenly the house did not feel so big after all. I could feel my husband in every room.

If you are having trouble in your relationship, figure out what Number is best for you as a couple and use simple math to pick the other Number that can alter your home energy. Or if you are single, you can put a Vibration on the door to help attract love into your life. It works!

CHAPTER 20

Personal Year Cycles: This Too Shall Pass

Harmony is pure love, for love is a concerto.

—LOPE DE VEGA

Every so often a client will express in the middle of a reading how frustrated they have recently become with his or her mate, even wondering if the marriage should continue. When I hear something like that, I instantly check the husband and wife's Personal Year Cycles, because there is a good chance that they are in conflict.

• FINDING THE PERSONAL YEAR CYCLE •

To find your Personal Year Cycle, take the month and day, and reduce it to one digit. Then add it to the World Number, which is the year reduced to one digit.

Let's use 2009 as an example.

Reduce the year to one digit to find the World Number: 2+0+0+9 = 11; 1+1 = 2. The World Number is 2.

Let's say you were born on January 2nd. Reduce the month and day to one digit: 1+2 = 3.

Add that to the World Number 2: 2+3 = 5.

So you would be in the Personal Year Cycle of 5.

Now, let's look at your partner's Personal Year Cycle.

Let's say he or she was born on December 8th: 1+2+8 = 11 = 1+1 = 2.

Add that to the World Number: 2+2 = 4.

The 4 and a 5 are considered a Challenge in Numerology. As you will discover later in this chapter, the Cycle of 5 means life is moving very fast and feels out of control. It's difficult to know if your life is what you want it to be. Suddenly, nothing feels quite right, even if it did before. Your mate in the Cycle of 4 may be worrying about the home and family, but because you are in the Cycle of 5, it seems like nothing is going quite the way you want it.

When you are asked a question, you become defensive. You feel your 4 Personal Year Cycle partner is controlling. These bad feelings occur because you are in Personal Year Cycles that are Toxic to one another.

As a result, someone in the personal year Cycle of 5 may feel that they want their relationship to end. I discourage people to leave a relationship while in a Personal Year Cycle of 5. I encourage them to wait a year to see what may happen next. After riding it out, you may find yourself in personal year 6 Cycle and say, "Wow, thank goodness I got through that," because the way you were feeling about your life was distorted by the Personal Year Cycle you were in.

• PERSONAL YEAR CYCLE DESCRIPTIONS •

Below are brief descriptions of each Personal Year Cycle, to give you insight into what Personal Year Cycle you or your partner are currently in and what to expect from them. After the descriptions, I will explain some of the more difficult Challenge Cycles and offer suggestions for how to cope when you find yourself and your partner in one of these. Just know that it is temporary, and knowledge is power. By knowing you are in Personal Year Cycles that clash, you cannot take that situation personally. Once you get through this year, you realize you will do much better as a couple in the future.

Personal Year Cycle of 1

If the person you are interested in is in a 1 Personal Year Cycle, you will discover they are really concentrating on achieving their own goals and looking at their personal success. You might feel a little disconnected as a couple, because your companion does not seem focused on you or your relationship. This is a temporary thing, a Cycle where they must look at all these things where they can improve on their life. By being aware of that, do not take it to heart. It is not personal. Encourage them to do things that will help them feel they are achieving. They might begin an exercise program, either at a gym or a place of their own devising. Provide them with some self-help books, so they can work on their spiritual and mental growth. They can improve their diets, with an emphasis on natural foods and good nutrition. If they smoke, this is the time to kick the habit. As they start to look and feel better, they will be elated to be in this Cycle of 1.

Personal Year Cycle of 2

If the person you are interested in is in a 2 Personal Year Cycle, you may discover that they are more sensitive than usual. You might see them get emotional, upset, or defensive in ways that you are not used to. It is the Cycle of 2 that encourages them to deal with all that emotion. As the partner, try to be understanding. If you find you are overly busy with your own life, take time out to treat them to a dinner or a weekend getaway. Your partner needs to feel strongly connected to you, so you must try to do your part to keep the two of you on track.

Personal Year Cycle of 3

If the person you are interested in is in a 3 Personal Year Cycle, they are going to want to express themselves. You might be used to a partner who is quiet and a bit reserved, and suddenly they want to talk. Please be open to it for the sake of your relationship. Know that they do need to express themselves in this Cycle; they might become a little silly and want to hang out with their friends more or be more sociable. They may take classes or do things that you are not used to seeing them do. Know that they are getting in touch with their inner selves and encourage it.

Personal Year Cycle of 4

If the person you are interested in is in a 4 Personal Year Cycle, this is a time to learn something new. You can help encourage them. Maybe they are in a dead-end job. Urge them to take a class to finish a degree or a course where they can get a certificate to increase their pay.

The Personal Year Cycle of 4 is about looking at income, finding ways for security, and also doing things in nature. You two should take trips where you experience the beauty of the world. All of nature's beauty has a profound effect on a person in this cycle. And it is good for you as a couple to share this together.

Personal Year Cycle of 5

If the person you are interested in is in a 5 Personal Year Cycle, you may notice that suddenly they seem scattered, or not as together as they were in the past, especially if it is an organized Life Path, like a 4 Life Path or an 8 Life Path. You might see that their life is out of control. Understand that this is something they are going through and it will pass. If you feel emotionally that they are not connecting with you, or they seem to misinterpret everything you say, it is like trying to live your life in the middle of a tsunami. Take a deep breath and stay calm.

It is best for the 5 Cycle people that you be sympathetic, especially if theirs is a Vibration that is used to being in charge. Suddenly they feel helpless, and if you can do anything to help their self-esteem, or to help them feel more grounded, that is the best thing you can do for them in this Cycle. One very good thing to do is to take a vacation together. Just make it peaceful and romantic. This can do wonders.

Personal Year Cycle of 6

If the person you are interested in is in a 6 Personal Year Cycle, it is time that individual take a look at the family. Perhaps you are the husband, and all of a sudden your wife says she really wants to become pregnant. The Cycle of 6 may include the need and desire to have a child. If children are in your plans anyway, I would certainly encourage a couple to start a family in this Cycle. This Cycle also encourages the desire to move. Maybe you are unable to because of the economy. You can refurbish the kitchen or the living room. This is a good Cycle to advance in your career. If your partner is in a Cycle of 6, encourage them to strive for a management position or to start a business. Really pay close attention to any contract that is signed in the Personal Year Cycle of 6.

Personal Year Cycle of 7

If the person you are interested in is in a 7 Personal Year Cycle, you will find that they are quieter than usual. Maybe they are usually sociable and like to talk to people, and you notice that they want to be alone. This makes you uncomfortable because it is not what you are used to. Just be aware of their Personal Year Cycle. This Cycle is about coming up with the answers to the bigger questions of life: figuring out who they are and what they want. You might want to provide them with some spiritual books to help them in their quest, like *The Prophet,* by Khalil Gibran, or *Where There Is Light,* by Yogananda. Do not force them to respond to you when they are quiet. This is about you believing that they are having a break through of some sort. By year's end they will feel better about themselves, because they will have more insight into their own life purpose. The Personal Year of 7 is also a really good time to travel.

Personal Year Cycle of 8

If the person you are interested in is in an 8 Personal Year Cycle, this is a good Cycle for them to focus on money matters. In the Affirmation Chapters 21 and 22, there are Affirmations specifically for the 8 Vibrations. Also, physical health can be an issue; encourage your partner to get a checkup. Watch how they drive because in a Personal Year of 8, if they do not pay attention, they are apt to get into an accident because they are not focused. So if the person you love is in a Personal Year Cycle of 8, help them pay attention to all the details. If you find they are more outspoken than usual, a little too in your face, you do not have to respond. The 8 Personal Year Cycle may be causing them some frustration. It will pass. With the right attitude, positive things can happen in this cycle.

Personal Year Cycle of 9

If the person you are interested in is in a 9 Personal Year Cycle, you may find that they are more involved with their original family and finding fault with a brother, sister, mom, or dad. During this Cycle, they may find themselves processing the past in a way they are not used to. Be a sympathetic ear and help them get through it by involving them in their current family.

Also, they might be thinking about your union and wondering what you two can do to improve it. It might seem as though they are dissecting what the two of you mean to one another.

If you find you are working too hard, or are married and too focused on the children, I suggest you slow down, because the Personal Year of 9 is also about clearing space for new beginnings. You do not want the person in the 9 Cycle to feel that you are not a part of the new beginnings. By helping them go through this emotional time of evaluation, they will be so grateful to you. By the time you move into the next Cycle, you will be stronger than ever as a couple and feel you have a more committed relationship.

• SOME CHALLENGING CYCLES •

There are certain Personal Year Cycles that seem to make a relationship feel unstable. It's entirely possible that you and your mate will never encounter these challenges together—it all depends on your birth dates. However, these challenging cycles may affect a friend or relative, and you will be able to help them examine the relationship problems they may face. I have seen people leave a relationship because they were in a Toxic Personal Year Cycle and then regret their decision the following year. If you are both in a Cycle that you're not thrilled with, just remember, as always, *this too shall pass*.

Some couples have a month and day that reduces to the same number, and because of this, they share the same Personal Year Cycle each year.

This is a good thing, in general, because it means you are going through the same cycle at the same time. Example: A couple born on 1/4 (1+4 = 5) and on 2/3 (2 +3 = 5) would share the same Personal Year Cycle. However, there are three Personal Year Cycles, in particular, that may feel difficult while you are going through them together. They are the 1,5 and 8. Study the descriptions of these Personal Year Cycles, and do what you can to avoid the Negative side of them. If you pay attention to these cycles when you are going through them as a couple, you will end up with your relationship in tact and stronger than ever.

Here is a list of other conflicting Personal Year Cycles that can make for a difficult year as a couple.

Personal Year Cycles 1 and 6

This can promote a power struggle, because a Personal Year of 1 means you feel passionately about what you believe and you do not want to give up your position. In a Personal Year Cycle 6, your partner is much the same way. They have a sense of authority, and they want to be respected. They want to have the last word. Now we have the clash of the Titans.

Before this New Year Cycle you may have had a healthy loving relationship, perhaps even a Soul Mate Connection as partners, and suddenly it feels like a tug of war. You are scared and depressed, thinking, "What happened to our relationship?"

If you are in a Personal Year 1, focus on winning in some way, not against your partner but in your life. Find a way to score a victory. Maybe you're out of shape. Work on getting physically fit. If your partner is in a Personal Year Cycle of 6, he or she needs to find a way to be in charge of something. It could be a home project, anything from painting a bathroom to a complete overhaul. Or maybe it is time to switch jobs or start your own company. The most important thing is not to get critical of one another. Instead, focus on the world outside your home. Do something that makes you feel victorious and keeps your relationship peaceful.

Personal Year Cycles 1 and 8

When you are in a Personal Year of 8, you have to watch your physical health. Once, when I was in a Personal Year of 8, my hands suddenly started to hurt. I had to put on braces to prevent carpel tunnel, and I have had friends whose backs have suddenly gone out on them during a Personal Year of 8. Psychic healers teach that lower-back pain points to issues with money. Since money is a part of the 8 Vibration's lesson in life, in the Personal Year of 8 sometimes the back can reflect this.

If you are in a Personal Year of 1 and your partner is in a Personal year of 8, it can be frustrating. The 8 starts feeling life is not fair, while the 1 is trying to go full speed ahead. You feel as though your partner is slowing you down.

Remember, the person in the 8 Personal Year needs to focus on his or her health. If they feel victimized, help them to take accountability for their situation so that they can take their power back. The person in a Personal Year of 1 needs to consider, "Okay, I am really working on me right now. Maybe I am being a little selfish and it is time to concentrate on my significant other, and be more loving."

Personal Year Cycles 2 and 5

If you are in a Personal Year of 2 and your partner is in a Personal Year of 5, you may feel emotional and need the love and support of your partner. Yet because he or she is in a Cycle of 5, everything is moving at warp speed, and they do not have any time to try to understand what is bothering you. That failure can cause you a lot of emotional pain. I have counseled people who are in a Personal Year of 2 and they will tell me, "I can't stop crying," or "I'm just feeling all these emotions I have never felt before." If their partner is in a Personal Year of 5, and intent on just doing his or her own thing, the partner in the Personal Year 2 can experience great pain during this cycle.

So how do you prevent this from happening? The 2s need to tell themselves it is okay to experience these emotions. When you move into your new Personal Year Cycle of 3 the following year, you are ready to laugh and have fun in the New Year.

The 5s need to understand that it is okay to not be in control of everything. They must learn to relax. Whenever I counsel couples in a Personal Year Cycle of 5, I suggest that they take a trip together and have some fun, because right now the 5 is a wild card and he or she does not have a lot of control. You should not break up with someone or make any other important changes in the 5 Cycle. Enjoy what you have and try to take care of yourself at this time.

Personal Year Cycles 8 and 5

When these Personal Year Cycles come together, all kinds of weird things can happen. The person in the 8 Personal Year feels that they are suffering or that life is unfair, and the person in the 5 Personal Year feels like a martyr. I have witnessed wonderful couples fall into this Toxic Personal Year Cycle and feel drained by each other. Suddenly you have two unhappy lovebirds.

So how do you overcome the problem? The person in the 5 Personal Year needs to stay busy. They should write everything down to help achieve their goals. Otherwise they will run out of time and find they have accomplished nothing.

The person in the 8 Personal Year worries about how to become financially secure. It is a money year, and actually a good time to look at that financial side of your life. If you lose a job, don't despair. Just move on. There will be something better for you. Keep an eye on your physical health as well. While you both tackle your challenge Personal Year Cycles, find ways to be loving with one another. If you make the effort, it will do you both a world of good to know you are not alone in all of this craziness.

Personal Year Cycles 3 and 7

The 7 Year Personal Cycle seeks a quiet place within. They want to know what they should do with their lives. This person should take long walks during this cycle, preferably near a lake, a river, or the ocean. When they return, they should pay loving attention to their mates, and listen carefully to what they have to say.

If your partner is in a Personal Cycle of 3, he or she is in a Cycle of communication. Your partner wants to have fun and engage in conversation with you. There is a chance the one in the 7 Personal Year will not have anything to say, upsetting their partner. You both may suddenly feel that you are no longer connecting and don't want to be in this relationship. Believe me, it will pass. These two Personal Year Cycles by no means reflect the truth of your life together.

Stay positive. The person in the 7 Personal Year is seeking a spiritual truth from within. If you are in a Personal Year of 3, find ways to enjoy your life while your partner goes through a period of introspection. Ultimately his or her self-awareness will benefit both of you. Do not feel as though your partner does not love you or does not want to spend time with you. You'll see a big change with the New Year. This is just a passing and clashing cycle.

Personal Year Cycles 6 and 7

This can be a difficult combination because the person in the 6 Personal Year wants to work on the job, home, and all the business aspects of life while the partner in a Personal Year of 7 has retreated and is deeply involved with himself or herself. They have become more quiet than usual and will not necessarily understand your needs. As with any other placement in your Chart when there is a 6 and 7 combination, these life cycles together can promote confusion. Just remember that this is part of the Personal Year Cycles, and it will be okay when this year passes. Let the partner in the 7 Personal Year focus on their spiritual side, and the 6 work on the business side of life.

Personal Year Cycles 5 and 6

These two are running at different speeds. It is like one is in a race car, and the other is in a luxury sedan. They are not made for driving in tandem. Your partner in a 5 Personal Year will want to speed ahead and be more spontaneous. The person in the 6 Personal Year Cycle will want to know exactly where he or she stands, asking, "What do you think about this?" or "What do you think about that?"

No matter what else, if you are in a Personal Year of 5, pay attention to the details because if you do not, your life will feel out of control. It is a very good time for the 6 to focus on home, family, career, and let the 5 have fun. Find a way to engage each other exclusively at least once a week. Listen to what each other has to say. If you are in a 5 Personal Year Cycle, just remind yourself, "This year is nonstop. I will surrender to it and know that it is going to be all right." One smart idea would be to take your spouse on a romantic weekend and get away from it all.

CHAPTER 21

Affirmations for Healthy Love

Truth is truth, we do but glimpse it.

—JOHN BETH REILLY

In order to have great love, we have to do some work on ourselves. There is a Positive and Negative side to every Number in Numerology, and your Life Path is the Number you need to focus on. To get your mind and body ready for real love, Affirmations are very important.

The mind is incredibly powerful, and it manifests whatever it believes. Affirmations allow you to reprogram your subconscious so you can achieve the life you really want to live. This is especially important when it comes to love. Each Life Path Number has a Positive and Negative side attached to it. When you find yourself living on the Negative side, you must begin to break the interior patterns that cause negative behavior. Affirmations can reprogram the subconscious.

For example, suppose that someone in your childhood told you that you were lazy. No matter how diligent you may be today, you may still be subconsciously repeating to yourself *You are lazy, you are lazy, you are lazy,* with the result, that no matter how hard you work, you never feel you are doing enough. You must replace that refrain with a positive Affirmation: *I am a hard worker, and I get the job done.*

An Affirmation is always couched in the affirmative, never in the negative—and it is also always in the present, never the future. You do not say, *I will be a better person*, you say, *I am a better person*. This chapter is dedicated to looking at the Toxic side to each Life Path and provides Affirmations so you can flip to a positive Life Path.

You should do Affirmations for 15 minutes a day. If you don't want to do them all at once, you can do them for 5 minutes in the morning, 5 minutes during the day, and then 5 minutes at night. Some people like to write out the Affirmation. I personally like to say my Affirmation out loud when I am driving, walking, or whenever I have a moment. Before my husband came into my life, I did a relationship Affirmation daily for 15 minutes a day, for six weeks. My subconscious was finally ready to accept a good man (yes, we keep them away), and after that, Charlie Youngblood showed up. From my own experience and the testimonials of thousands of clients, I can tell you that Affirmations work.

I have laid out Affirmations for you by the Life Path Number. Read through all of them. You have six Numbers in your Personal Chart, so if you read an Affirmation under a Life Path Number that is not yours, but it really rings true to you, use it. If you find you are living on the Negative side of your Number, I suggest you do the Affirmations in your Life Path category that will open you up to a healing love relationship.

1 Life Path

The downside of the 1 Life Path is that they can be hypercritical of others, and also too critical of themselves. This can interfere with attracting a satisfying love relationship.

Here is an Affirmation to counteract this bad habit:

"I release all judgment, and embrace the love in everyone."

They can also be workaholics and are so busy that they cannot seem to settle down, or get emotionally connected to another person.

Here is an Affirmation to heal that part of a 1 Life Path:

"I welcome a loving partner to share my life. Love flows from me, and I attract love wherever I go."

2 Life Path

There are two pitfalls for the 2 Life Path. The 2s can feel needy and fear that their partners do not love them. They become too dependent on their partners, and that is not healthy; or they can be so hurt by a failed love that they shut down and do not want to connect with anyone.

Here are Affirmations with which to work on that:

"I am complete within myself, and I welcome a loving partner."

"Love is ever new. I am open to a healthy love right now."

3 Life Path

The 3s in love are all about sharing their thoughts, but they can say things that they regret. The 3s verbally express what they think and feel, but sometimes they forget to listen to their partners.

Here is the Affirmation to help them:

"I listen to my partner with an open, loving heart."

If the 3 is not using their creative energy and is feeling frustrated, they may take it out on their partner. This Affirmation on the next page will ensure that you protect your love:

"I share love and laughter with my partner every day."

4 Life Path

The downside of the 4 is that they can be judgmental of their partners and sometimes feel that if others are not doing it their way, then they are doing it wrong. They have to be more open to how we all differ, and they need to learn to let go.

Affirmation:

"I appreciate my partner, and I respect our differences."

If 4s are in an unhappy relationship, they believe they must stay once they have made a commitment. Sometimes the cost is too high and the relationship will destroy them. Here are two Affirmations that could rid them of the truly destructive relationship:

"I trust the truth of love, and I accept the change it brings."

"I release you, live your life in peace, as I am living mine."

5 Life Path

The Negative side of the 5 Life Path is that they can have a hard time settling down. A good Affirmation for this trait is:

"I am where I should be at this moment; I embrace the here and now."

On the Negative side of their Vibration, they are often bored and restless. They may fall madly in love, and then get over the person and want to let them go.

Here is an Affirmation to end that bad habit:

"I deserve and give unconditional love, and I am ready for a lasting love."

A 5 is a considerable source of light and can attract unwanted people into their lives. Here is an Affirmation to help avoid this:

"I am a loving, healthy person and I attract a mate who is my loving, healthy equal."

6 Life Path

The 6s feel the need to control and believe that if they do not do so, nothing will get done. That can be upsetting to their partner.

So this Affirmation is to help break this pattern:

"I trust my partner as I trust myself; our love is a constant blessing."

The 6 also needs to give up the belief that, if life is moving along effortlessly, then it is too good to be true. The 6s are so adept at damage control, they do not know how to relax. Here is an Affirmation to help release that Negative programming and help the 6 truly believe that good things are possible and, indeed, are the normal state of life:

"I am at peace knowing that all is well. This is a perfect day."

7 Life Path

If the 7 does not find a spiritual base in which they believe, they can become cynical. Here are two Affirmations to help them end their cynicism:

"I trust my inner truth. It never fails me."

"My thoughts create reality and are a force for positive change."

Number 7s sometimes have a hard time sharing themselves with their partners. This Vibration may shut down emotionally, or just want to be left alone, which will make their partner feel rejected.

Here is an Affirmation to open the 7 up to more effective communication:

"I love you in my silence, and now share my love with words."

8 Life Path

The 8s have to deal with financial issues. If they are making money but do not feel secure, they become workaholics and think that just giving material things to themselves and others is enough. That is simply not the case. Here are two Affirmations to break that pattern:

"I share my heart, body, and soul with you. I love you in every way."

"I take the time to speak of my love for you, and I am grateful for all you bring to me."

When an 8 gets defensive, they are often blunt when they are hurting, and might unfairly criticize their partners. In doing so they can destroy what otherwise could be a great relationship. Here are two Affirmations to stop that behavior:

"I release the past with love, and on this day, I begin anew."

"I trust you as I trust myself. I am filled with love, which I share with you right now."

9 Life Path

This Vibration often comes into a relationship with issues of abandonment that cause them to worry that the relationship will end. So, they either will not open up emotionally to their partners, because they fear they will be rejected. Or they will not ever fully trust their partners. So here is an Affirmation to help them be more trusting of their relationship and their mates:

"I give pure love, and pure love is given to me."

The 9 also has a difficult time asking for help. They often feel that they have to take care of things themselves. As a result, they can be overwhelmed. If they feel alone in a relationship, here are Affirmations to help them have the courage to ask for help, and make the relationship more complete. Repeat them to yourself and you will quickly find your inner defenses crumbling:

"I can openly share my feelings because I trust you completely."

• LOVE AFFIRMATIONS FOR THE • NATURAL MATCH CATEGORIES

The 1, 5, and 7 Life Paths

The 1, 5, and 7 Life Paths are cerebral and constantly processing everything, so it is not uncommon for them to turn their partners into a science project as if they are putting them under a microscope. They see everything that is flawed about their partner and then they let them know about it. That can destroy any love relationship. Even though we love someone very much, it is human nature to start shutting down if the partner starts judging us constantly. One can reach the point where the partner is no longer affectionate or loving, but instead constantly on the defensive. I have found the 1, 5, and 7 Life Paths need to be careful about how they respond to their partners. Thinking those critical thoughts are one thing. After all, your thoughts are your own. But I suggest you be aware of the fact that you are spending too much time scrutinizing your partner. Your beloved is not a bug in a jar.

For those who are too much in their minds and over critical:

"I speak of you with love, a love that does not measure."

"I give you all that I am, and I accept all you have to give me."

The 2, 4, and 8 Life Paths

Creating a solid security base is a major issue for the 2, 4, and 8 Life Paths. No matter how well off they may be, they can still feel impoverished. This is especially true for the men. Often they will not want to marry their lovers because they feel financially insecure, even though they are completely loved and wanted. Since they will not commit, they lose what could have been a great love.

It is important that the 2, 4, and 8 Life Paths remember that financial security is a part of their Numbers, and they should find a way to share the money and make it flow easily. Because they are so worried about their future, they just keep it in the bank or let it slip through their fingers. Establish a balance. Save some for your descendents, give some to others, and have a fun with the rest.

For those who worry about not having enough:

"You are my greatest treasure, and I am always here for you."

"We are one with the infinite abundance of life."

The 3, 6, and 9 Life Paths

The 3,6, and 9 Life Paths are natural counselors. You will rarely meet a 3, 6, or 9 Life Path who does not feel called upon to give advice or help people. They do need to avoid attracting a partner who is literally their patient. They tend to attract a partner who is broken in some way, and they believe they can make the person better. That is not true, nor is it healthy. When we seek someone to love, we should try to attract a partner who is an equal, someone we can respect and learn from, someone who is striving to achieve their goals to be a success. Not an individual afflicted with chronic problems or who has childish needs.

The 6 is a nurturer and parent to all. The 3 wants to make sure you are okay. The 9 is the old soul, who does not want people to think they need anything. Again, this group of Numbers has to be careful not to attract a mate who needs to be saved, because it does not make for a healthy love relationship.

For those who want to attract a worthy lover:

"I welcome a mate who loves and cares for me."

"We are strong together and our love is unconditional."

CHAPTER 22

Affirmations to Attract Great Love

I am my beloved's, and his desire is toward me.

—THE SONG OF SOLOMON

If you want to improve a love relationship, the Affirmation below can help make the relationship you are currently in healthier or invite the right person into your life. So you have nothing to lose by doing this love Affirmation right away! This chapter applies to people who are married as well as those who are single and looking for love. People tell me that soon after beginning this Affirmation they began to notice the positive things that their partners do that they just didn't notice before. I have underlined the key points that matter most. Go through the pros and cons of your love relationships and personalize this love Affirmation to suit you.

I welcome a life partner who loves and cares for me, who is <u>financially stable</u>, takes care of their <u>physical and spiritual health</u>, who embraces

<u>commitment</u>, and sees me as his or her equal. Together we are strong, and our <u>unconditional love is boundless</u>.

Below is the same Affirmation with blank spaces for you to fill in and personalize.

I welcome a life partner who loves and cares for me. Who is _____ _____, takes care of their _____, who embraces _____, and sees me as their equal. Together we are strong, and our _____.

For a relationship Affirmation to work and to really reprogram your subconscious mind, you must find a way to do the Affirmation a full fifteen minutes each day, and remember, you can break this time into three five-minute sessions.

Here are some more love Affirmations for you to try. Instead of attaching them to a particular Life Path number, I decided it would be best if you went through all of them, and use the ones you feel apply to you.

For the Numbers who have trouble letting others in:

"I trust you with my Love, as I trust my Love for you."

For those who cannot articulate their sexual needs and desires:

"I love to give and receive pleasure."

For those who are self-conscious of their bodies:

"I am beautiful to my loved one and (he/she) is beautiful to me."

For those who suffer from performance anxiety:

"Sex is free expression. I embrace each moment as it comes."

For everyone:

"As my body responds to my lover, our souls are responding to our love."

For those who feel there is no love in their lives:

"Love is within me; it flows out into the universe and comes back to me in abundance."

A Peek into the Bedroom:

Your sexuality is the Creator's greatest gift to you. It is the joyous abandonment of self in the sex act that creates life on this planet, so it must be very well thought of by the Creator. We are created in joy, and we have been created to experience joy in the sex act. Does this make you a little nervous? Do you feel like cringing? Let me tell you what makes you cringe. It is not sex. It is the abuse of sex.

Because sex is so powerful, indeed the very basis of our being, the abuse of that same sexuality has the power to deeply wound us. From adultery to the whole list of damaging sex addictions, I firmly believe that the people ensnared in any unhealthy sexuality are those who deep down think that sex is a bad thing. This must change if you are going to enjoy a complete partnership with another man or woman.

Sex in marriage is the ultimate expression of Love. We need all the touching we can get, from hugs, to massages, to holding hands. But a marriage without intimacy is no marriage at all. Sooner or later, one or the other partner will be so frustrated that the individual will look for love elsewhere. If you are having any problems getting physical with your partner, you can begin to change that by reprogramming your inner beliefs about your sexuality.

A powerful Affirmation:

"My sexuality is a gift to me and I lovingly share this gift with you."

This Affirmation will help us embrace this truth. However, if you have a more serious problem, a real sex addiction, get counseling or join Sex Addicts Anonymous, and begin this Affirmation right away:

"My sexuality is in healthy balance with my wholesome life."

(Remember you recite your Affirmations as though what you want is happening right now)

Keep in mind, to get results, you must repeat the Affirmation for no less than 15 minutes a day. As discussed in the previous chapter, it is through repetition that we reprogram our subconscious mind. As you will discover, it is so worth it!

CHAPTER 23

The Fascinating Numerology of Power Couples

The inner progressiveness of love between two human beings is a most marvelous thing; it cannot be found by looking for it or by passionately wishing for it. It is a sort of divine accident, and the most wonderful of all things in life.

—SIR HUGH WALPOLE

Barack and Michelle Obama

Barack Obama	Michelle Obama
DOB: 8/4/1961	DOB: 1/17/1964
14542*/ 3 Attitude	99982*/9 Attitude
Destiny Number: 1	Destiny Number: 7
Maturity Number: 3	Maturity Number: 9

In 2009, Barack Obama became the first African American president of the United States. He has inherited this office in one of the most challenging times that any president has had to face. There is, however, one blessing and source of strength that he can truly count on, and that is his wife, Michelle Obama. These two have an unbeatable connection in Numerology, and I am sure that this bond will play a huge part in his role of Commander-In-Chief.

Their Life Path Numbers are both a 2, and the 2 Vibration is the Number for love. So when they made this commitment, they knew they were in it for the long haul. This explains why so many people comment on their chemistry and obvious delight in each other. Before their Life Path Numbers reduce down to the final digit 2, they both have the Master Number 11 (1+1 = 2), which tells me they are intellectual equals. I am sure that they are mentally stimulated by one another, as well as physically.

When I look at Michelle's chart, I see she has four 9s, and the 9 is the number of completion in Numerology. It is considered a wise number, and sometimes people will feel intimated by that number. A person with a 9 Vibration can often have their words misconstrued and can come off as condescending without meaning to. I believe quite a bit of that took place during the campaign to the point where Michelle took a step back so as not to steer any attention away from her husband's potential victory. She would not let the media make her a distraction.

The 8 Birth Day Number in Michelle's chart tells me she is tougher and more outspoken than her husband. As First Lady, we will definitely hear from her, because you cannot be born on an 8 day and not have strong convictions. It is interesting to note that Hillary Clinton was also born on an 8 day, and we certainly heard from her as First Lady.

With four 9s in her chart, it also tells me that family is the most important thing to her, and she will always be extremely protective of them. I believe this has been evident whenever someone has been critical of her husband, and she has spoken out to defend him. You can see her loving maternal instincts when she is with her children. All those 9s would also explain her close relationship with her mother and having her move into the White House with them to help with the children.

The Soul Number 1 in Barack's chart shows his competitive drive and how he was able to win the presidency. Not to mention the fact that he also has a 1 Destiny Number, which tells us he has always been very driven to reach for the brass ring. Well, one would argue that there is no brass ring greater than becoming President of the United States. Michelle Obama has a 7 Destiny Number, which is about finding your spirituality. Michele was the one who originally brought Barack Obama to the Unity Church in Chicago. Her faith is extremely important to her.

Another blessing for this couple is that their Maturity Numbers also has a Natural Match connection. Barack's Maturity Number is a 3, which means he feels called to motivate and uplift others. This Vibration really showed itself when he was motivating thousands of young people to get involved with his historic campaign. Michelle's Destiny Number is a 9, which lets us know that she feels called to do some great humanitarian work to effect a real change. As first lady, she will certainly have the platform to do just that.

I cannot foretell what Barack Obama will accomplish as President. But by looking at his Personal Numerology chart, I can say that whatever decisions he makes as president, he will sincerely believe it is what's best for the country. The other thing that is clear after studying their charts is that it is no accident that they are, and will continue, making history together.

Tim McGraw and Faith Hill

Tim McGraw	Faith Hill
DOB: 5/1/1967	DOB: 9/21/1967
17812*/6 Attitude	13438*/3 Attitude
Destiny Number: 3	Destiny Number: 2
Maturity Number: 5	Maturity Number: 1

This Power Couple's Attitude Numbers are examined in full in Chapter 10, on Attitude Numbers. Here we will examine the rest of their Charts. The Soul Number is a 1 Vibration for both of them, and the 1 means to strive to be the best at what you do. Just look at this team! They actually broke all records a few years back when they made $80 million in one summer, during one of their tours together.

Tim's Life Path Number is a 2, which gives him the gentle spirit of a man who really values the love in his life. Faith welcomes that sensitivity and her Life Path 8 makes their Life Path Numbers a Natural Match. She would be the tougher of the two, which brings me back to a well publicized story that some woman tried to grab her husband's crotch while he was performing; Faith went on mike and said, in front of the audience, "Somebody needs to teach you some class, my friend. You don't go grabbin' somebody's husband's balls, you understand me? That's very disrespectful."

It is typical of an 8 Life Path to be protective of their partner, and Tim would appreciate that quality. As we discussed previously in the Attitude Number Chapter, Tim McGraw has a 6 Attitude, which gives him the fathering energy. Taking care of his kids is a joy to him, and he has three daughters who he says are the light of his life. This 6 Energy would also make Faith Hill feel cared for and loved. She has a 3 Attitude, which is a Natural Match to his 6 Attitude, but the 3 also encourages her to communicate her feelings. Faith must express herself whether it is through singing, acting, or writing lyrics. She is strong enough to achieve many things. Tim is the best possible partner to help and encourage her and not be remotely jealous of her success.

It doesn't get much better than when you have a Natural Match, like a loving 2 Life Path and an 8 Life Path, which are both business-minded Vibrations that work hard to establish prosperity and a secure foundation. These two sing together and go on the road together, and at the same time are nurturing parents. Faith says that in order to keep their marriage strong, they have vowed to never let three consecutive days pass without being with each other.

When you look at Faith's Destiny Number you see that it is a 2. Tim's Life Path Number is also a 2. When that pattern appears in a couple's Numerology Comparison Chart, it means that they are part of each other's destiny. When Faith met Tim, she knew instinctively that this man represented a major turning point in her life. His Destiny Number is a 3, and the 3 Vibrations need to express themselves, and it can be through performance. She has three 3s out of her six Numbers. It would be criminal if she could not express herself through a creative, verbal outlet.

Now, let's look at their Maturity Numbers. Her Maturity Number is a 1, and his is a 5. Again, these numbers are considered a Natural Match. That tells me that when they are old and gray, they will be able to travel and enjoy the world, look at all the beautiful things that are in it, and continue using their energy in a powerful way because the 1 and the 5 have so much light, intelligence, and ability to stay active. They really did pick a winning hand from a Numerology perspective when they found one another. They have only one Challenge Number in Numerology, and one Challenge Number means you can overcome anything. This is a really strong relationship.

Will Smith and Jada Pinkett Smith

Will Smith and Jada Pinkett Smith are a fascinating case study in Numerology. If you lay out their Numbers with the names they use today, you get:

Will Smith	**Jada Pinkett Smith**
DOB: 9/25/1968	DOB: 9/18/1971
98874*/7 Attitude	72999*/9 Attitude
Destiny Number: 8	Destiny Number: 3
Maturity Number: 3	Maturity Number: 3

I have already used Will and Jada as the Personality Number example, and we will further explore their Charts here.

The Numbers 4, 7, and 8 are a Challenge to the Number 9. You can see that Will Smith has a 4, a Double 7, and an 8 Destiny Number, so that shows you this union takes some work. However, Will Smith's Soul Number is a 9, and Jada Pinkett Smith has four 9s out of six Numbers in her chart. That tells me that it felt like a lightening bolt hit when Will met Jada. His Soul Number 9 is content every time he is with her—because those 9s are coming from her Birth Date, not her name. Actually, her Birth Date Numbers made him notice her. Those four 9s in her chart also tell me that she would be a great parent. This is such a blessing for Will and makes it possible for him to concentrate on his career because he knows his children are well taken care of.

There's a lot there for her, too. If you notice, she has a 7 in her Soul and he was born on a 7 Day with a 7 Attitude. The 7 Day is the appearance Number. And that means when she looks at Will, her Soul is fulfilled. Everyone knows this is one of the most dynamic couples in Hollywood and, in fact, the world. Every time Jada Pinkett Smith and Will Smith appear together, you cannot take your eyes off of them. They are beautiful, of course, but what you are really seeing here are two people whose Soul Numbers are fulfilled through their relationship. Another reason Will Smith loves Jada is that she is upfront and in your face. Will Smith has been so incredibly productive, from being a successful rapper, to his TV show *Fresh Prince*, to having massive hit movies. He has made over 2 billion dollars in the entertainment industry!

Jada keeps him grounded, and he counts on her strength. Once Will Smith was talking about Jada's influence on his life, and he said, "You are so much stronger when your partner is strong. I honestly believe there is no woman for me but Jada. Of all the women I have met, and there have been a few, no one can handle me the way Jada does. Once you feel someone locked in on you, it's no contest. As fine as other women can be, and tempting sexually, I am not going anywhere. This is it. I cannot imagine what anyone else can offer."

It is also a trademark of Will's that there is no major swearing or gratuitous sex in his movies. He's a wholesome man. And that I believe is the result of the many 7s in his chart, because 7 is the spiritual Number. So again, I think this is a relationship based on mutual respect. And because their Numbers are so different and there are quite a few Challenges, they have learned to compromise and fully understand the role each plays in the relationship.

The Number 2 in Jada's Chart tells me how sensitive she is to Will and his needs. Since they do share the Number 7, I think their spirituality will become an even bigger part of their life. Will Smith has always talked about religion. Some people have asked him if he adheres to Scientology, and he says he respects all faiths and he is trying to embrace and learn as much as possible about all of them. This, too, makes perfect sense because of the double 7 in his chart. The fact that they share the same Maturity Number will prove to be a huge gift for them as a couple.

To get the Maturity Number, you add the Life Path Number and the Destiny Number together, and then reduce them to one digit. In Will Smith's case, his Life Path Number is a 4, and his Destiny Number is an 8 (4+8 = 12 = 1+2 = 3). Will's Maturity Number is a 3. Jada Pinkett Smith's Life Path Number is a 9 and her Destiny Number is a 3 (9+3 = 12 = 1+2 = 3). Jada's Maturity Number is a 3. So they share the Number 3, and 3s serve to motivate and inspire other people. Will Smith has said that he wants to do whatever he can to help people in need, to set up charities and be involved so that they make a difference for people in trouble. With Jada, not only does she have that Maturity Number 3, but with all of her 9s, that is exactly what makes her happy: to know that she is changing the lives of people who really need help.

A final thought on Jada. The 9 is considered the Number of Completion. Jada has four 9s in her chart, and it would make sense that someone as successful as Will Smith would instantly realize that Jada is a very special lady. Their journey together, despite all of the Challenge Numbers in their relationship, has been well worth it because they make an unbeatable team, a Power Couple that is an inspiration for all of us.

Heidi Klum and Seal

Heidi Klum	Seal
DOB: 6/1/1973	DOB: 2/19/1963
83219*/7 Attitude	64114*/3 Attitude
Destiny Number: 2	Destiny Number: 4
Maturity Number: 2	Maturity Number: 8

In 2004 Heidi Klum was in a relationship with Flavio Briatore, the international business mogul. She found out she was pregnant in the autumn of 2003 and proudly announced to the world that she was expecting. On the same day she made the announcement, a photo appeared depicting Briatore kissing jewelry heiress Fiona Swarovski. Devastated, Heidi resolved to raise her baby as a single mom. Shortly thereafter, she met the love of her life, Seal.

This was in early 2004. They started dating, and he was perfectly fine with the fact that she was pregnant. He has said that within weeks he was so in love, he would always be with her. He has always treated Heidi's baby as his own. A year later, they got married and now they have two more children. As of this writing, Heidi has announced she is pregnant again! Everyone talks about how this is a magical couple and how much in love they are, which is expressed in their Numbers. They like to renew their wedding vows every year.

When your Birth Day Number is the same as the person you meet, an instant attraction takes place. Heidi was born on a 1 day, and so was Seal (19 = 1+9 = 10+1+0 = 1). Seal said when he met her originally he said to himself, "Wow, whoever is with that woman is such a lucky guy," not knowing her circumstances. It was a few months after her breakup with Briatore that they met again, and that is when they started dating. Seal is a 4 Life Path, and the 4 is a very responsible and reliable Number. Heidi had not made a good choice in the previous relationship and she needed stability. She could not have done better than picking Seal to be her life partner.

The name Seal, which is the name he goes by, has a 6 Vibration in his Soul, which means that having children would complete his soul, so it is evident that children are important to him. Heidi has a 2 Destiny Number, which means she is all about finding a love relationship with whom she can share her life. As a 9 Life Path, not only is she an old-soul Number, but she has also been incredibly successful at everything she attempts. She is one of the world's most recognizable supermodels, an actress, TV reality show host, a designer, a painter, and she is able to use all of her gifts. In Seal, she has found a partner who is not jealous or who competes with her. He wants her to be successful. She has a show on television called *Project Runway*, which helps young men and women break into the modeling world. That would be her 2, a Vibration that loves to help everyone. The 2 is also made happy by being a mother, and her 1 Vibration made sure she lost her baby fat and that she could return to modeling within eight weeks of giving birth to her second child.

Seal has said, "I was taken aback when I met her. I thought she was the most beautiful woman I had ever seen." And "Apart from being my wife, she is also my best friend." Seal is famous for his magnificent voice and was inspired in 2008 to create an album that contained soul music by such greats as Sam Cooke and Otis Redding. When he heard the song *A Change is Gonna Come*, he cried because it was a civil rights anthem, and it just seemed so appropriate in that we had just elected our first African American president.

Seal has a 6 Soul Number and Heidi has an 8 Soul Number, which are compatible in Numerology. I think the fact that Seal has a 6 in his soul made him willing to take on Heidi's unborn baby when they first met. He was happy to become an instant father, and now having two more children with Heidi and another one on the way has been a dream come true. The 8 in Heidi's soul is business minded, planning for the future, doing what it takes to be victorious, and Seal completely supports her in this endeavor. They both have a 3 Vibration, which reflects laughter and communication, so it is easy for them to express and share what they are accomplishing in their life together.

As for Heidi, her motivation is to create enough income to make a difference and do things to improve the world we all live in today. And Seal joins her in that effort. Her 9 Life Path makes her a philanthropist. She has done work with the American Red Cross and the AIDS Foundation. Heidi knows that there is no true success unless others benefit from it as well. Seal is the same way. Seal, with his 4 Vibration and his need for family and home, feels so grateful to have all this love in his life. He says that Heidi is an inspiration to him, and because they look at life with the same philosophy, we are all lucky that they found each other, because this Power Couple is taking steps to change the world for the better.

Bill Clinton and Hillary Clinton

Bill Clinton	Hillary Clinton
DOB: 8/19/1946	DOB: 10/26/1947
68512*/9 Attitude	55183*/9 Attitude
Destiny Number: 6	Destiny Number: 6
Maturity Number: 8	Maturity Number: 9

I discussed Bill and Hillary Clinton in my first book, *Glynis Has Your Number*, but so much has transpired since then, I feel their relationship warrants a Numerology update. When I look at Bill and Hillary Clinton's Charts, I see they have a Soul Mate Connection in Numerology. You determine that by looking at the Six Main Numbers in the Chart, and they share the Numbers 1, 5, and 8. They also have the same Attitude Number 9, which means that when they go through a Personal Year Cycle, it is the same Cycle at the same time. The 5 Vibration implies that there's never a dull moment in their lives. The 8 Vibration means learning the hard way.

Also, the 8 is the politician Number. How appropriate. Truly, we always knew Bill Clinton was a politician, but Hillary has certainly come into her own as a Senator of New York and now as the Secretary of State. I saw that during the 2008 primary season, Bill and Hillary Clinton became such an amazing team when Hillary was running for President. That's because they were both in a Personal Year of 1, which is the Cycle that encourages winning. Hillary appeared at rally after rally and continued to campaign, even when many suggested that Hillary step aside for Obama. "I am not a quitter," she said. Neither is Bill Clinton, and they continued to compete. By the end of the contest, Hillary was ahead in the popular vote, but the Superdelegates put Barack Obama over the top. He became the nominee and is now President of the United States of America. Through the years, people have often said, "Well they definitely have a connection, but is it a marriage of convenience?" I say "no." According to the Numbers, they love each other deeply. It is both an intellectual connection and a Soul Mate Connection. I was deeply touched when Hillary came to the podium at the Democratic Convention, and Bill Clinton watched her with tears in his eyes. You could see him mouthing the words, "I love you, I love you, I love you." He meant it. I believe that going through triple bypass surgery was a message to him to stop his shenanigans and realize that she and daughter Chelsea really are a blessing for him.

I can feel the Clintons' fierce ambition and determination. I would not be surprised if Hillary Clinton runs for president again. And if not Hillary, perhaps Bill and Hillary are grooming Chelsea for the position. Hillary's and Bill's Destiny Number is 6, and the 6 Vibration is powerful. When you have a 6 Destiny Number, people automatically look up to you. The fact that they have an identical Destiny Number certainly tells me that these two will be together until the end, and that their love is genuine. And yes, it's all in their Numbers!

CHAPTER 24

Glynis Shares Her Secrets!

We are all born for love...it is the principle existence and it's only end.

—BENJAMIN DISRAELI

• WHAT I LEARNED THAT PYTHAGORAS • DID NOT TEACH ME

Through my many years of counseling and own observations, I have had many break throughs in recognizing Number patterns that come up again and again. In this chapter, I will share some of these break throughs with you.

The Full Moon and the 2 Vibration

Although most of us realize a full moon has an effect on us, those with a 2 Vibration in their Charts are even more affected. I have a 2 Attitude and at some point each month, I find myself feeling as though something is weighing me down, and I can't shake it. When I feel that, I just look up at the sky to find the glow of a full moon and say to myself, "Okay, I get it. It is nothing real. Just the full moon messing with my emotions."

If you consider the fact that the Number 2 represents love, and feels deeply, it is not surprising that the full moon can have such an impact. Time and again, people who are 2 Life Paths—or someone born on a 2 day, someone with a 2 Power Name Number, or someone with a 2 Destiny—will say to me, "Oh, those full moons just put me in a tailspin." Some will say, "Well, I feel compulsive" or "I suddenly crave sugar." Or another shares, "I just feel like drinking alcohol and cannot seem to stop, and I normally don't drink at all!"

If you or your partner has a 2 in your chart, pay attention to that full moon when it comes around, so you don't fall into the trap of bad behavior. Don't blame yourself, thinking your life is not working, because nothing is wrong with you. Also, do not allow compulsive behavior just because your emotions have spiraled out of control.

Let's say you are married to a 2 Life Path, and he or she is acting strangely—a little too defensive—or getting upset with you. Look out that window and check for a full moon. Do not take their behavior personally; know that it will pass. It's just a little something between a 2 Vibration and the full moon.

When the Life Path and Attitude Number Are a Natural Match

I have found that when you and your partner have a Life Path and an Attitude Number that are a Natural Match, it means that your needs are very similar. If these needs are met, you can expect a companionable life.

When the Birth Day Number and Life Path Numbers Are the Same

If you are born the same day as your Life Path number—for instance born on a 3 day and have a 3 Life Path—that means "what you see is what you get." You are basically an open book, and you will tell people what you think.

When a Person is Born on a Day That is a Challenge to Their Life Path Number

If somebody is born on a day that is a Challenge to his or her Life Path, you don't know exactly who that person is. A good example of that can be found among people born on an 8 day who have a 3 Life Path. The 8 Birth Day makes them appear as an 8 to others, and this façade is quite unlike their 3 Life Path. Some people might think these people are all about business, and straightlaced, but behind their cool façade is a Life Path 3 who enjoys keeping things lively and upbeat.

Hillary Clinton is a good example of a person born on a day that challenges their Life Path Number. Considered cold and aloof, people discovered she had a great sense of humor during her campaign for president. She even went on *Saturday Night Live* to make fun of herself and brought down the house. It was the fact that, though she was born on an 8 day, a more businesslike Number that people were used to seeing, she actually has a 3 Life Path, which is a Vibration known for its humor. If you are born on a Birth Day Number that is a Challenge to your Life Path Number, let others know who you really are.

The Mirror Numbers

If you and your partner have the same Birth Day Number and Life Path Number, but they are reversed, it is like looking in the mirror. Example: You are born on a 4 Day and have a 7 Life Path. Your mate is born on a 7 Day and has a 4 Life Path. The good news is if you get in an argument, you can quickly end it because it is like a mirror reflection. It is your same vibration reflecting back to you, and if you change your tone, you can easily return to a peaceful, loving relationship.

Soul Mate Connections

Three out of the Six Main Numbers in common are considered a Soul Mate Connection (not counting the Attitude Number). That means that whether the connection is good or bad (remember every Number has a Positive and Negative side), the connection is forever. Your Soul Mate is the one you learn from. This combination can result in a great relationship, or the opposite, where you say, "Boy, I'll never do that again."

Either way, you have to realize this person is in your life for a reason. Ask yourself, "What am I bringing into this relationship and vice-versa?" Then ask yourself, "Am I happy?" You have to decide whether you are in a Positive or Negative Soul Mate Connection. It is common for people in a Soul Mate Connection to feel obligated to stay in the relationship, no matter how unhealthy it is. If they end it, they feel drawn to reunite with that person. The information discussed will help you break that pattern once and for all.

Sharing the Same Attitude Number

Another great thing in a love relationship occurs when your Attitude Numbers are the same. For example, my dear sister Vanessa was born October 12 (1+0+1+2 = 4), so she has a 4 Attitude Number. Her husband, Adam, was born May 17 (5+1+7 = 13; 1+3 = 4), and he has the same 4 Attitude Number. These two have been through many changes in circumstances and geography. The good news is that every time two people with this configuration go into a new Personal Year Cycle, they share the same Cycle at the exact same time. They have the ability to grow together. Vanessa and Adam are very close and have been married for twenty years.

Problems between a couple can develop when you are in a Personal Year Cycle that is completely the opposite of what your partner is going through. For example, you are in a Personal Cycle of 2, so you are looking for love and more of a connection. Let's say your partner is in a Cycle of 5, which means he or she needs more personal space than usual. The person in the 5 Personal Cycle feels out of control. During that Cycle he or she may not be happy. If you don't understand what Personal Year Cycle you are in, it can actually hurt an otherwise stable relationship.

You need to make a note of your Personal Year Cycles and tell yourself, "We are going to get through this difficult time, and by next year, we will be back on track." This subject is thoroughly covered in Chapter 20.

Need Help? Call 9,1,1

When I see somebody who has a 9, 1, 1 in their Numerology Blueprint—maybe their name breaks down to 9,1,1 or they have 9,1,1 as their three Numbers from their actual Birth Date—other people call on this individual for help when they have problems. People with this Number pattern attract those who want to be rescued or given advice. When I have counseled people with the 9, 1, 1 series in their Numerology Blueprint, I have found that they have become drained because they feel so responsible for everyone in their life. They need to learn to set up boundaries. If you or your mate has a 9,1,1 in your Personal Numerology Chart, remember it is okay to say "No." A wise old woman once told me, "'No' is a complete sentence." I love that! Keep this in mind.

The Exact Same Name Numbers: WOW!!

If your first and last names contain the exact same three Numbers as the other person's, this can be fortuitous indeed. I have always found that these couples have a wonderful connection. I had a client who said that he would never get married again because his first wife had broken his heart. Then he met a woman who had his exact three Name Numbers; he had a 3 Soul Number, a 3 Personality Number, and a 6 Power Name

Number, and so did she. He worked up the courage to commit to her. They married and are both happy in their love. He made sure she did not take on his name when they married, because he did not want to destroy their perfect Name Number Connection. The wonderful outcome gratified me as a Numerologist, because I was aware of his struggle with his first marriage and had seen his heartbreak.

To be clear, if you are a woman and you have a first and last name that has the same three Vibrations as your partner's, *do not change your name when you marry*. Why would you want to change something that is such a wonderful gift? Keep the name that gives you an amazing connection. Never alter a Natural Match of three numbers in a name comparison. This topic is thoroughly covered in Chapter 18.

Sharing the Same Birthday Numbers

You might meet someone who shares your Birth Numbers. Maybe you were born on a 2 day with a 2 Life Path, and you meet someone who was born on a 2 day with 2 Life Path. You are going to be drawn to this person, because you'll have an instant, subconscious recognition. *But I have to warn you here, the pendulum could swing either way.* As we know, each Number has a Positive and a Negative side. It is just like twins; you often hear about the good twin and the evil twin. Sometimes one twin will choose the Negative side, just to rebel against the other twin. If you share Birthday Numbers with someone, carefully study their Numerology and find out which side of their Numbers they are living on—especially if the numbers are at odds with each other.

This is also useful when you study people who possess any of the same Numbers as you do. If you observe a flaw in a personality that bothers you, it may be a negative trait inside you that you fight against. This Numerological "twin" can really help you know yourself better. And if you both live on the Positive side of your Numbers, you two will bond for life.

Using 11:11 for Love

Take advantage of 11:11 when you see it on the clock. It can be 11:11 in the morning, it can be 11:11 at night; you should deliberately pay attention to it every day and use it, for that whole minute, you should concentrate on what it is you want: a wonderful person to share your life with, the financial security that you need, the home you really want for your family etc. If your relationship is in trouble, you can spend that minute saying, "That my partner and I start to understand each other better and know that we love each other and will always be there for each other." It is really remarkable how well it works when you spend one solid minute asking for what you want when the clock says 11:11.

One of my clients wrote me a while back and told me that her husband had left her. She had become too focused on her career, and when it came to intimacy, she was just too tired and did not even want to make love. So she took advantage of 11:11. She spent every day saying, "My husband realizes that it is worth trying again. He comes back and gives us a second chance. When we are together, we do engage each other, and I am aware of his needs, and he is aware of mine." She did this for several weeks, and he finally called and said, "I do want to meet for dinner and talk." Sure enough, they were able to get back on track, and almost three years have passed since I last heard from her. I remember how happy she was, crying and laughing at the same time, saying that she could not believe how well the mantra worked. I believe that the magic of 11:11 worked, and also that whatever we really want will occur if we keep our focus.

A Triple Number in Your Chart that is Different from Your Life Path

Any time there is triple Vibration in your chart, it means that the Number is a big part of who you are. *Pay special attention if these repeating Numbers are not the same as your Life Path Number.* As I have noted before, your Life Path Number is the Number you must fulfill in order to be happy. The tripling of any Number has the same effect, magnifying the impact of that vibration. If a different Number is repeating itself in you or your partner's chart, read about that particular Number throughout this book to gain more insights. I'm going to give you three examples: the triple 6, 8, and 9.

A 6,6,6 Configuration

Let's say you have a 4 Life Path and there are three 6s in your Chart. It then becomes important for you to pay attention to the 6 Vibration as well, because it is a big part of who you are. Contrary to what some people may think, by the way, these numbers have nothing whatsoever to do with any evil force. A 6 is magnetic; we are drawn to people with 6s in their Charts because they have a commanding presence.

The downside of the 6 Vibration is that when things are going too smoothly, they may become edgy, waiting for the other shoe to drop. But when, or if, everything falls apart, they call out, "Okay, I'm here to the rescue. I can fix it." These folks need to learn to say the words, "It's going really well in my life, and I welcome this."

An 8,8,8 Configuration

These people are far too hard on themselves. They've got to develop a healthy relationship with money, and above all else, learn to take advice. All those 8s can produce a real stubborn streak and can also turn you into a workaholic. The 8 is business minded, which is magnified when you've got a triple 8 Energy. These triple 8s can vent quite easily. I have never met a triple 8 who does not flare up when they are stressed.

Louise L. Hay and other New Age teachers say that what we don't deal with mentally will eventually attack us physically. I agree wholeheartedly.

So the triple 8 has to be careful that their bodies are not under attack because they haven't dealt with their inner turmoil. Triple 8s should put all their thoughts out there in the open. It's good to write them out, or pick up an audio cassette player and shout out everything that is troubling them. They should get in touch with what they are actually feeling, play the tape back once, and then erase it. This simple exercise releases internal turmoil and can do wonders for overall health.

A 9, 9, 9 Configuration

If you love someone whose chart contains the repeating Numbers 9, 9, 9, you have to make it your business to study their original family. See if he or she was adopted, felt abandoned by their mom and dad, or felt too responsible for them. You've got to see what has happened in the past to understand what will happen in the future. If you have a 9, 9, 9 in your own chart, it means you are the one who has to overcome your past. Whatever you are hanging on to, you've got to let it go. If you still feel too responsible for your original family, again it is about establishing your boundaries and saying, "I'm not always going to be there for you. I need to have my life too." It doesn't matter your birth order. You can be the eldest, or the youngest of the family. If you have a 9, 9, 9 in your chart, people will automatically count on you more than they do others.

The 5 and 2 Connection

When I see a 5 and 2 in someone's Birth Numbers, I know that they have inner conflict. This is particularly strong when the 5 and 2 come from their Birth Date Numbers. Let's say it is a person who is a 2 Life Path and was born on a 5 Day, or a 5 Life Path born on a 2 Day, or it could be someone with a 2 Attitude, born on a 5 Day. That combination in their Blueprint is something I take note of. What it means is they have an ongoing battle within themselves. Their 2 says, "I want love. I want a relationship, I want someone I can call my own." But their 5 says, "Do not control me. I can barely breathe, and I need to get out of here." The way to keep their relationships healthy is for someone with these dueling vibrations to go on vacations when they can, or to be by themselves for a while. Otherwise, they will feel entrapped and stuck in an unhealthy situation.

If you have a 5 and 2 in your chart or you are in love with someone with a 5 and 2, make sure you take trips together whenever possible. If you need to be by yourself, you can take a thirty-minute time-out to a nearby nature retreat, or enjoy a movie matinee. Doing this allows you to keep some sense of freedom. Otherwise, the drama will come charging into your relationship.

If you love someone with a 5 and 2 in their Personal Numerology Chart, don't take these "escapes" personally, even though you might sometimes feel rejected. Especially since the 2 part of them makes them seem so dependent on you. You may find yourself saying, "But I thought you wanted me. I thought you needed me." That's still true, but sometimes the 5 Vibration takes over and says, "You have got to give me space." This really isn't about you. It is about an inner struggle. When that happens with a partner whom you love, be prepared. Understand that they are battling within themselves because of the duality these two Vibrations have inside one person.

Easy as 1, 2, and 3

When 1, 2, and 3 is in someone's Birth Numbers, whether in their Birth Date or in their Name Numbers, that person should proclaim, "My life is as easy as 1, 2, 3!" The reason is that the 1 promotes ambition; the 2 is the ability to love; and the 3 is the ability to express oneself with humor and style. When you have that winning combination—1, 2, and 3—the sky is the limit!

CHAPTER 25

Some Final Thoughts on Love

Love is an act of faith, and whoever is of little faith is also of little love.

—ERICH FROMM

In the final episode of *Sex and the City,* there was a scene that took place that brought tears to my eyes. It summed up exactly what I believe is true about love, and what I want everyone to have in their life.

The scene takes place in Paris, where the character Carrie is with her boyfriend, Aleksandr. She has left New York to be with him. She is a writer, and when she goes to a Parisian bookstore, they recognize her, think she is amazing, and want to throw a party on her behalf. That same night, Aleksandr has a party showcasing his artwork. He makes it clear how much it matters to him that she come to his art gallery show. So she chooses his party over hers to please him.

So there she is at his party, in her party dress, sitting on a bench, while he is talking to everyone but her. She suddenly realizes how completely alone she is and is upset by his rejection. When they finally return to the hotel room, she tells him that he completely ignored her, she was there for him, and it did not even matter. While they are talking, he moves his arm in such a way that it seems he hit her. Although you can tell that it was not intentional, it does not matter; she is shocked back to reality. She realizes this relationship is wrong for her, and as she is leaving him, she declares,

"I'm looking for love. Real love. Ridiculous, inconvenient, consuming, can't-live-without-each-other love."

Those words sum up what is possible. Some of us will stay in an unhappy and basically loveless relationship because we cannot bear to be alone. Why settle for the semblance of love, instead of the real thing, when you don't have to?

Take in these beautiful words from Khalil Gibran's *The Prophet.*

When love beckons to you, follow him,
Though his ways are hard and steep.
And when his wings enfold you yield to him,
Though the sword hidden among his pinions may wound you.

Gibran explains how difficult love can be, and what a blessing it is too. To know love is to know God's heart.

If you don't choose to go for that deeper love, he declares,

But if in your fear you would seek only love's peace and love's
pleasure,
Then it is better for you that you cover your nakedness and
pass out of love's threshing-floor,
Into the season less world where you shall laugh, but not all of
your laughter, and weep, but not all of your tears.

Khalil Gibran's words are so true. There are levels of love, and some of us are more capable than others of completely giving our heart to another person. But if we pursue someone who cannot match us, our thirst will seem unquenchable. If you find another person who is mostly a Natural Match, or has Compatible Numbers to your own, or whom you can understand through their Personal Numerology Blueprint, then you can have this wonderful love that we all seek and deserve. *And I am rooting for every one of you.*

APPENDIX A

Suggested Reading

The Five Languages of Love. Dr. Gary Chapman

The Power of Intention. Dr. Wayne Dyer

Blink, Malcolm Gladwell

The Power of Now , Eckhart Tolle.

Where There is Light, Paramahansa Yogananda

Appendix B

Bibliography

Allen, Dr. Patricia and Sandra Harmon. *Getting to I Do*. New York: Avon Books Trade Paperbacks.

Anderson, Peggy, ed. *Great Quotes from Great Leaders*. Franklin Lakes, NJ: Career Press, 1997.

Behrendt, Greg and Liz Tuccillo. *He's Just Not That Into You*. New York: Spotlight Entertainment, 2004.

Blyth, Laureli. *The Numerology of Names*. Australia: Kangaroo Press Pty Ltd, 1995.

Evers, Rev. Anne Marie and Laurel von Pander, LSI, LSC. *Affirmations, Your Passport to Lasting, Loving Relationships*. North Vancouver, B.C. : Affirmations-International Publishing Company, 2001.

Gibran, Kahlil. *The Prophet*. New York: Borzoi Book, Alfred A Knoph, Inc., 1923.

Gladwell, Malcolm. *The Tipping Point*. New York: Little, Brown and Company, 2002.

Gray, Urna, Marlo Gray. *Numerology for Newlyweds*. New York: St. Martin's Paperbacks, 1997.

Haye, Louise L. *You Can Heal Your Life*. Carlsbad, CA: Hay House Publishing, 1984.

Lerner, Rokelle. *Affirmations for the Inner Child*. Deerfield Beach, FL: Health Communications, Inc. 1990.

Miller, Dan. *The Life You Were Born To Live*. Novato, CA: H.J. Kramer, New World Library, 1993.

Ruiz, Don Miguel. *Prayers: A Communion with our Creator*. San Rafael: Amber-Allen Publishing, 2001.

Chart Comparisons for Yourself, a Friend, or a Family Member

The following pages are provided for you to practice charting. Make sure you use the name you go by day-to-day.

Example:

Michael Smith: Michael Smith likes to introduce himself as "Mike Smith," so it is the name Mike Smith that he would use when doing a Personal Numerology Chart Comparison.

CHART COMPARISON	Name	Name	Number Connection
SOUL NUMBER			
PERSONALITY NUMBER			
POWER NAME NUMBER			
BIRTH DAY			
LIFE PATH			
ATTITUDE NUMBER			

Destiny Number: _____ _____

Maturity Number: _____ _____

CHART COMPARISON	Name	Name	Number Connection
SOUL NUMBER			
PERSONALITY NUMBER			
POWER NAME NUMBER			
BIRTH DAY			
LIFE PATH			
ATTITUDE NUMBER			

Destiny Number: _____ _____

Maturity Number: _____ _____

CHART COMPARISON	Name	Name	Number Connection
SOUL NUMBER			
PERSONALITY NUMBER			
POWER NAME NUMBER			
BIRTH DAY			
LIFE PATH			
ATTITUDE NUMBER			

Destiny Number: _____ _____

Maturity Number: _____ _____

CHART COMPARISON	Name	Name	Number Connection
SOUL NUMBER			
PERSONALITY NUMBER			
POWER NAME NUMBER			
BIRTH DAY			
LIFE PATH			
ATTITUDE NUMBER			

Destiny Number: _____ _____

Maturity Number: _____ _____

CHART COMPARISON	Name	Name	Number Connection
SOUL NUMBER			
PERSONALITY NUMBER			
POWER NAME NUMBER			
BIRTH DAY			
LIFE PATH			
ATTITUDE NUMBER			

Destiny Number: _____ _____

Maturity Number: _____ _____

CHART COMPARISON	Name	Name	Number Connection
SOUL NUMBER			
PERSONALITY NUMBER			
POWER NAME NUMBER			
BIRTH DAY			
LIFE PATH			
ATTITUDE NUMBER			

Destiny Number: _____ _____

Maturity Number: _____ _____

The Pythagorean Number System

1	2	3	4	5	6	7	8	9
A	B	C	D	E	F	G	H	I
J	K	L	M	N	O	P	Q	R
S	T	U	V	W	X	Y	Z	

EXCEPTION:

Sometimes the **Y** is a consonant, and sometimes the **Y** is a vowel. Here's how to determine which is which:

If the **Y** is **next to a vowel** (A, E, I, O, U) it is considered a **consonant**.

If the **Y** is **next to or between two consonants**, it is considered a **vowel**.

Example:

Lynn: The **Y** is a **vowel** because it is **between the two consonants** L and N.

Judy: The **Y** is **next to the consonant** D, and so it is considered a **vowel**.

Joy: The **Y** is **next to the vowel** O, so in this case, the Y is a **consonant**.

Note: if your name has a suffix, such as Jr., Sr., III, you do not include them when you break down the name.

Example:

If you go by John Smith III, you only break down John Smith.

Notes

_____

_____

_____

_____

_____

_____

_____

_____

_____

_____

_____

_____

_____

_____

If you would like more information on getting a personal reading, more books and tapes, or dates for a workshop with Glynis McCants, write for a pamphlet:

ADDRESS: Glynis Has Your Number
           PO Box 81057
           San Marino, CA 91118-1057

EMAIL: numbersladyinfo@aol.com

OFFICE: 1-877-686-2373
FAX: 626-614-9292

WEBSITE: www.numberslady.com